LONGEST JOURNEY

A History of Black Lewisham

Deptford Forum Publishing Ltd
441 New Cross Road
London SE14 6TA

First published 1995

Design by Ed Fredenburgh
Cover by Nïxx
Edited by Jess Steele
Picture research by Karen Bray
Picture acknowledgements on p218
Printed by Redwood Books Ltd, Kennet House,
Kennet Way, Trowbridge, Wiltshire BA14 8RN

Published with financial assistance from London
Borough of Lewisham Race Relations Committee

ISBN 1 898536 21 X

British Library Cataloguing in Publication Data
A catalogue record for this book is available from the
British Library

Contents

Foreword

OUR LONGEST JOURNEY

Longest Journey: A History of Black Lewisham documents the continued presence of a black community for whom 'home' could have been Africa, the Caribbean or Britain. It tells of the struggle of African-Caribbean people to build a community and to 'belong' to the area once known as Kentish London, now South East London, and primarily to the present day borough of Lewisham. Many of the stories in the more recent section are told through the voices of black Lewisham, not just to contradict a history of imposed voicelessness but to offer that too often invisible community a published presence.

I have come to see our history as a journey in which black people have the illusion of arrival only to find that they must move on, perhaps in another direction, however reluctantly or with a sense of not being quite ready, so that the travelling itself appears to be unending. It is this metaphor which lent the title *Longest Journey* as the shape of the collective history.

While the term 'black' refers to a number of communities, including the growing communities within the borough from the African continent, limited research time dictated that the book would focus on the African-Caribbean community in Lewisham. There is a particularity about the relationship between African-Caribbean people and 'the British'. The process by which Africans became African-Caribbean was one of enforced and degraded transportation from a place that was home, Africa, to an unrelenting, bestial and widespread labour camp in the Caribbean which involved a denial of language, culture and liberty. While this experience certainly affected the subsequent development of Africa, the focus on African-Caribbeans tells the story of a people who survived bitter enslavement, disenfranchisement and dispossession. How the early relationship affected and continues to affect current relationships in South East London is crucial to the history being pieced together.

The method used for compiling the history was, in part, the standard one of archive search, scouring newspapers and books for frequently small accounts and items of local interest with significance for black history. Extensive use has also been made of personal taped interviews to give substance to the post-Windrush period and to give space to a people largely denied a public voice. The interviews brought out the histories of local black individuals and of projects which supported African-Caribbean community life. Oral history warrants no special justification in the life of the black community. It has been a sustaining force used to teach the young, hold communities together and to remember the past despite systematic attempts to make people forget. Thus a traditional source of evidence has been used here partly to balance the lack of black testimonial evidence from the earlier period.

It must be said, however, that many black people in the Lewisham of the mid 1990s were reluctant to be interviewed, not because they did not wish to tell their stories though sometimes their part in the history seemed to them insignificant. More alarmingly and indicative of the continuing vulnerability of black people in British society, several people did not wish to be identified in my re-telling of their story. For this reason, some of the names have been changed and the focus on individuals has been underplayed.

Because *Longest Journey* concentrates on local black experience it does not focus on the part played by individual white employers, colleagues, allies and co-workers of black people, although it is acknowledged that white individuals and institutions have sometimes played substantial roles in supporting black people. The same may be said about allies from other ethnic groups.

While the present day London Borough of Lewisham provides the boundaries for the history, it seemed unnecessarily artificial to keep too strictly to those boundaries since to do so would be a denial of both inner city reality and the movement which has been part of the process of settling. So, while Lewisham and its constituent parts are foregrounded in the history, the modern area of South East London forms an important backdrop.

Longest Journey is divided into four parts. The first describes the establishment of Atlantic slavery and the relationships developed by British merchants in pursuit of wealth through human cargo. The trade in Africans generated a mythology that would inform racist perceptions for centuries afterwards. These perceptions, in turn, became institutionalised, operating against those forcibly brought out of Africa who found themselves, however temporarily, living part of their lives in the area. We glimpse the black poor of London and the south east at a time when slaving wealth raised the status and lifestyle of white slave owners and enriched local and national prosperity.

The second part tells of resistance to slavery's appalling conditions and the long struggle to dismantle it. The beginnings of widespread acknowledgement of common humanity and equality emerged from the recognition of the wider significance of slavery by many of the 19th century radical movements. In this lengthy period the black presence was largely and paradoxically an 'invisible presence'.

Part Three reveals an increasingly visible black presence after the end of slavery when the movement of black people to South East London was more or less voluntary. We track some of the early travellers to the area and explore the experiences of those who responded to Britain's call to arms in defence of the Empire. This part ends with the response to post-war economic needs which attracted mass voluntary immigration, bringing relatively large numbers of black people to settle in Deptford Lewisham.

The final and longest part, 'Putting Down Roots', tells the story of African-Caribbean people's early attempts to settle in Lewisham, redefine their goals and reach for self-defined dreams and visions against the odds. There are chapters about growing up black in South East London; about racism in all its local manifestations from the colour bar at a Forest Hill pub to the horrors of the New Cross Fire and about setting down the roots of a black community. The missionary heritage of the Caribbean did not prepare newcomers for the hostile reception they found within Christianity in 'the motherland'. Such rejections led to the growth of Lewisham's pentecostalist churches and contributed to the appeal of Rastafari. They caused some to abandon religion and others to move into previously unknown faiths such as Buddhism. Lewisham's black community is feeling the loss of those who return to the Caribbean or move elsewhere, sometimes tired and demoralised, at other times with renewed conviction. Chapter 17 tells of the younger generation and the struggles faced by those who will be the black adults of the new millennium. The final chapter portrays a diverse community of the 1990s, still facing old struggles but beginning to realise the dream of self-determination.

Longest Journey documents the survival of a people and the growth of a community, its adjustments and re-adjustments in the face of racial hostility both institutionalised and personalised. It tells of a community's resistance to this hostility, how individuals and groups find strategies to deal with negation and denial, hard times and abuse, adversity and continued trouble, whether within the systems provided or despite them. In each part of the story certain themes recur: denial of rights, freedom and justice, repatriation, exploitation, criminalisation and the assertion of a collective will against these forces. *Longest Journey* is black history but it is also British history. There is no contradiction.

Thanks are due to so many who have given support and encouragement along the way: Sue Mead, Sharon Joseph, Charles Warren, Les Back, Dr Elsie Warren, Viv Golding, David Killingray, Patrick Addo and Mary Boley. I also need to thank all of those ordinary and extraordinary survivors, contributors to Lewisham's history who have added to the collective knowledge, sometimes in the bravest circumstances and uncertain about the value of their contribution.

While researching the history, I was privileged to come to know so many people. There is one person, Metrina Mitchell, whom I would specially have wanted to see this work. Sadly, she died before it was completed but her sheer zest helped me through some of it.

This book is dedicated to my extended family, some of whom I have discovered or rediscovered in the borough of Lewisham, to my children Kofi and An'yaa who made the documenting of this history of 'belonging' an urgent task and to the children of Lewisham who in the new millenium will seek to know each other's stories. Ours is a history which has brought us to the capitals and big cities, the ports and docks, and it is here on the banks of the Thames that the story begins.

Joan Anim-Addo, September 1995

BEFORE THE WEST INDIES

"A people without the knowledge of their past history, origin and culture is like a tree without roots" MARCUS GARVEY

Long before the geographical area known now as the London Borough of Lewisham came to be so called, long before the Caribbean or the West Indies came to be conceptualised at all by local inhabitants of the small settlements along the Thames and its tributaries, a Roman legion halted and made ready to camp locally along the banks of the Thames within easy reach of running water. A Roman camp at Southwark stretched in a line of forts from the Thames at Lambeth to the River Ravensbourne at Deptford Bridge.

At this time, some 2,000 years ago, Rome enjoyed mutually beneficial contact with Africans, as Greece had before. It was a period characterised by Roman expansion, well before Atlantic slavery came to dominate African perception of Europeans and vice versa. Within the Roman ranks were African soldiers. Whether among these Africans were men who delighted in crafting wood or whether a homesick youth had brought with him a memento of his homeland is not known. What is known is that someone carried in his pack a carved artefact that would provide the link between Africa and south eastern London dating back to a conquering Roman army of occupation.

2. This miniature wooden spoon handle, carved in characteristic African style, was found near Southwark Bridge. Nearly 2,000 years old, the carving is evidence of African soldiers in the ranks of the invading Roman army.

The earliest history of the contact of Africans with the South East London area is indicated in an archaeological find dating back nearly 2,000 years.

This evidence is a miniature carved wooden figure fitting comfortably in the palm of an adult hand. The small shape is a head, carved with characteristic African style and markings. It was found near the northern end of Southwark Bridge. "Only 3.3 centimetres high, the head acts as a handle decoration at the top of a serving spoon. Carved in the latter part of the first century AD, the spoon was perfectly pre-served because it lay for almost two millennia in waterlogged conditions."

The name Depeford, a version of the more familiar Deptford, is believed to have arisen after a settlement of Romans who knew the area as Vadum Profundum, the Latin for 'deep ford'. Deptford was occupied by the invading Romans, including African soldiers. Roman finds in the area include tesselated pavement, urns and door carvings.

An African presence in several other areas outside London is already fairly well documented. For example, there was thought to be a 500-strong regiment of African soldiers based in Carlisle. Further south a tombstone was discovered and is now held in the Roman Fort Museum, South Shields. The case has even been made that the mystery of Stonehenge lies in its African construction. Taken together with other finds indicating evidence of Africans in Roman Britain and given that the soldiers are believed to have forded the creek at Deptford, the 'Negro head' marks an important African connection in the area's black history.

The centuries since the Romanus Africanus period witnessed a number of waves of migration of African peoples to London's south east, especially following the English penetration of Africa and the beginning of trade in enslaved Africans. It is from these beginnings that the African-Caribbean relationship with South East London developed.

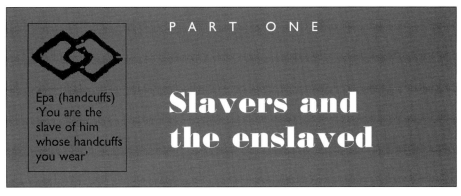

PART ONE

Epa (handcuffs)
'You are the
slave of him
whose handcuffs
you wear'

Slavers and the enslaved

1

THE OPENING SHOT

"Alas for Africa and the sufferings of her desolated millions." J.J.THOMAS

From 'Roman' Africans marching through the marshlands, our story must now jump more than a thousand years to the court of King Henry VII, the first Tudor king, when we can next find evidence of a local black presence. Africans were introduced into the south east in the 16th century by royalty. In the early 1500s Henry VII's court at Greenwich added a particularly exotic note to the pageantry to which special guests were treated. Court gatherings involved lavish banquets, courtiers in fashionable clothes, wining, dining and dancing.

Black Presence in the Tudor South East

Among the court musicians entertaining guests in the palace at Greenwich was a trumpeter who stood out from the others, not necessarily because he was the best

3. Trumpeters at the court of Henry. VII. John Blanke, in the second row, was something of a novelty in 16th century Greenwich

musician of the group but because he was black. This faithful trumpeter, a source of particular fascination to visitors of the court, would have been one of the earliest black people to visit the south eastern area of London in Tudor times, but others were to follow.

After the king's death, this same black trumpeter served the next monarch, Henry VIII, and was rewarded with an income of eight pence a day. He was known as John Blanke, an imposed name with none of the features of African naming systems which were often elaborate. For example, in the Akan tradition in the 'Gold Coast' of West Africa (currently Ghana), children would be given two or three names which they had earned and which told of their personal history. Over the next 500 years, one of the first losses endured by Africans in their relationship with Europeans was that of name.

Henry VIII's action in establishing the first royal dockyard at Deptford was even more important to the black history of the area than his father's palace. Deptford held no particular merit as a town until its development as a naval centre by the crown.

This towne, being a frontier between Kent and Surrey, was none of estimation at all, until that King Henry the eighth, advised (for the better preservation of the Royal Fleete) to erect a storehouse, and to create certaine officers there.
WILLIAM LAMBARDE, 1570

Catherine of Aragon was another royal figure who brought Africans to England. When she arrived at Deptford on 9th November 1501 to marry Henry VII's eldest son, Arthur, her retinue included two African slaves. This is the first record of enslaved Africans in Deptford's history.

Whether enslaved or free, early Africans living or visiting locally in the 16th century are unlikely to have experienced life in the West Indies. Africans were not sent to labour on Caribbean plantations until the 17th century. Those taken as slaves in the latter half of the 16th century were often treated as curiosities or exotic specimens rather than the 'beasts of labour' they were to become.

However, in Spanish-held territories in the Caribbean, developments were already afoot which would lay the foundations of racial slavery. Bishop Bartholomew Las Casas observed that attempts to enslave the indigenous Arawaks in the Caribbean to labour on Spanish planatations had led to huge numbers of deaths. He wrote advising Spain to replace indigenous Amerindians with more robust African slave labourers. After this holy man's intervention the importation of Africans as labourers into the Americas began from 1503. English plantation slaveholders later refined this pattern to maximise the economic exploitation of Africans.

As Atlantic slavery developed economic muscle, the words 'blackamoor' and 'black' became interchangeable with the term 'slave'. The word 'Moor', which can be traced to the Roman invasion of West Africa, came to indicate Black African in Tudor England (see Shakespeare's 'Othello'). Thus the slaves lost the dignity, not only of their personal names but of the country they came from – 'African' being replaced with 'Moor'.

Desperately Seeking Africa

Around 1530 English seamen, including many from London, began to challenge the Spanish cartel which guaranteed Spain and Portugal exclusive rights to African trade. Foremost among them was William Hawkins, father of John Hawkins. The involvement of the Hawkins family is important in any consideration of the English part in New World slavery. Several of the well-known national figures were also central players in the local history of Deptford and nearby Greenwich.

Between 1530 and 1532, William Hawkins made at least three voyages to Guinea, as the west coast of Africa was known. In time, enslaved Africans' reference to Guinea came to signify Africa, the home continent. What was the fatal attraction of Africa?

Hawkins pioneered travel to Africa with trade in mind. His outward journey in 1530 was a success. Though he could not boast of gold, he had traded in ivory and other rare goods.

[Hawkins] touched at the river of Sestos upon the coast of Guinea, where hee trafficked with the negroes, and took of them elephants' teeth, and other commodities which that place yeeldeth. RICHARD HAKLUYT, 1589

4. The 'Gold Coast', known then as Lower Guinea. African traders were known to pay for their purchases in gold dust.

Early in the 16th century adventurers like the elder Hawkins sailed south in wooden boats to trade in exotic commoditiies. Trade rather than the acquisition of slaves was the priority. 'Elephants' teeth', today known as ivory tusks, would alone have been a sufficiently exotic and financially rewarding cargo. Gold, however, was the especially appreciated prize of that period in African trading. This led to the naming of the 'Gold Coast' in the area known then as Lower Guinea. In that area African traders, tantalisingly for Europeans, were known to pay for their purchases in gold dust. To the early 16th century imagination, the 'Great Ocean Sea', seemingly boundless, yielded territories to be exploited by whoever dared. Ultimately these private ventures provided the prospect of excitement, adventure and financial reward. While the navy needed to 'press', that is to force seamen to enlist, privateers offered inducement in a share of the booty that would attract a queue of volunteer seamen.

Out of 16th Century Africa

The expansion of the Spanish Empire between about 1340 and 1470 could be traced by its outposts along the African coast. When British expansion followed it was spearheaded by private adventurers seeking to wrest from Spain some of the riches she had made, and continued to make, through direct contact with Africa.

It was first realised about halfway through the 15th century that the Portuguese had a lucrative deal with West Africa. It was known to involve gold. Portugal claimed a crown monopoly of this trade and had built a fort at Elmina on the coast of Ghana as early as 1481. Before long, nationals from other European countries were seeking access to the trade. By the time of the English interest in Africa later in the 16th century, African people to be used as slaves were certainly a most sought after 'merchandise' for Europeans. Gold and slaves became the main prizes, along with ivory, wax, dye-woods and condiments such as pepper.

Before 'peaceful' trade in enslaved people was established, Europeans attempted to acquire Africans as slaves by raiding their homes. In 1446 a group of Portuguese slavers who used the 'raiding' strategy suffered such a memorable defeat at the hands of Africans skilled in marine warfare that they issued warnings to fellow venturers. European survivors of such disasters learned the approved methods of securing trading

5. European traders were met by organised groups defending the waterways. The coastal Africans had an established maritime culture. Small, specialised African crafts were initially able to repel Europe's sophisticated maritime war machinery.

partnerships. By 1525 advice had filtered to most upcoming seamen on the etiquette of trade, including a warning for ships to wait until properly signalled by officials. "The presence of African naval craft along most of the coast seems to have deterred recurrence of a raid-and-trade pattern...although, of course, the policy of refraining from attacks on Africans was not always followed."

Traders were met by organised groups skilled in defending the waterways, particularly the rivers leading upstream into the heart of Africa. The coastal Africans, they found, had an established maritime culture. Their skilled handling of the canoe was a speciality. Naval forces consisting of small, specialised African crafts were initially able to repel Europe's sophisticated maritime war machinery.

While rumours of gold were an important initial impetus to enterprise with Africa and slaves became of paramount significance, other items of trade should not be overlooked. Hides, camwood, indigo, cotton, resin, soap and ivory from elephants and hippos also attracted London sea traders and their merchant backers to West Africa. Hawkins, Fenton and other pioneering seamen found on the coast of Africa local people skilled in the manufacture of trading commodities such as pepper and cloth. They found African traders, manufacturers and skilled artisans in organised communities but this was not widely reported. The distorted representation of African lifestyle and patterns of existence was given prominence in the century to follow, as English slave trading took root.

London and Deptford Lead the Slaving League

According to Kenneth Andrews: "A feature of the shipping engaged in West Indian privateering which may cause surprise is the overwhelming predominance of Londoners. There are forty-one ships mentioned herein whose port of origin has been traced; thirty-one were from London."

The Royal Dockyard at Deptford played a significant role in London's privateering ventures. In 1553 *The Primrose*, built two years earlier at Deptford, was one ship in a small fleet setting sail on a venture to Guinea which would be the first contact between the English and the African kingdom of Benin. *The Primrose* was loaned by the navy and sailed with two other ships *The Lion* and *The Moon*. This notable journey represented collaborative enterprise involving crucial trading information from an exiled Portuguese knight, the business interests of a group of London merchants and the young adventurer, Martin Frobisher. Frobisher is more usually associated with Arctic voyages but he spent some of his formative years along the West African coast. As a mere youth of 14, Frobisher sailed on the 1553 trip with Thomas Wyndham, another pioneer of the Guinea trade. Although the English traded according to plan, it was to be a fatal journey, with illness and death rampant. The adventurers returned having lost one ship and 100 men.

Whether from the resilience of youth or sheer single-mindedness, Frobisher was undaunted. The following year he set off on a return trip to West Africa, this time with John Lok. He returned nine months later having been imprisoned in Guinea. During the period 1559-62 he appears to have been involved in plans to build a fort on the Gold Coast. In the following 10 years, he was arrested three or four times for piracy. Frobisher's regular trips indicate an important source of financial backing. His uncle, Sir John Yorke, was a leading member of the Muscovy Company, a successful trading company of the time. In 1576 Queen Elizabeth I watched Frobisher sail from

Deptford in an acclaimed voyage to find a north west passage to China.

Deptford acted as a gathering place for those interested in sea voyaging, many of them actively seeking royal patronage or financial backing from wealthy London merchants. The networking within this group, of which John Hawkins became a key figure, would have been fairly intense.

Deptford's ancient parish church of St Nicholas dates from the 12th century and is the earliest recorded church within the present borough of Lewisham. Named for the patron saint of seafarers, it celebrates seamen such as Hawkins. Within the church stands a statue of the second William Hawkins, brother of John Hawkins and fellow pioneer of English slave trading. At the south side of the church an inscription, in translation, reads:

> To the sacred and perpetual memory of William Hawkins...He made many long and distant voyages...This monument was erected by his sorrowing brother, Sir John Hawkins, knight, treasurer of the Royal Navy, on the 7th day of October, in the year of Our Lord 1589.

Also buried at St Nicholas' church and with a memorial there is Edward Fenton whose trade for slaves in Sierra Leone is well documented. Fenton believed that his request for slaves in 1580 stimulated warfare among Africans, so eager were they to provide a supply of enslaved peoples for trade with Europeans. Fenton was John Hawkins' brother-in-law, the two having married sisters, Thomasine and Katherine Gonson.

English Father of the Atlantic Slave Trade

John Hawkins, who lived in the Treasurer's House at Deptford Dockyard, could be considered the 'English Father of the Atlantic Slave Trade'. On his first slaving trip in 1562 Hawkins was able to combine trading activities for the two chief commodities of the period. He took gold from Lower Guinea and at least 300 slaves from Upper Guinea, 1,000 miles away. Portuguese sources insist the figure was nearer 900.

In 1562 Captain John Hawkins had the backing of his father-in-law, treasurer of the Admiralty and several London merchants. Hawkins' trading in West Africa, which audaciously flaunted protocol laid down by Spain, established the lucrative triangular slave trading link for England. Hispaniola was his trading stop in the Caribbean and he returned to England in August 1563 with ships laden with pearls, ginger, sugar and hides. Spanish authorities suggest that he also had gold. Hawkins' first slaving venture certainly proved a financial success and it is not surprising, given the trail of slavers which followed, that Benin and the Niger delta in Africa came to be known as 'the River of Slaves'.

Impressed by Hawkins' first expedition, Queen Elizabeth I supported his next through the loan of The Jesus of Lubeck, a 700-ton vessel purchased by Henry VIII for the navy. Ships of such size were rarely used for slaving. However, such a vessel would prove worthwhile as a boast of English power.

Records of this expedition indicate the manner of acquiring Africans for slavery that was to enrich England for centuries to come and correspondingly depopulate and impoverish Africa.

> The men of the fleet were kept busy going ashore every day to capture the negroes, burning and spoiling their towns, and many were taken...By the 21st

December, the raiding parties had taken all the negroes they could find and had also carried on board as much fruit...

The expedition was borne in vessels that were among the best England supplied. The small fleet was manned by no less than 170 skilled seamen, many of whom joined armed raiding parties on the African coast. The English emerged triumphant in terms of slave seizure, but not without loss of life. While ransacking for gold in a raid on one village, Hawkins' men were attacked and sent hastily back to their crafts.

6. Crest of John Hawkins, Deptford resident and Treasurer of the Navy. His coat of arms showed three black men shackled together by the neck.

Thus we returned backe, somewhat discomforted, although the Captaine in a singular wise manner, with countenance very cheerful outwardly, as though he did little weigh the death of his men, nor yet the great hurt of the rest. RICHARD HAKLUYT

Hawkins had lost seven of his best men and gained ten enslaved Africans. Many more of the English seamen had been hurt. On 19th January 1565 the slaving fleet left Africa for the Caribbean.

Hawkins profited financially and his reputation soared. In the wake of the financial success of such an operation other trips were planned. Hawkins rose in stature within the slave trading circles of the day and, indeed, became a national figure. Hawkins' coat-of-arms showed three black men shackled with slave collars. His crest depicted a black man captive and bound.

On his third slave hunting expedition in 1567 Hawkins was accompanied by Francis Drake. On this occasion the Queen's investment had increased to two ships. Hawkins described his third voyage to the West Indies in 1568:

Now had we obtained between four and five hundred Negroes, wherewith we thought it somewhat reasonable to seek the coast of the West Indies; and there, for our Negroes, and other our merchandise, we hoped to obtain whereof to countervail our charges with some gains. Whereunto we proceeded with all diligence, furnished our watering, took fuel and departed the coast of Guinea the third of February.

This expedition also proved profitable. Slave trading in Africa and the Caribbean was lucrative indeed.

Another source of income to seamen of rank was the taking of 'prizes', namely enemy ships. Often these ships were the subject of legal disputes. Caribbean waters were a rich source for such prizes. Towards the end of the 16th century Sir John Hawkins was still involved with these prizes but most often from the safety of a desk. Writing from Deptford in 1593, Hawkins certified to the Admiralty that a ship taken from the French in the Indies was laden with fish from Newfoundland, a portion of which the French could have claimed at the time. He wrote:

The kyng of frances servant beyng the [ambassador] toke a porcyon of the fyshe for the kynges ryght...& this ys all that I know of this matter, but that my lord thomas payd for the ship & her fornyture to her majestie & the Rest of the partners... this I leve to trouble you from Deptford the Last of July, 1593. Your very lovyng friend, John Hawkyns

Sir John Hawkins, dealer in enslaved Africans and treasurer of the Queen's navy, died on 12th November 1595 near San Juan de Puerto Rico in the Caribbean.

Deptford Connections and Royal Support

Together with his uncle, Sir John Hawkins, whom he trained alongside, Drake was a pioneer of the English slave trade. In the slaving expedition of 1568, while Hawkins captained *The Jesus of Lubeck*, within the fleet the little known captain in command of *The Judith* was Francis Drake.

Drake's family is well connected with slavery and with Deptford. It was here, after a sumptuous dinner on board his ship *The Golden Hind*, that Queen Elizabeth I allowed Drake to be knighted. Concerning Drake's link with the Caribbean it has been said that he is the personification of that period. "The incarnation of this phase of Caribbean history is Sir Francis Drake. Born...of a father who was both a strong Reformation man and a kinsman of seamen, bred and reared among ships and sailors, Drake personified the Elizabethan age, its growing sense of nationalism, its confidence in 'this sceptred isle...this precious stone set in the silver sea'."

In December 1585 Sir Francis Drake was appointed to command an expedition to the West Indies which marked the beginning of open war with Spain. His mastery of combined operations enabled him to capture Santo Domingo (Hispaniola), Cartagena (on the Caribbean coast of Colombia) and St Augustine in Florida.

Elizabeth I felt Drake's low birth and independent temperament made him unfit for supreme command in the fight against the Spanish Armada in 1588. Though he had been personally responsible for collecting and maintaining the fleet, Drake loyally ceded the command to the Lord High Admiral, Charles Howard of Effingham, a resident of Deptford Green. Drake remained his chief tactical adviser throughout the campaign.

In 1595, after a period of disgrace following the failure of his expedition to Corunna and Lisbon to destroy the remnants of the Armada, Drake was recalled to naval service to share command of another West Indies expedition with John Hawkins. He arrived in Dominica with a fleet of some 40 ships. Among these was *The Swallow* which had been part of Hawkins' first slaving expedition. The captain of another vessel of the fleet, *The Primrose*, was Vice Admiral Martin Frobisher. This expedition failed when Spanish defences proved too strong. Drake died of fever off Porto Bello on the Caribbean coast of Panama, where he was buried at sea on 28th January 1596.

In 1589 Walter Raleigh had recruited volunteers for his crew at Deptford. He had business connections with John Hawkins and Martin Frobisher. In 1595 he commanded a small fleet of four ships seeking El Dorado or the Golden Land of Guiana. Lord Howard was one of his main supporters, contributing his own ship *The Lion's Whelp*. Raleigh would have been a regular visitor locally. He was a great grandson of Baron Edmund Carew of the Carew family of the Hundred of Blackheath.

On 5th February 1595 Raleigh set sail for the Caribbean. In a decisive attack on Spanish-held Trinidad, the Governor was captured and, with the assistance of native Indians, Raleigh reconnoitred the nearby mainland for possible sources of gold.

At home Elizabeth I and her court required persuading of the feasibility of a colony so vulnerable to Spanish attack as Guiana would be. At the time there was little crown interest in setting up colonies in the Caribbean. The significance of Raleigh's trip was not widely appreciated. Even the samples of gold he brought back were doubted. Raleigh wrote of the wonders of the new land:

> Guiana is a country that hath yet her maidenhead, never sacked, turned, nor wrought; the face of the earth hath not been torn, nor the virtue and salt of the soil spent by manurance, the graves have not been opened for gold, the mines not broken with sledges nor the images pulled down out of their temples. It hath never been entered by any army of strength, and never conquered or possessed by any Christian prince.

Raleigh used the printed word carefully and with powerful effect. His description of El Dorado contrasts with the reality of a violated West Africa, already sacked and torn by Raleigh's fellow seamen in their pursuit of great wealth across the Atlantic.

In 1616 Raleigh was released from a long imprisonment in the Tower of London to organise another trip to El Dorado. He commissioned Phineas Pett of Deptford Dockyard to build The Destiny. On arrival in Guiana, Raleigh was very ill and sent his hothead son Wat to lead the voyage upriver, reminding the men of their promise to King James I to avoid confrontation with any Spaniards they might meet. When the Spanish attacked Wat retaliated, sacking the fort of San Thome where he was among the first to die. Raleigh was devastated at the news and returned to England without the cherished gold. He was arrested in a dramatic river trip from Greenwich when he entrusted to the wrong party his secret plans of escape from Britain in the summer of 1618. He was tried in closed court and beheaded in October 1618.

Cornelius and the Lee Connection

A short carriage ride from Deptford at St Margaret's in Lee, the first recorded entry of a black person in the parish registers of the Lewisham area was made in 1593. It concerned the burial of 'Cornelius, a blackamore' on 2nd March 1593. Nothing else is known of this African buried in the 16th century on English soil. His occupation, age and employer remain a mystery but the lack of information raises a number of questions. Was Cornelius brought into England by Drake, Raleigh, Frobisher or Hawkins? Given the evidence of the interconnections among the seafaring fraternity, it is likely that Cornelius not only arrived with one of London's slave trading pioneers but that he went into the service of a local family with whom they were associated.

It is not surprising that the earliest recorded parish entry for a black person in the present Lewisham area relates to Lee. The area was an important residential area for influential families such as the Annesleys, who lived in their ancient seat at the Manor House in Lee. Bryan Annesley, a friend and legatee of Admiral Sir John Hawkins, died a gentleman pensioner of Elizabeth I.

Sir William Harvey witnessed Bryan Annesley's will and later married Annesley's daughter, gaining the Annesley land at Kidbrooke. In 1595-6 Harvey was captain of

The Bonaventure which had been built in 1561 and used as a privateering merchant trading ship for many years. Rebuilt in 1581, the ship served as Drake's flagship in the West Indies in 1585-6.

The picture emerges of a busy and businesslike London with expanding commercial activity but essentially a small and closely connected network for which Kentish London was an important base. The distinction between 'slavetrader' and 'discoverer' was entirely blurred at this time. The famous names which have come down to us are often to be found together both on journeys and in legal and personal documents sent from Deptford or Lee. The ships themselves, the majority built or fitted out at Deptford for their maiden voyages, often returned to Africa after repair in the area's dockyards. The Manor House at Lee, along with a number of other large houses in the area, reappears as the residence of further local worthies involved in slaving activity in later centuries.

The Elizabethan Numbers Game

Towards the end of the 16th century the routes taken by slaves and traders begin to be marked by records of their deaths far from home. Thus while John Hawkins was buried in Caribbean waters, local burial registers are an important source for the presence of black people like Cornelius.

Africans had become part of the London population, particularly in seafaring centres such as Deptford. Royalty and the nobility supported African servants and slaves, yet it would appear that many Africans fell on hard times in London. In 1596 the Privy Council noted their presence as a burden.

Her majestie understanding that there are of late divers blackamoors brought to this realm, of which kinds of people there are already too manie, considering how God hath blessed this land with great increase of people of our own nation...those kinde of people should be sent forth of the land.

The Queen's open letter sent by the Privy Council to the Lord Mayor and aldermen referred specifically to ten 'blackamoors' recently brought into the country by a seaman, Sir Thomas Baskerville. Presumably many seamen were engaged in this lucrative activity, since ships' captains were allowed part of their payment in slaves while involved in such trading.

These black people brought into the country through ports like Deptford established a presence not favoured by the crown. This resulted in a proclamation in 1601 which demanded that all 'negroes and blackamoors' be speedily expelled from England. Suggesting that the Africans had crept into the kingdom since the troubles between Britain and Spain, the crown appointed an agent, Casper van Senden, to supervise their deportation.

What place did black people have in English affairs? It seems that the black presence in areas like Deptford, Greenwich and Lee in the 16th century was largely a by-product of Anglo-Spanish preoccupations. Spanish sources of gold in Africa and their treasure routes in Caribbean waters were to be intercepted. Alongside the potential financial rewards, blocking these routes would impress upon Spain the might of its enemy. Early slavery appears almost as a byproduct of this political tension and lust for gold. In the palace at Greenwich and in the residences of the wealthy in areas such as Lee, black servants and entertainers played a part in confirming the status of the rich and influential. As a group, they remained isolated, subject to the whims of their masters or employers.

7. Burial register for 1593 at St Margaret's Lee, showing 'Cornelius a Blacke a more buried ye second of marche'

The black presence in Britain is relevant to the Lewisham area despite the scarcity of evidence about early black lives locally. From the specific information and the general picture we may glimpse the contribution black people were beginning to make: early entertainers at court, providers of stimulating diversity, the cause of increased shipping activity and with that the growth of Deptford, and also workers, servants and slaves.

2

THE WEST INDIAN CONNECTION

"Consider slavery - what it is - how bitter a draught and how many millions are made to drink it." IGNATIUS SANCHO

Ambitious merchants and well-placed, wealthy individuals became increasingly interested in trade with Africa during the 17th century. For merchants trading with Portugal who in turn traded with Africa, the huge profits to be made must have seemed all the more alluring for being one step removed. England, like much of Europe, was excluded by Spain from direct trade with Africa or, indeed, with Spanish colonies. Undeterred by national treaties, determined privateers and their merchant financiers, many from London, sought loopholes to the lucrative African trade.

By 1602 a number of prosperous merchants were actively engaged in West Indian trading. Deptford Green resident, Lord High Admiral Charles Howard, Baron of Effingham and later Earl of Nottingham, seems to have been very keen on the possibilities that Guiana offered. Howard had already supported Raleigh and in 1602 he became involved in promoting the initiative led by Charles Leigh to Guiana. The venture proved disastrous and most of the party died. However, persistent attempts to explore Guiana led to the first English success at crop planting in the Caribbean. Early success, though short lived, was achieved through tobacco growing in Guiana, before Virginia tobacco dominated the market and before Raleigh's return trip to the Caribbean region so enraged Spain and hastened his own dramatic end in 1618.

Supplanting Spain in 'The Indies'

'The Indies' were associated in the 17th century mind with opportunities for the quick acquisition of riches and fortune. It was popularly held that the main source of these was the plunder of Spanish galleons for gold. But English merchant traders, like other Europeans before them, did not stop at precious metals. They raided the African coast for people, whom they shipped like livestock and sold as slaves. Noblemen and merchants vied for profit in the trade. The Royal African Company which came to monopolise the English slave trade was dominated by noblemen. Sometimes competitors in the trade co-operated and in the history of Lewisham's African Caribbean connection, three men played a key part. They were Arthur Annesley Earl of Anglesey, George Monck who rose from the ranks of soldier and sailor to become Duke of Albemarle and Captain-General of the Kingdom, and the merchant Maurice Thomson who lived in Lee.

Spain incited strong feelings of envy, anger and frustration among 17th century English expansionists, excluded from trade with Africa and the colonising of Caribbean territories. Sir Benjamin Rudyerd's speech in the House of Commons on March 17th 1623 was explicit.

Now let us a little consider the enemy we are to encounter, the King of Spain. They are not his great territories which make him so powerful, and so troublesome to all Christendom. For it is very well known, that Spain itself is

but weak in men, and barren of natural commodities. As for his other territories, they lie divided and asunder, which is weakness in itself; besides, they are held by force, and maintained at an extraordinary charge...

No sir, they are his mines in the West Indies, which minister fuel to feed his vast ambitious desire of universal monarchy: it is the money he hath from thence, which makes him able to levy, and pay soldiers in all places; and to keep an army continually on foot, ready to invade and endanger his neighbours so that we have no other way, but to endeavour to cut him up at root, and seek to impeach or supplant him in the West Indies!

Such rhetoric in the offensive against Spain was taken up by many enterprising and adventurous men of the period. Among them, not insensitive to the prospect of financial gain, were London merchants like Maurice Thomson. For a number of these, events in 'the Indies' and particularly early settlements of fellow English people in the Caribbean offered unparalleled opportunities for trade and profit.

Along the chain of Caribbean islands, from the tip of Florida in the west to the southern American mainland border which came to be known as Guiana in the east, early attempts at settlement were hazardous. In the eastern Caribbean, native Caribs of the Windward Islands proved a warlike and successful deterrent to occupation of islands like St Lucia and Grenada.

St Christopher, the 'Mother Colony'

A group of settlers, fewer than 20 men, financed by London merchants had landed in St Christopher in January 1624. In spring 1626 Maurice Thomson, who later lived in Lee, fitted out three ships commanded by Captain Thomas Warner for a pioneering voyage to establish the settlement at St Christopher. Among Warner's cargo were 60 enslaved Africans bound for the Leeward Island 'St Christopher in the Caribbees', today the island of St Kitts.

When Warner established the first English colony in St Kitts, his stated interest was the planting of tobacco. Having submitted a proposal outlining the possibilities for developing a tobacco plantation there, he obtained the necessary and coveted Royal commission appointing him governor of St Kitts, Nevis, Barbados and Monserrat.

Warner's little convoy appears to have tried an abortive attack on Spanish-held Trinidad before arriving at St Christopher on 4th August 1626. The 100 colonists then began the task of tobacco planting. A month later they were devastated by hurricane which destroyed the houses, crops and two of their ships. Despite these losses, in 1627 Thomson and his business partner jointly brought into England, among other goods such as indigo and ginger, some 9,500 pound weight of tobacco.

Following English settlement on St Christopher the English and French ceased their fighting over colonial rights to the island and formally partitioned the 68 square miles of this tiny island. The French occupied both ends while the English inhabited the middle. This was the first permanent English settlement in the Caribbean.

Planter activity gradually replaced buccaneering in the pursuit of profit in the Caribbean. It is suggested that at least 30,000 people left the British Isles on colonising expeditions to the Caribbean during the reigns of James I and Charles I (1603-1649). Success followed these merchant-led ventures. By the end of the period St Christopher, Barbados, Nevis, Antigua, and Monserrat had been settled. Maurice Thomson would later leave property in many of those islands in his will.

St Christopher, the 'mother colony' of the English West Indies, survived as an English settlement only through the alliance with the French against the Spanish and the native Caribs. Together, French and English decimated the Carib population in a relentless campaign which heralded the new settler era. It was an ominous forerunner of the fate that would befall the ancestral people of the whole region.

The small settler colony in St Christopher was just the beginning of English colonisation in the West Indies. The race was being led by merchants, among them powerfully connected London traders such as Maurice Thomson.

Thomson's trade in enslaved Africans to St Christopher represents one of the earliest recorded English transactions of this nature destined for an English settlement in the Caribbean. How was Thomson in a position to supply slaves? In 1618 James I had awarded a charter to the Guinea Company which was still trading on the Gold Coast in 1649-50. Its monopoly was renewed in 1651. This information came to light in 1686 when the Royal African Company found itself in a legal wrangle with Denmark about land near Cape Coast, West Africa. An affidavit revealed that one Thomas Crispe was, until 1649, 'chief factor' for Maurice Thomson and three other members of the Guinea Company. A factor was a commercial agent. In the West African context this meant a period of residence, with attendant health risks, in the area known as the 'white man's grave'. It also meant managing a more or less fortified territory which functioned as a collection point and storage for enslaved people. Maurice Thomson, through his factor, was evidently an established merchant in the 'African trade'. West Indian trade could be seen as an extension of this.

Local history records refer to Maurice Thomson as a Merchant Taylor. Thomson's merchant profile, however, shows him to be one of London's more high-powered and tenacious merchants, seizing the opportunities of the time and eager to invest in the new trade. He was said to have traded equally in the East and West Indies, Virginia and Guinea. Although not an isolated entrepreneur, Thomson was one of the earliest with South East London links.

These merchant adventurers sometimes clashed over land rights in the newly claimed Caribbean lands. Another London merchant had spearheaded the colonisation of Barbados but Thomson, with access to critical Caribbean information, invested in the island which was set to become the most valuable of all British Caribbean possessions. A dispute over his right to land there was settled favourably and his wealth secured.

Native Peoples

The native peoples of the Caribbean – Caribs, Arawaks, Ciboney and others – responded variously to the arrival of successive groups of Europeans. Raleigh's 1595 account refers to Arawacans, Tivitivas and Ciawani and Waraweete. Raleigh's party, unlike many who followed, found the native peoples generally co-operative.

However, the Caribs (who gave the region its name) built up a reputation for warlike territorial defence while the Arawaks appeared more peaceful. In any case, the native peoples represented a serious threat to the English colonisers.

When the Spanish arrived in Barbados, they had first to defeat the Caribs who repelled advancing colonisers in many territories, including Dominica. In St Christopher, however, as described above, the English and French decimated the native

Carib population by combining forces in a ruthless campaign. The Caribs were initially as wary of the Africans as they were of Europeans. Yet as increasing numbers of enslaved Africans were brought to Barbados, the more fortunate escapees were able to take refuge with Caribs in St Vincent. In time a distinctive group of Black Caribs emerged through African-Carib intermarriage. Their notoriety in warfare proved, if anything, more alarming than that of the original Caribs.

It was on behalf of the Arawaks that Las Casas made his famous appeal at the beginning of the 16th century. However, in Trinidad, Arawaks did not conform to the norm of gentle natives but drove newcomers away with a ferocity as memorable as any Carib attack. In English Jamaica there was some joining of forces between the freed Spanish slaves and native Arawaks when the Spanish fled from the British.

Bondservants and the Tobacco Age

Early experiments in Caribbean settlements relied heavily upon the introduction of commercially viable crops and an intensive labour force. Tobacco provided the focus for the former and bonded servants largely satisfied early demands for labour. Thanks to Raleigh, Thomson and Warner, the period 1600-40 would be remembered as the tobacco age.

However, the importance of Barbados to merchants, planters and to England depended overwhelmingly on slave labour. Tobacco soon gave way to sugar cane as the money-making crop on the island. Sugar production required much larger plantations and a larger labour force than tobacco. Gangs of labourers were required at each stage from planting, cutting and transporting the cane to loading the hogsheads of raw sugar onto ships bound for Britain. The population of the island changed correspondingly. It is estimated that by 1643 the population of Barbados included 6,000 blacks and at least 25,000 whites. Seven years later, in 1650, when the main crop was no longer tobacco but sugar cane, there was a significant increase of 37,000 blacks and a substantially decreased white population of 17,000. Of the white population, approximately one third were indentured servants.

Cromwell's Western Design

During the spring of 1652 Oliver Cromwell stood among the important figures visiting Deptford Dockyard to witness the launching of two ships, *The James* and *The Diamond*. Local squire and prolific diarist John Evelyn recorded the event:

> *1652, March 15th, I saw The Diamond and The Ruby launch'd in the Dock at Deptford, carrying 48 brasse canon each. Cromwell and his Grandees present with greate acclamations.* JOHN EVELYN

Meanwhile, Lieutenant-General George Monck, who would later bring Charles II home from exile, was distinguishing himself in the subjugation of Scotland. Doubtless his success in this matter was directly related to his later role in Cromwell's 'Western Design'. There is little information indicating exactly when Monck became involved in Caribbean affairs. It is known, however, that his relation, Thomas Modyford was one of the early investor settlers in Barbados and in 1654 Monck sent prisoners to the island as indentured servants.

Monck had been considered as a possible commander for the western expedition but even his advisory role allowed him a central decision-making part in early English

8. Barbados around 1650 at the beginning of the sugar boom.

A Scale of five Miles

Caribbean history. Cromwell, hoping to engage Spain at her most vulnerable point and one that could prove lucrative, sought armed action in Caribbean waters. Monck, on becoming a key adviser to this project, included his relative, Modyford, as well as his colleague, William Penn.

'Western Design' was the scheme of conquest to effect England's plans for involvement in the West Indies. Central to the plan was the capture of Santo Domingo (now Haiti). To this end William Penn and Robert Venables were appointed to lead a joint army and consequent naval attack in the north western Spanish-held Caribbean. In 1653 William Penn was made General of the Fleet.

Maurice Thomson, thought to be a personal friend of Cromwell, was appointed commissioner in the Navy and Customs in 1654. This and his network of contacts may explain why he was a key named figure in Cromwell's expedition to the Caribbean. In August 1654 Penn, Venables and Thomson, together with 10 other commissioners were notified of their positions.

We have chosen, constituted and appointed, And doe hereby constitute, chuse and appoint you to bee Our Commissioners for the Ordering and manageing of the designe and undertaking aforesaid, according to the Instructions now given unto you.

As one of the first investor planters in Barbados, Modyford's knowledge of the Caribbean had attracted Cromwell's interest. Later, with Monck's assistance, he became Royal Governor of Jamaica.

An estimated 3,000 recruits were needed for the expedition to 'the Indies'. In the first instance a call for volunteers from English regiments released more undesirable characters than had been anticipated. Since this method failed to produce the necessary numbers, the decision was made to add to the fighting force by beat of drum. Of those gathered in this fashion it was said they were

hectors and knights of the blade, with common cheats, thieves, cutpurses, and such like lewd persons, who had long time lived by sleight of hand, and dexterity of wit, and were now making a fair progress unto Newgate, from whence they were to proceed towards Tyburne.

Despite a disappointing recruitment drive, Penn and Venables set sail in command of the surprise attack on Spanish-held Caribbean territories. The attack was central to Cromwell's plan. Robert Venables was accompanied by his new bride, who turned out to be the source of discontent between the General, his men and his colleagues as the couple appeared to honeymoon while troops waited to do battle.

As General of the Fleet, Penn's leadership was restricted to the seamen while Venables was responsible for activities on land. Barbados was the designated first stop. The commanding officers intended to gather more recruits on this English-settled island and, if necessary, from St Christopher. Store ships sailed from Deptford, stocked with goods from the Red House stores where Pepys Estate now stands.

General Venables' instructions were flexible, so as not to circumscribe actions he would deem necessary in Caribbean waters. He was to co-lead with Admiral Penn Britain's expansionist thrust 'beyond the line'.

The design in general is to gain an interest in that part of the West Indies in the possession of the Spaniard, for the effecting whereof We shall not tie you up to a method by any particular instructions, but only communicate to you what hath been under our consideration. Two or three ways have been thought of to that purpose. The first is to land upon some of the Islands, and particularly Hispaniaola, and St John's Islands, one or both... The gaining of these Islands, or either of them, will as we conceive amongst many others have these advantages.

In case it shall please God to give you success, such places as you shall take and shall judge fit to be kept, you shall keep for the use of Us and this Commonwealth, and shall also cause such goods and prizes as shall be taken to be delivered into the hands of the said Commissioners, that so they may be brought to a just and true account for the public advantage.

The task of further recruiting from the islands proved daunting, challenging the combined skills and experience of both leaders. The planters were reluctant to give up their workforce as a volunteer army and even the keenest recruits were unimpressed by the poor equipment offered by Cromwell's leaders who were themselves sorely tried by the delay in food and equipment expected daily from naval supplies at home.

A sailor named Henry Whistler served, possibly as Sailing Master, on Penn's flagship. Whistler kept a diary from which valuable information of the period may be drawn. English Barbados was a source of some wonder to him.

Our English here do think a negro child the first day it is born to be worth 5 [pounds], they cost them nothing the bringing up, they go always naked: some planters will have 30 more or less about 4 or 5 years old. They sell them from one to the other as we do sheep...This island is the dunghill whereon England cast forth its rubbish, rogues and whores and such like people are those which are generally brought here. A rogue in England will hardly make a cheat here: a bawd brought over puts on a demure act, a whore, if handsome makes a wife for some rich planter.

Josiah Child wrote in similar vein.

...loose, vagrant people, vicious and destitute of means to live at home (being either unfit for labour, or such as could find none to employ themselves about, or had so misbehaved themselves by whoring, thieving or other debauchery, that none would set them on work)

The settlers themselves left few records of these early days. Seeking rapid profit, struggling to survive or labouring under indenture, there were few among them with any literary interest or skill.

Despite great efforts, only an army of raw recruits could be mustered. Alongside those undesirable elements recruited at home, the settler contingent included bondservants and freedmen already in the West Indies, armed with the plantation tools and with no training or uniform. This doubtful selection formed Protector Cromwell's forces in the Caribbean. Altogether a force of 7,000 gathered for action in this initial assault upon Spain in the West Indies.

The attempt upon Santo Domingo in Hispaniola in 1654 failed miserably with the loss of an estimated 1,000 British troops to a mere 40 Spanish. The fleet of 30 ships remained in the West Indies.

English Jamaica Under Army and State

In the following year the large military naval expedition made a dawn landing in Spanish Jamaica. The day after their arrival they invaded and effectively occupied the town of San Jago de la Vega (now Kingston). This was a critical moment in Caribbean history. The British state, supported by its army and navy had arrived in the region and won a signal victory over Spain. The prize was Jamaica.

Cromwell's response to the capture of Jamaica was a proclamation "giving Encouragement to such as shall transplant themselves". There was also promise of land: "Twenty acres besides lakes and rivers for every male of twelve years old and upwards, and ten acres for every other male or female." The hoped-for rush from the British Isles did not materialise but many already in the West Indies were induced to move to Jamaica. Thomas Modyford, who had enjoyed great success as a founder planter in English-settled Barbados, moved to Jamaica. The success of the sugar plantations in Barbados had been outstanding and the annexing of Jamaica would allow substantially more acres for the crop.

By the end of 1656 the English population of Jamaica was estimated at 1,500. The African slaves abandoned by the Spanish remained mainly in their hideouts in the mountain areas. The determined English efforts to supplant Spain in the Indies had finally met with success. Founded in bloodshed in 1655, the Jamaica taken by Cromwell's fleet was a base for English pirates waiting to attack Spanish ships. Port Royal became a place of infamy, celebrated as the 'Sodom of the Indies'. Colin Ward's *A Trip To Jamaica* called Port Royal "the dunghill of the universe", populated by prostitutes, convicts and drunks.

The Jamaica wrested from Spain held many possibilities for profit for the incoming group. Soldiers under Venables had gone to the area to fight in the tradition of their Elizabethan forefathers. Seamen and soldiers alike looked forward to prizes to be gained and booty to be salvaged. Nonetheless, there was a willingness to explore the possibilities of family life in the region largely absent from the plans of those in the previous century. Indeed, the main excuse given by General Venables for taking his new wife with him was that they were considering whether they might settle there.

The inheritance of Jamaica, however, contained seeds of resistance and rebellion which took root from the earliest days of English occupation. In the face of war with the English on Jamaican soil the Spanish freed their slaves to fight the invading forces. Warring Africans met the English forces; still more took to the hills to engage in guerrilla activities, establishing a culture of resistance known as maroonage.

With the conquest of Jamaica, Britain's expansion and trade abroad was set for record growth. Among those influencing the course of events was Arthur Annesley, first Earl of Anglesey. In the period of unprecedented expansion of British trade abroad, Anglesey was among officials responding to petitions and documents from West Indian merchants and planters. On 24th April 1660 a commission from General Monck and the Late Council of State for the Government of the Island of St Christopher was signed by a number of Privy Council members including Arthur Annesley, president. The petition came from "merchants and others interested in and trading to the English Plantations in America". These included Maurice Thomson, Anglesey's father-in-law. Marital ties between the Annesley and Thomson families were further strengthened by the marriage of Maurice's son John to Anglesey's daughter.

Among the posts Anglesey later held was that of Treasurer of the Navy. In March

1677 a charge order for transporting soldiers and passengers to Jamaica also bore signatures which included Anglesey's. In 1678 he was still a key member of the Privy Council.

Jamaica became a sugar-producing island around 1664. In the meantime political figures in London sought an infrastructure which would regulate the activities of the English in the West Indies. In January 1666 Deptford diarist John Evelyn was presented to Charles II by George Monck, recently created first Duke of Albermarle. Evelyn became involved in the emergent infrastructure for colonial government when, on 26th May 1671, he took the oath to the newly constituted Council for Foreign Plantations, established to provide advice and counselling to the King on the governing of the new colonies. The Royal African Company was well represented within the group. George Monck, instrumental in setting up the Council for Foreign Plantations, was involved in the Royal African Company and was one of the shareholders and beneficiaries of the charter to the Royal Adventurers. Not only did he reap profits from the buying and selling of slaves, he was also granted a share in the Bahama Islands. His son Christopher, an MP at 17, was appointed Governor-General of Jamaica and died there in 1688.

Deptford's Naval Role in the West Indies

Samuel Pepys was Secretary to the Admiralty from 1673 and was a frequent visitor to Deptford Dockyard. By the late 1670s the number of ships in West Indian ports had increased as the need for defending English colonies became a priority. Marauding European groups of different nationalities practised a 'finders keepers' system which was sometimes close to terrorism as far as planters were concerned. Naval ships were instructed by the Admiralty to remain in the Caribbean. Instructions to ships' captains were usually signed by Pepys himself.

One of the veterans of that early naval era in the West Indies was Christopher Myngs whose death was recorded in Pepys' diary. It was Myngs who led a 900-strong unit to avenge the earlier defeat in Hispaniola and capture the second largest town in Cuba. He returned to Jamaica triumphant. A keen fighter of the Spanish, Myngs was later knighted by Charles II.

Captain Young of Deptford also gained distinctions in this era. He is remembered by local diarist, John Evelyn as

a sober man and an excellent seaman... he was the first who in the first war with Cromwell against Spain took the Governor against the Havana.

Admiral George Legge, Lord of the Manor of Lewisham, was appointed Governor of Ports and Master of Ordnance in 1673. By then Jamaica's need for protection with a strong British naval presence had been well established. The new colony had begun to benefit from the mercantile experience of sugar planters who made a lucrative move from Barbados. Jamaica held more enslaved Africans than the Leeward Islands. George Legge commanded the Royal Fleet in 1688. He was later created Baron of Dartmouth. His only son, William, was to see action in the West Indies.

Vice Admiral John Benbow, an experienced merchant seaman and naval commander owned property in Hughes Fields, Deptford and lived for a time at Evelyn's manor house of Sayes Court. Benbow saw service in Jamaica as a squadron commander for which he was promoted. On returning to further service in 1701 in

Port Royal, Benbow was involved in "one of the most painful and disgraceful episodes in the history of the British navy" which won him praise as a hero but cost him his life. Effectively deserted by a number of reluctant members of his fleet, Benbow was mortally wounded. His monumental inscription at Kingston Cathedral Church reads:

Here lyeth interred, the body - of John Benbow esqr., Admiral - of the white: a true pattern of English courage who lost his life - in defence of his queene and country, november ye 4th 1702 - in the 52nd year of his age - by a wound in his leg, received - in an engagement with Mons. Du Casse, being much lamented.

St Nicholas' church in Deptford also bears a memorial to Admiral Benbow.

Developing Trade in the New Colonies

Once the supplanting of Spain had been accomplished in Jamaica, the profits of long-destance trading in crops became clear. 40,000 tons of tobacco was sent with Penn's fleet which returned to England in 1660. This was not the best quality tobacco available on the market and prices in England reflected this. However, a new trend to 'settlements' and to the stimulus of trade through the introduction of new crops had taken place. Since naval ships returned to Deptford, the new crops would have been unpacked, stored and handled locally, mainly through the Red House warehouses on the site of Pepys Estate.

The commercial failure of tobacco grown by English settlers resulted in diversification into sugar cane. A mere 19,000 pounds of sugar was sent back on the naval ships with the tobacco mentioned above. Before long, however, sugar became the single commodity that seemed most likely to satisfy the English quest for profit. Neither 'prest' labour nor bonded servants could satisfy the demand for the cheap and plentiful labour needed for sugar production. Demand grew for workers to be trained into a rigorous factory-style regime. It was met by the supply of large numbers of enslaved Africans. By 1686 Jamaica was exporting 7,000 tons of sugar to England.

Agents for slave trading companies in key areas like Jamaica and Barbados were often also governors of the islands. Most governors were sent out on naval ships which usually returned to Deptford where crews were paid off and the ships surveyed, repaired and fitted out for another voyage.

Prest Labour

The crews often included men press-ganged on quays and streets of naval towns like Deptford. These were known as 'prestmen' and some were detained to serve on West Indian plantations. Thomas Wilson was one young Deptford man press ganged in that period. He sent word to his family in October 1675 that he had been a servant for four years and asked for money to buy his freedom. The story goes that, out late and rather the worse for drink, he had fallen asleep in the Deptford area and woken to find himself on board ship. He described himself to his family as having been "sold as slave to a planter" in the remoter area of northern Jamaica. He was sent £20 to purchase his freedom.

Climactic adjustments, settler conditions and tropical illnesses each took an exacting toll on the new influx of people to the Caribbean. Among them a kinswoman of Maurice Thomson's, Katherine Rokeby (nee Thomson), who was only 19 years old when she died in April 1666. She was buried at All Saints Chapel in Barbados. The monumental stone laid in her memory reads

> *Under this stone lyes the body of Katherine, late wife of John Rokeby, merchant, daughter and coheiris of Christopher Thomson, late of this parish, gent...who departed this life ye 15th April, 1666, in ye 19th year of her age.*

Slaves and Sugar

The establishing of settler colonies was to affect the history of the Caribbean region, but it was the change of trading commodity from tobacco to sugar that created the demand for labour which would strip West Africa of so many able-bodied men and women. In port areas such as Deptford and in the homes of the wealthy nearby, the Africans put into service were always young and able-bodied. Only the fittest Africans were chosen and only the healthiest of them survived the traumas and conditions of the Atlantic crossing. To be sure of a 'good price', the Royal African Company preferred boys and young adults. The preference for males is reflected in local parish registers. From the 17th century onwards hundreds of thousands of Africans were transported as slaves to meet English demands for cheap labour. Through an excessively traumatic and dehumanising system, they produced sugar to sweeten the lives of those who could afford to buy the product, thereby enriching the planters and their agents. In the south east sales of sugar at good prices would also bring extra income to captains of ships bringing the goods into local ports, their agents and local tradesmen.

The shift to sugar drastically affected the enforced movement enslaved Africans brutally transported to the West Indies in the 'Middle Passage' of the triangular slaving route from England to Africa to the Caribbean and back to England. The voyage was "a veritable nightmare. Overcrowding was most common and there are records of 90-ton ships carrying 390 slaves in addition to crew and provisions. These crowded

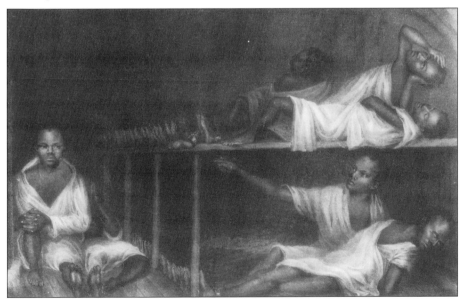

9. This painting gives some impresson of conditions on board the slave ships crossing from Africa to the Caribbean in the infamous 'Middle Passage'. Sickness was rife in the stinking holds.

conditions increased the incidence of disease and epidemics. Hunger strikes and mutinies added to the burdens of the voyage and it was not unusual for half the human cargo to die en route."

Sugar production, introduced into Barbados in 1640, transformed economic activities in the Caribbean. Its profit capacity was, at the outset, linked to the cheap labour of large numbers of people. To this end, a rise in the African population from 1,000 to 20,000 was engineered in the first 11 years of sugar production on the island. Within a further 20 years the African population had doubled to 40,000.

In London during 1662 the Guinea Company's grant finally ran out and was not renewed. That year Maurice Thomson paid hearth tax on the second largest house in the village of Lee. He was one of the wealthiest men in the area. His newly purchased house was in the top tax band, measured in those days by the number of chimneys. His house had 15. The date of Thomson's death is uncertain but it is given by a local historian as 1676. Not surprisingly in view of his Caribbean dealings, Thomson left property scattered around the Caribbean, in St Christopher, Barbados and Antigua.

The Royal African Company took over the role of the Guinea Company and came to dominate the slave trade. Several members of the Company were co-members with John Evelyn of the Council for Foreign Plantations and were, therefore, strategically placed for their trade in enslaved Africans. In January 1663, on the granting of a new charter, slave trading was officially stated as an aim of the company. In the eight months to March 1664 the company delivered 3,075 enslaved Africans to Barbados. In the period from 1673 to 1689, it sold 26,245 Africans into slavery in Barbados alone.

Pepys' Black London

The paucity of material on the life of black people in London during the 17th century makes for immense difficulty in the documentation of the black experience. However, a glimpse through Pepys' diary gives both a record and some indication as to the reasons for such lack of material.

Trade on the scale which developed in the West Indies of the late 17th century required settlement by whites. It also required movement back and forth to the motherland by planters, merchants, naval personnel and their families. Accustomed to a lifestyle dependent on cheap serving people in the new colonies, settlers and their families travelled with their slaves. In addition, sea captains were allowed to bring in an allowance of slaves. Thus, another wave of black people were introduced to Britain through the ports, principally London.

As the ship weathervane on Deptford Town Hall reminds us, the area was a thoroughfare for ships and shipping. Ships were built and launched, refitted and repaired, unloaded and restocked on the Deptford waterfront. Many of those enriched by the African Caribbean trade began and ended each trip at Deptford. They brought with them slaves, symbols of wealth. Deptford became a key area for these newly arrived individuals whose number would increase as the trade developed. Still other slaves may have found themselves in the vicinity via other routes. As sales or gifts, black people may also have come through a number of other ports before reaching Kentish London.

Black people were certainly a topic of interest, at least among those with naval or nautical connections. Pepys recalls several bouts of drinking which included the swapping of stories about blacks and slavery.

Among other things, he and the other Captains that were with us tell me that Negros drowned look white and lose their blacknesse – which I never heard before.

A range of services were cheaply provided by black people, many of whom proved themselves to be valuable domestic help. Pepys confirms his personal experience of this in the following entry:

and for a cookmaid, we have ever since Bridget went used a blackmoore of Mr. Batelier's (Doll) who dresses our meat mighty well, and we mightily pleased with her.

On 27th March 1661 Pepys reflected on his first attempts at dancing. To make up the numbers required for the dancing figure, the masters of the household prevailed upon two black domestics to join in.

At last we made Mingo, Sir. W. Batten's black, and Jack, Sir W. Pens, dance; and it was strange how the first did dance with a great deal of seeming skill.

Mingo is also recorded as entertaining the guests with a parrot and delivering messages, including one which helped Pepys to hide from visitors who were seeking him out with a view to possible arrest.

These domestic details show Samuel Pepys, a gentleman of his times, conforming to the social trend in which such well to-do citizens had within their households black servants, or indeed, slaves. While Pepys' diary offers us the minutest detail of white London life, how Doll, Mingo or Jack viewed their service in 17th century London is nowhere recorded.

Black people were often treated as curiosities. Pepys records a visit to Sir R Viner's, the proud owner of an opulent residence with window cases, door cases and chimneys remarkable for having all been made of marble. On a conducted tour

he showed me a black boy that he had that died of a consumption; and being dead, he caused him to be dried in an oven, and lies there entire in a box. And so to dinner...

That the subject of blacks was a contemporary issue in such 17th century circles is very clear. This was of heightened interest to those involved in trade and nautical matters, the circle within which Samuel Pepys moved.

Entered in the Register

While English people like Katherine Rokeby were dying and being buried in the Caribbean, Africans were dying and being buried in Britain. Some had arrived on slaveships at a number of different ports; others had come from the Caribbean with planters, merchants or officials visiting or returning from the West Indies. A key difference was that for the families of Africans taken into slavery, there was virtually no chance of them ever being traced. There would be no monumental inscriptions like that for the 19 year old member of the Annesley family.

Recorded in the late 17th century burial register of St Nicholas' Church, Deptford, however, are the following deaths of Africans, their family names irrevocably lost:

4 April	1676	Affee, a black
13 December	1678	John Punch
23 May	1690	Jane Williams, a black
11 March	1695/6	A Moor
17 November	1696	Richard Murrey, black

No other details are given but it may be that one of the group managed to keep his own name. Affee, which does not seem English, bears some resemblance to the name Kofi in the Akan tradition. This would suggest a connection with Ghana.

On several counts Deptford was central to the African-Caribbean trade and the black presence in the South East London area. Firstly, there was the crucial link through the navy. In the late 17th century naval vessels sailed to and from the Caribbean, carrying the slaves of those becoming accustomed to the new lifestyle evolving in the Caribbean. Sea captains brought with them their allowance of slaves to be sold, left as gifts or disposed of at will. Secondly, Deptford remained a port of some significance to trade with Africa and the Caribbean. A steady black presence became established locally at the same time as esteemed members of the local community were building up increasing profits from the slave trade.

To a great extent, despite their increasing numbers, blacks remained largely invisible in 17th century Kentish London. Isolated in employment, they remained mainly within the homes of wealthy individuals. This growing black presence, largely as servants, reflected Britain's increased involvement in the Caribbean and her trade in enslaved Africans.

The Monck-Thomson-Annesley triangle indicates ways in which local relationships developed which were used to exploit Africa and Africans. The financial benefits reaped were subsequently invested in the mother country to enrich individual families, purchase status positions and support local economies as well as, in the longer term, general national prosperity. Such was the basis of the relationship between Britain, Africa and the Caribbean in the 17th century. The next chapter looks more closely at how local wealth produced through the enslavement and degradation of Africans supported the lives of white masters at the expense of the black poor and dispossessed.

MANOR HOUSES AND THE BLACK POOR

"Oppression I can bear with patience, because it hath always been my lot; but when to this is added insult and reproach from the authors of my miseries, I am forced to take up arms in my defence, and to abide the issue of the conflict." ROBERT WEDDERBURN

We have seen how black people began to be brought into Lewisham areas such as Lee and Deptford as a result of a national thrust towards quick profits. Enriched slaving merchants used their new profits to buy land and titles, symbols of status and power.

The Manor House at Lee

In Henry VII's reign the manor house of Lee was set in 575 acres of arable land, an area larger than some West Indian islands. Between that period and the early 1700s the land was bought and sold many times over. In the 18th century, when so many ships left Deptford for Africa and the West Indies, many who amassed fortunes through slavery invested in property which reflected their status and wealth.

The actual buying and selling of slaves was only one of many ways to make money out of slavery. Fortunes were also reaped through shipping. Great sums grew from commission agencies supplying the growing population in the West Indies with a range of commodities from manacles to foodstuffs. Plantation owners bought their labour cheap and sold their sugar as competitively as the market allowed. Despite fluctuations, profits were enormous. London merchants were foremost among those to profit from slavery, handling some 75 per cent of the sugar imported. They were the 'upwardly mobile' of the era and their lavish carriages, social gatherings, fashionable clothes and the constant attendance of their black slaves marked them out as newly rich. With titles added where possible, they became members of the landed gentry. Many bought safe seats in Parliament.

When Wealth Survives

A number of local residents profited directly from the African Caribbean connection. John Thomson, son of Maurice Thomson, kept the lease of Lee House for three years after his father's death. Like many whose wealth was founded on slavery, he became a member of 'the mother of parliaments', a knight and was later made Baron Haversham. His wife, Frances Annesley, was a member of that other old Lee family mentioned in the previous chapter. The signature of her father, Arthur Annesley, Earl of Anglesey, is to be found on many documents affecting the governing of newly founded colonies in the West Indies, including petitions from Maurice Thomson and other merchants.

William Coleman also came to live in Lee. He was a factor or agent based in London who specialised in West Indian trading. In effect, merchants like Coleman gave credit to individual planters, handled their goods and dealt with their supplies for a commission. Coleman took up residence at the Manor House Lee around 1750. Already

66 when he bought the property, Coleman made a number of further property purchases which extended the family estate locally. In February 1748 part of Lee Farm had been added. In April 1766 more land was acquired.

Coleman's wife, already deceased when he moved to Lee, had been related to one of the Deputy Governors of St Christopher. As a young man in the 1720s, Coleman had been the London agent for the West Indian proprietor and planter John Pinney and his heirs. Pinney was a plantation owner in Nevis, a sister island of St Christopher. It has been suggested that Pinney himself may have been associated with Lee. There is insufficient evidence to be sure but the Lee Church Rate Book records a Mr Piney in the village from 1761 and other Piney family members are buried locally.

John Pinney, a respected and responsible planter active in political affairs in Nevis, treated his slaves in the manner of the times. Profit through sugar was the first consideration. Pinney is reputed to have

> made his (black) boiler test the sugar before striking by dipping thumb and forefinger into the scalding syrup to see whether the sugar that stuck spun a thread of the right consistency.

10/11. Francis Baring, who built the Manor House at Lee (below), was the most famous of the many slaveholding men who lived on the estate in the 18th century. Baring is said to have made his first money out of dealing in slaves while still a very young man of 16.

Thomas Lucas was nephew and partner to William Coleman. Their business partnership was known as Coleman & Lucas. The firm continued a business relationship with John Pinney in Nevis until 1773. It is thought that the property purchased at Lee was an investment in favour of Lucas. When Coleman died, some 88 years old in 1771, his chief heir was Thomas Lucas whose inheritance included not only the manor house at Lee but also property in the West Indies. It was partly due to Lucas' recommendation to Governor Woodley that the younger John Pinney was appointed a seat on the council of Nevis.

Planters had political as well as economic power in the West Indies. They also became involved in politics in London and the south east. Thomas Lucas was elected an MP for Cornwall in 1780, became treasurer of Guy's Hospital in 1764 and its president in 1775. When he lost his Parliamentary seat four years later, one of the new MPs for his area was Francis Baring who also succeeded him in his residence at Lee.

Lucas established a family tomb at St Margaret's, Lee. His first wife was buried there in 1756 and his second wife in 1776. On his own death in 1784 most of his property passed to his third wife, Eliza, who subsequently married John Angerstein of Greenwich, taking her inherited property into her marriage with him.

Francis Baring was apprenticed to the leading Manchester and West Indies merchant Samuel Touchet. Said to have made his first money out of dealing in slaves while still a very young man of 16, Baring's rise in the financial world made his a household name. Like many merchants of the time, he dealt in a number of trades. He joined the Baring family linen and wool business based in Exeter and London and developed it into a merchant banking house, a route taken by a number of successful businessmen. He was made a baronet in 1793 and three years later he purchased the manor house and estate in Lee. He later enlarged the estate and built the present Manor House. By 1815 Baring's had become the top merchant banking house. The bank has been in the international spotlight in 1995 when a single broker, Nicholas Leeson, caused its bankruptcy. Baring Road, Lee runs from the South Circular to Grove Park.

The Slavers of Blackheath

Some 20 merchants lived around the edge of Blackheath in the 18th century, several of whom were closely involved in the slave trade and slave plantations. William Innes of Grotes Place was a leading West India merchant and supporter of the slave trade. Thomas King of Dartmouth Grove was a partner in the firm of slave agents Camden, Calvert & King. Francis Abbatt, perhaps best remembered for founding the Blackheath Golf Club, was also a shipping merchant and made much of his wealth shipping slaves.

Samuel and Thomas Fludyer were partners in a well-known firm of warehousemen and merchants. They traded widely as West India merchants and were designated as such in the Universal Directory of 1763 which was intended to assist "foreigners to avoid dealing with warehousemen who call themselves Merchants, whereas their proper business is to supply the Retailer".

In 1744, Alderman Samuel Fludyer purchased the prestigious Dacre House in Blackheath and, some years later, added a cherry orchard to the estate. In 1747 the wealthy alderman is reputed to have spent the considerable sum of £1,500 on his campaign to be elected for Parliament. He was elected MP for Chippenham in 1754 and no doubt used his influence in the House of Commons on behalf of the West

Indian planters and fellow merchants. Thomas Fludyer was knighted and in 1757 Samuel was made a baronet. In 1761 he was Lord Mayor of London.

Probably the most famous of the Blackheath businessmen was John Julius Angerstein, founder of Lloyds of London. A cautious businessman, Angerstein appears to have made much of his wealth through East Indian trade but he inherited extensive West Indian business interests through his wife's earlier marriage to Thomas Lucas. He owned a third share in a slave estate in Grenada, one of the islands ceded to England at the end of the Anglo-French Seven Years War (1756-63).

Angerstein built Woodlands House at Blackheath between 1772 and 1774, the year he formulated the general policies on which Lloyds is still based. Angerstein's painting collection became the foundation for the National Gallery. His family remained at Woodlands until the 1780s.

12/13. John Julius Angerstein, slave trader, art lover and founder of Lloyds of London. Below is Woodlands House which, like Baring's Manor House, was put to use in the 20th century as a local history centre.

He was MP for Camelford from 1796 to 1802. He died in 1823 and is buried at St John's church, Blackheath. His son John Julius William Angerstein, born in 1801, rose to Colonel in the 4th West Indian Regiment.

The grand residences of both Francis Baring and John Julius Angerstein came to be publicly owned in the

20th century and shared a similar use. Frances Baring's Manor House was Lewisham's Local History Centre until 1994 and is still in use as a branch library. Angerstein's Woodlands houses the Greenwich Local History Centre.

Iron merchant Ambrose Crowley, who moved to Greenwich in 1704, made a fortune producing manacles, ankle irons and collars. These were indispensible, for the securing and transportation of slaves both within Africa and during the traumatic and lengthy 'Middle Passage', the Atlantic crossing from Africa to the Caribbean.

Duncan Campbell, the overseer of the prison hulk system and another Greenwich worthy, was a plantation owner in Jamaica. He was an uncle of Captain William Bligh's wife. For four years he employed Bligh in the command of ships carrying plantation goods, sugar and rum, between Jamaica and Britain. Campbell recommended Bligh for the command of *The Bounty*.

Mutiny and the Breadfruit Tree

When Britain assumed a presence in Caribbean waters, a role was created which could not be retained without a degree of policing. Thus, a good many naval officials saw service in the Caribbean. In 1750 William Coleman took possession of the Manor House, Lee from a Captain Limeburner who had served as captain of the frigate *Seahorse*. Limeburner was successful in anti-privateering duties, realising many a seaman's dream by capturing a Spanish prize, *Le Galgo*. Captain Limeburner died in December 1750 and is buried at St Margaret's Lee.

The frequency of mutinies on slave ships is unsurprising given the large number of seamen pressed into service, captains legendary for discipline based on the whip and the harsh conditions both on board ship and on the sweltering slave coast. One mutiny, which took place on *HMS Chesterfield* off the coast of West Africa in 1748 involved the lieutenant of marines, a gang of carpenters and other crew members. Gastrill, the ship's boatswain, recovered the vessel from the mutineers. For six weeks he took charge and finally delivered the slaver and the imprisoned mutineers to Barbados. Gastrill was rewarded by being appointed Master Attendant of Woolwich Dockyard and in 1776 he became Lieutenant at Deptford Yard.

Like Gastrill, Captain William Bligh also knew mutiny at first hand but his most important role in the service of West Indian trade was to introduce the breadfruit to the Caribbean. The breadfruit tree was of enormous benefit to the planters in their quest for economical sources of food for their slaves. It required little land and grew in plentiful supply. It also used less labour than the 'ground provisions' like plantain and yams, favoured by the Africans. The tree bore its large fruit, the size of a man's head, all the year round.

14. Breadfruit tree, cheap food for slaves

The king having been graciously pleased to comply with a request from the merchants and planters interested in his Majesty's West India possessions, that the bread fruit tree might be introduced into those islands, a vessel proper for the undertaking, was bought, and taken into dock at Deptford, to be provided with the necessary fixtures and preparations for executing the object of the voyage...The ship was named the Bounty: I was appointed to command her on the 16th August 1787. WILLIAM BLIGH

Feeding an enslaved labouring force cheaply was a practical matter for the planters whose property contemporary law declared them to be. Bligh's first attempt to get breadfruit trees from the South Seas needs to be seen in this light. While enlightened governors saw self-sufficiency in individual territories as desirable, the profit motive made many planters and merchants direct their labour force exclusively towards sugar production, avoiding any substantial investment in food crops.

The Inhabitants are so Intent upon making of Sugars which it seems turn to better Account, that they Chuse rather to Purchase those Commoditys (flour, bread, corn, beef, pork, butter, salt-fish, rice, staves, lumber and horses) from their Neghbours than to employ their own Slaves in that work. GOVERNOR ROBERT HUNTER TO THE BOARD OF TRADE, 1731

Imported food arrived from Britain, America and Ireland. After a period of war embargo during the American Revolution and a succession of hurricanes which devastated plantations, thousands of slaves died. Representation was made to the British government. The planters estimated that 15,000 slaves died in the seven years to 1787 mainly due to the famine caused by hurricane. Undernourished and poorly housed, slaves fell prey to diseases. The catastrophic loss of slaves combined with tightening regulations imposed by Britain concerning the subsistence of the slave population stirred the planters to action. They wanted to find ways of feeding slaves that would not tie up too much land in food crops. An Act of 1788 required plantation owners to plant at least one acre of land for every four slaves for the provision of food, although the number of slaves living off each acre was subsequently increased.

Bligh, who had sailed with Captain Cook on his third trip, served on a warship in the American War of Independence. Like many seamen of the time, he also enjoyed a spell in the merchant marines. Bligh's first botanical trip, commissioned by the British government and sponsored by West Indian planters, is notorious for having come to a mutinous and abortive end. On returning to London in March 1790, Bligh was exonerated by court martial and voted 500 guineas by the House of Assembly of Jamaica. Bligh lived in what is now Lambeth Road, near to the present Imperial War Museum as a GLC plaque testifies.

In March 1791 Bligh set off again, this time with two large ships and a detachment of marines. His mission was to take breadfruit and other plants to the West Indies and also to collect and distribute plants on the way and back. In February 1793 the expedition arrived at Port Royal, Jamaica and some 347 breadfruit trees were landed. By August the ships had returned from the South Seas expedition and lay anchored at Deptford.

The planting of breadfruit trees in the West Indies was considered a great success by Britain and the white West Indians. However, no-one had consulted the Africans who were destined to be the chief consumers of the breadfruit. It was, therefore, a long time before its culinary value was generally appreciated since the African palate proved more discriminating than had been anticipated.

The negro, however, who is a pretty good judge of the substantial benefits of vegetable production, regards this stranger with cold apathy; except as a novelty, he prefers the cultivation of his more productive and substantial plantain, and his more palatable and nutritive yam. JOHN STEWART, 1808

Growing Black Presence in the South East

Throughout the 18th century the number of black people in South East London was growing. Contemporary estimates of black people in London varied considerably and debate about the figures continues. In 1723 the *Daily Journal* reported

a great number of Blacks come daily into this city so that its thought in a short time, if they be no suppress'd the city will swarm with them.

The correspondent did not suggest a figure for those "great numbers". In the 1760s the *Gentleman's Magazine* guessed at 20,000 while the *Morning Chronicle* suggested 30,000 in Britain. Scholars are still assessing and reassessing the numbers but it is clear that the growing number of black people in South East London was part of a general trend. From St Nicholas', Deptford the burials recorded in the parish registers show a nearly twofold increase on the previous century.

13 January	1719/20	John Peterson, a negro from New Street
16 July	1719	Thomas Cestus, a negro servt to Wm. Sherwin, surgeon, The Green
27 April	1721	Enos Cross, a negro from the Red House
29 September	1724	Serica, a black servant to Mdm. Benbow, deceased
16 October	1724	Thomas Berry, a negro mariner
28 February	1742/43	Michael Quorey, a negro, per Towne
18 October	1759	Peter, A negro
24 December	1771	Wash Roberts, a black
31 December	1785	William Brown, a blackman

Of the registered black deaths for the parish of St Nicholas', Deptford during the 18th century only Serica, the black servant of Madame Benbow, was female. The reason for so singularly fewer recorded female deaths must be that the local black population was overwhelmingly male.

Negro Mariners

As well as the familiar servant status, the occupations given for the group above include that of mariner. In 1724, for the first time in Deptford's history, a black seaman appears in the records. As the distinction between slave and servant was blurred in the case of Africans in service, so too was that between seaman and slave.

The burial register of St Paul's Deptford gives two entries for May 1783.

| 20 May | 1783 | William Talar, a black of Red House Wharf |
| 25 May | 1783 | John McCoy, a black drowned |

It is likely that William Talar worked at Red House Wharf, which since 1742 had been the official victualling yard for the Royal Navy as well as providing storage and provisions for merchant ships. This local connection means that Enos Cross could have been not, as we might think, from a local property with the name Red House but also a worker at the Victualling Yard. And what of John McCoy? Was his drowning an occupational hazard, an accident or something more untoward? These questions show the qualities of parish registers for black history, both the frustrations and the sense of discovery.

The number of black people living in the area increased with the building of the Royal Hospital for Seamen at Greenwich. This was founded by William III and Mary II to house over 2,000 sailors from the Royal Navy who, because of old age or infirmity, could no longer earn their living at sea. Black sailors were among its residents and they were also treated at the Dreadnought Seamen's Hospital moored off Deptford.

15. Royal Dreadnought Hospital ship, moored off Deptford. Along the side is painted the slogan 'For Seamen of all Nations

What is believed to be the first book written in English by a black man was the Narrative of Briton Hammon published in Boston in 1760. Hammon served on both merchant and military ships and spent six weeks in the Greenwich Hospital for Seamen with a dangerous fever, alongside many other West Indian and Lascar sailors. After gaining his freedom Hammon eventually re-settled in America. He greeted his freedom with a biblical reference.

And now, that in the Providence of that God, who delivered his servant David out of the paw of the lion and out of the paw of the Bear, I am freed from that long and dreadful captivity. BRITON HAMMON

Black Soldiers Join the London Poor

During the American War of Independence many blacks served the British, having been promised their freedom. The first 300 soldiers formed the Royal Ethiopian Regiment with the slogan 'Liberty to Slaves' on their uniforms. Despite poor treatment and American efforts to woo them, 10,000 joined the British. They were used as shock troops, as cavalry, as guides, spies and couriers. The Black Pioneers were used as labourers. At least 14,000 were evacuated when the British left America, thousands more fled to Canada. Hundreds of discharged black soldiers arrived in London. The Commissioners for American Claims were less generous to them than to white loyalist refugees and as a result many joined the ranks of London's black poor. By 1786 there were at least 1,144 black people [?] living in London.

The presence of black people in Britain became significant, especially in London and ports like Bristol, Cardiff, and Liverpool, as a direct consequence of Britain's involvement in the Atlantic slave trade and its colonial expansion, including the American colonies which were also served with slave labour. Slaves were constantly resold and the Kentish London area was frequently one of many temporary homes in the longest journey.

Between 10,000 and 15,000 black people lived in London during the 18th century. Significant black communities are thought to have been concentrated in Mile End, Stepney, Paddington and the St Giles area. Some of these would have been runaways and freed slaves. They were banned from taking apprenticeships by London's Lord Mayor in 1731. Many of the black population shared an impoverished existence with thousands of whites.

Norma Myers estimates that at least 5,000 black people must have been living in London at any one time during the late-18th century. Figures vary considerably from one source to another. Concentrations of black people would have been more visible in one area rather than another.

Through Deptford to the Horn Fair

During the 17th and 18th centuries there was an annual Horn Fair held at Charlton. People met at Cuckold's Point near Deptford, then marched through Deptford and Greenwich to Charlton with horns of different kinds on their heads. The following account from 1700 describes the scene at New Dock near Deptford.

Having past by a great Number of these Condescending Mortals, we came to a Field which led to the Entrance of the Dock, about a Stones Cast on this side of which, were a parcel of West-Indian-Creoleians, lately come on Shore, Cooking in the open Air, and English Porker after the Indian manner...

Arriving in Deptford, the writer comments on the local seamen's wives who *live upon Publick Credit till their return, who if it were not for the Benevolence of a well-disposed Neighbouring Knight, and a few more Charitable Worthy Gentlemen, they might, tho' married, grow Sullen, like the Negro women, for want of Husbands, and pine away because Nature is not supply'd with due Accomodation.*

The Suffering Black Poor

I am happy to find that some humane persons have interested themselves in favour of the poor Blacks, whose wretchedness the streets of London too *plainly bring to view. Among these poor sufferers, it should be remarked, that the Lascars and other East Indian mendicants demand your pity only; but that the African Negroes have an actual claim on our justice: They, or the greater part of them, have served Britain, have fought under her colours, and after having quitted the service of their American masters, depending on the promise of protection held out to them by British Governors and Commanders, are now left to perish by famine and cold, in the sight of that people for whom they have hazarded their lives, and even (many of them) spilt their blood. Britain, though unfortunate in her last contest, has yet preserved her honour inviolate. Those who quitted estates and offices for her sake, have found her non ungrateful to such steady friends – And shall these poor humble assertors of her rights be left to the agonies of want and despair; because they are unfriended and unknown? – Forbid it, honour! – Forbid it, justice and gratitude! – There is, I am told a township in Nova Scotia settled and inhabited by Negroes, in the same predicament with the Blacks who daily perish in our streets. Would it not be a deed of real charity, and of use to society, to send these poor creatures to their countrymen at this settlement? Gratitude, humanity, and politics join to excite the attention of the public towards a set of people the most thoroughly wretched; and at the same time the most innocent, of any who have ever merited the appelation of vagabonds.* THE PUBLIC ADVERTISER, JANUARY 1786*

The ranks of the black poor were increased by impoverished Lascar seamen. In 1786 a 'Committee of Gentlemen' was established to organise relief for the Lascars and this was extended to the black poor. Later renamed the Committee for the Black Poor, by April 1789 it had helped 460 people and by September, it was helping nearly 1,000, largely funded by the Government. But who were the black poor?

Servants would occupy a place in that category, particularly when their employment was insecure. Black women were frequently employed as servants. With the 1731 restrictions on apprenticeships for black men, the possibility of skilled employment was closed. There was also a group of black individuals who 'belonged to' a specified employer. These inhabited a twilight world between slavery and wage earner. While some had slave collars to remind them of their status, others served on board ship as common tars who shared a precarious existence with white seamen. Provision for the support of the poor in the 18th century was severely limited. When black people were perceived either as property or as servants, concern for their pauper existence is hardly to be expected. The battle had first to be won for black people to be respected as humans with even notional rights.

On the other hand, those who profited from the misery of the slave trade which removed black people from their homes, families and cultures, transferring them to an unrelenting role of service and labour, enjoyed an enhanced lifestyle. British West Indian plantations, valued at £50 million in 1775, were worth £70 million only three years later. This wealth gave access to rewards and positions of power at the same time that black people, lynchpins in the creation of that wealth, were denied the only meaningful right of the period – the right of settlement. This 'ancient right' allowed the white poor parish relief in the place where they had been born. Ripped from their place of birth, London's blacks had no access to this safety net.

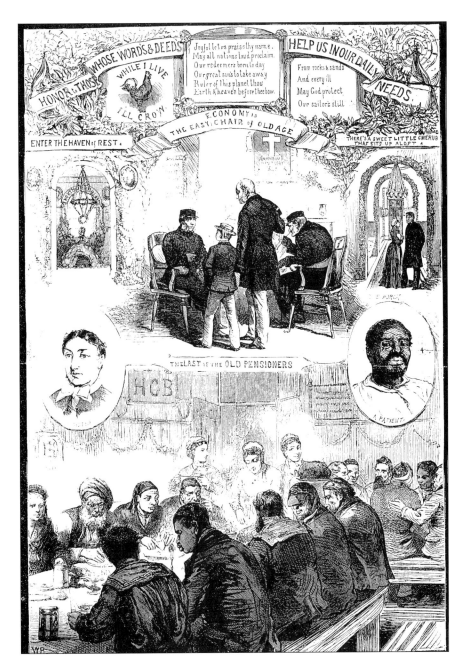

16. *The Royal Hospital for Seamen at Greenwich, housing over 2,000 elderly or infirm sailors from the Royal Navy. The mixture of races shows that naval service was one version of the journey to South East London.*

PART TWO

Aya (fern)
'I am not
afraid of
you.'
Symbol
of
defiance

The fight for freedom

4

RESISTANCE IN LONDON'S SOUTH EAST

"I would rather die upon yonder gallows than live in slavery" SAM SHARPE

Pockets of resistance to the conditions and institution of slavery were to be found among the black poor. Anti-slavery action ranged from the small-scale acts of individual slaves, such as running away, to the more concerted and influential protest of black individuals with a published voice. Several examples of 'anti-slavery resistance' may be found locally, some surprising. Baptism, for example, is not usually considered an act of resistance but, as adopted by enslaved Africans, it showed an intention to undermine the institution of slavery. Running away, in contrast, involved no such ambiguity and many a runaway would have added to the ranks of the black poor.

Appropriation of goods, open revolt, engagement in legal proceedings and civil disobedience all played a part. While each of these served a limited purpose, the increasing use of an informed, public voice was to have wide-reaching effects.

Baptism

In the parish register of St Mary's, Lewisham are the following entries for baptism:

5 November	1717	Charles Nevis, a black adult moor
5 November	1717	Anne, a black Moor adult
24 March	1750	James Purcell, a black servant to Mr Purcell at Mr Boydes at Lewisham, aged about 32 years.

At St Margaret's, Lee the following baptisms took place:

30 April	1710	Francis Lee, a black boy belonging to Major Ascough
13 June	1725	Belinda Charleton, a black maid lodging at Blackheath
11 July	1737	John Cuffey, a negro manservant of Mr Collett

In 1750, the year that James Purcell was baptised in Lewisham, the following item appeared in a London newspaper.

Last Saturday two daughters of Major Askew, formerly Deputy-Governor of Jamaica went to Deptford, in order to embark there on board the ship Mermaid

for Jamaica together with the four blacks the said gentleman brought over with him, who were lately christen'd at St George the Martyr, the air of this country not agreeing with the young Gentlewomen; not long since their mother and another Daughter who came over from thence, died here.

In contrast to the white population, most of the baptised black people were adults. There is little research evidence which compares baptism in metropolitan areas like London with equivalent practices in the West Indies. It is likely, however, that baptism seemed more attractive in London where freedom seemed more possible.

There are 17 entries of black baptism for the period 1783-1812 in the Lewisham area. The figure represents one per cent of the total number of baptisms for the locality. Using these baptism figures alone, a projected minimum one per cent local black population is suggested.

Why were these adult Africans keen to be baptised, sometimes in opposition to their masters' wishes? On one level this evidently demonstrates a willingness to embrace Christianity. On the other hand, misunderstanding about the nature of Christianity cannot be ruled out, particularly around the meaning of the idea of salvation.

He that believeth and is baptised shall be saved; but he that believeth not shall be damned. BOOK OF COMMON PRAYER

This was a crucial part of the Christian message to black people in preparation for baptism as older converts. Through baptism, slaves became 'heirs of salvation'. It is difficult to determine how this message could be comprehended by people in bondage or in constant danger of bondage, unless salvation was understood in terms of some kind of freedom. Add to this the general knowledge based on a legal ruling of 1677 that blacks as infidels could be purchased and sold and it can be understood that, for some blacks, baptism was a logical act of resistance.

Francis Lee: 'Belonging' and the Denial of Family

But what of Francis Lee, the only black child in the group? The only detail known about him is that he was "a black boy belonging to Major Ascough". The destruction of African families displaced in the Caribbean can be seen here. It is not known how old Lee was, whether he was acquired in Africa, on board ship or on Caribbean soil. What is known is that his mother and father, as slaves, had no claims, rights or responsibilities to their offspring.

Born to slave parents, the young Francis Lee entered the same world of denial of basic rights. As slaves, children could be sold at any moment. They could be removed from one plantation to another or from one country to another. To be a child slave was to be denied precisely the family circumstances universally held to be nurturing to the human young. Consider the characteristic physical bonding of West African mothers and their young ones, still depicted in carvings and sculptures of the 20th century. The child is not swaddled and laid aside but carried, kept in place on the mother's back as she goes about her domestic routine by a strategically placed cotton wrap. Often this practice, still evident among the African population in areas like Lewisham, was enjoyed by the child until he or she was displaced by a newer sibling. Even then, older girls would assume the role of baby carrier. The misery for parents and children on denial of such taken-for-granted family rituals can be imagined.

Major Thomas Ascough is indicated as the master or owner of Francis Lee. Whether Francis was sent to London by his master who had been stationed in Jamaica since his arrival there with Venables and Penn, or whether he travelled with him on a visit to London is a matter of conjecture. The Major Askew mentioned earlier, whose daughters returned to Jamaica from Deptford in October 1750, is likely to be of the same family.

Runaways

For each slave arriving in London freedom must have been a desire, at least some of the time. Many would have known or heard of those who, in favourable circumstances, seized the opportunity and ran away to freedom.

Port areas and towns in Britain would have appeared densely populated to slaves more used to rural or provincial settings. To some, this was an opportunity that could not be ignored to make a bid for freedom. The prospect of freedom in foreign territory such as South East London, away from the rigours of plantation subsistence and persistent physical abuse, would be worth the hazards. These were well known. The ultimate penalty was death. More usually, there was a severe beating. Despite this, many slaves tried to run away both in the West Indies and on English soil.

The prospect of physical abuse was seldom far away as the following newspaper item illustrates.

Dec. 1772: On Saturday a Captain at Deptford beat his Negro boy in so cruel a manner, that he died yesterday by the bruises he received. The Captain has absconded.

Was this an unusual case? The incident, recognised as murder by modern standards, was not generally held to be so in 1772. The essential distinction, upheld by the courts in the case of black people jettisoned in mid-Atlantic with shipowners making consequent claims for insurance on their cargo, was that enslaved Africans were chattel not unlike horses. The boy beaten to death was legally held to be the property of the Deptford captain. Had the captain beaten to death someone else's slave compensation could be claimed by the wronged master.

This fatal story illustrates the precariousness of slave life whether abroad or on local soil. It is hardly any wonder that some black people resorted to running away. Hope lay in the possibility of employment, however menial. It lay in avoiding the whip, a legendary symbol of slavery. A whole culture grew out of the use of the whip, the material for which was chosen with particular care. The skins of animals were often used for such instruments of torture. The hide of the Manatea or seacow, described as having skin an inch thick, was used by the white West Indians in thongs for punishing slaves.

Black Convicts

It is difficult to assess how frequently slaves stole from their masters. Certainly when they were caught, the penalty was exacting. Billy Blue and John Caesar were two seamen who paid a steep price for gaining criminal records.

Before the British settlement of Australia in 1788, political dissenters and criminals were transported to America and the West Indies. After the American War of Independence ended in 1783, penal transportees were sent instead to Australia including hundreds of black people. John Caesar and William 'Billy' Blue, both of whom lived for a while in Deptford, were among the earliest convicts. Caesar, "a powerfully built negro" was convicted at Maidstone in March 1785 and held on one of the Thames prison hulks until the First Fleet sailed for Botany Bay in 1787. On arrival Caesar was sent to labour in chains on Garden Island in Sydney Harbour. Australia's first bushranger, Caesar managed to escape in April 1789 with a musket, some rations and an iron cooking pot. He survived for 19 days by steeling from the settlements on the mainland. When he was caught he returned to the island but escaped again, stealing a canoe from 'the blackfellows' (Aborigines). After a month he was caught and banished to Norfolk Island. Five years later he fled into the woods and by the end of January 1796 a reward of five gallons of rum was offered for his capture. In February he was ambushed and shot dead by bounty hunters in a place known, ironically enough, as Liberty Plains.

Whether Billy Blue came to England via the West Indies or from America or indeed Canada is not known. The national identity of blacks during the era of slavery was, in any case, a very fluid matter. Blacks were sold and re-sold in different countries, even sometimes when they were freedmen but did not have the documentation to prove

17. Billy Blue who lived at Deptford, was convicted of stealing sugar from a West Indian ship to feed his chocolate-making business. Transported to Australia, he became a trusted ferryman and watchman, known affectionately as 'The Old Commodore'.

themselves. What little we know of his early life comes from a petition he sent to Governor Brisbane in 1823 when he was 89 years old. He said he had been in the service of George III and was a marine in the British attack on Quebeck in 1759. During the wars of American Independence Blue was a 'spie or guide' for the British army, suggesting perhaps that he was of North American Indian ancestry.

Billy Blue was a 'lumper' at Deptford dockyard and was convicted in 1796 of stealing sugar from the Lady Jane Halliday, a West Indian ship. He was said to have had a chocolate-making business and was therefore considered a dangerous sugar-thief. He spent almost five years in the prison hulks before transportation. In 1804 Blue lived in a small hocks on the Rocks, a raucous area of taverns and straggling settlers' houses. When his sentence was served he married another convict Elizabeth Williams and acquired the license to ply the ferry in Sydney Harbour. Governor Macquarie, a frequent passenger on the ferry, dubbed Blue 'Comodore of the Fleet' and he was known afterwards as 'The Old Commodore'. Macquarie appointed Blue as Watchman at Sydney Cove and granted him 80 acres of land to the north of the harbour, now known as Blue's Point.

In 1818 Billy Blue was convicted of smuggling rum, but he was pardoned for this and a number of other offences because of his special relationship with the Governor. 'The Old Commodore' became a legend in his own lifetime and as he aged became increasingly eccentric. He would sometimes make his passengers row themselves across the harbour. He died in 1834, leaving the property at Blue's Point to his children.

Open Revolt: Mutiny on the Zant

In Britain, black people frequently lived isolated from each other, often in the households of the wealthy. Seamen, however, lived or worked in communities with others sharing similar difficulties and at the mercy of tyrannical masters. It is the stories of seamen like John Caesar that often provide examples of black people in revolt.

Stories of mutiny aboard slave ships were well known among naval and merchant seamen. Some black people had the opportunity in 18th century South East London to work on board ship. One black seaman, a 'free Negro', was employed as an ordinary seaman or 'common tar' on The Zant in 1721. He lived in Deptford and is remembered for having

...bred a Mutiney that we had too many Officers, and that the work was too hard, and what not.

This 'free Negro', it would seem, was not only involved in the mutiny but instigated it. As a result of his subversive action, several people turned against the captain and were known to have 'muttered' against his authority. One or two indiscreet seamen had even let it be understood that they "often wished that the said Ship was in the hand of Pyrates".

The captain of the ship had the black seaman promptly removed and he was subsequently detained on a man-of-war.

This action shows the breadth of 'resistance behaviour' in a range of circumstances affecting black people of the period and is a reminder that the perceived differences between freed men and slaves were not always indicative of status, community or lifestyle. Frequently, these imposed differences masked a shared community with a common bondage.

Legal Proceedings

The cases of John Caesar and Billy Blue offer examples of black people caught up in the process of the law through prosecution. But slaves sometimes sought engagement in legal proceedings during the period of slavery in order to improve the conditions of their existence. That they did so may be seen as both a tremendous act of faith and an act of resistance, challenging all they had learnt about African hopes of human rights at the hands of their white masters.

The case of Jonathon Strong was not local but it drew the attention of many who were to become important in anti-slavery action. It also focused interest on the commitment of the activist, Granville Sharp, who became involved in seeking justice for the victim. Jonathon Strong was a slave who was beaten by his master but survived. In 1765 he was found on the doorstep of Granville Sharp's brother. The Sharps took him to hospital where they paid for treatment. Two years later, having recovered from the near fatal beating, Jonathon was discovered after his master hired two professional slave hunters. Arrangements were made for his sale to another captain whose ship was bound for the West Indies.

18. Granville Sharp

Jonathon had taken the precaution of getting himself baptised, believing literally, as many of the enslaved did, that this would free him. When detained in jail on trumped-up charges, he sent to his godparents for help. Later he wrote to Granville Sharp, soliciting his legal help in the matter. The case was widely publicised.

While the Jonathon Strong case is not directly part of our local history, the case of the unnamed boy beaten to death at Deptford shows how vulnerable slaves were everywhere. A number of miscellaneous Deptford press cuttings confirm that such an incident was not rare. Several of these notices refer to captains sailing from Deptford. It was, in fact, the kind-hearted Sharps who were still a rarity.

Avoiding Resettlement

Deptford played a central part in the Sierra Leone Resettlement plan. As a solution to the 'problem' of the black poor, the scheme was devised with the help of the Royal Navy to re-settle hundreds of London's black population in Sierra Leone on the west coast of Africa.

Sierra Leone was an important a slaving area and there was great reluctance to accept an offer involving another sea voyage back into possible slavery. Also, blacks arriving from America had passed on information about a location of freed black people in Nova Scotia where a number of black loyalists had already settled. Some black people found the prospect of settling there more attractive than the unknown Sierra Leone.

Months passed and increasing pressure was placed upon the black poor to take up the resettlement offer. There were threats of arrest for begging under the Vagrancy Act. The public was urged to stop giving alms to the black poor.

Although opposed to the scheme, the leading London black activist, Olaudah Equiano, agreed to become commissary of provisions and stores for the journey. People began to board the navy ships *The Atlantic*, *The Belisaurius* and *The Vernon* waiting in the Thames at Deptford. Richard Weaver was one of the first would-be settlers to embark at Deptford and he was later selected as the first Chief in Command or Governor of Freetown.

As the months dragged by, 50 of those on board died from cold and disease. Many changed their minds and left the ships, especially after Lord George Gordon advised their leaders to reject the scheme.

> *We hear that some of the leaders of the seven hundred poor Black who had signed an engagement to go to a Free Settlement on the coast of Africa, submitted to the new system, intended for their government in Ethiopia, to the consideration of the Right Hon. Lord George Gordon, and requested his advice and opinion on the subject, before they sailed from England. His Lordship advised them not to go.*

Seven hundred had signed the agreement but, though the ships had been waiting since the end of October 1786, only 259 were aboard a full month later. Over 60 per cent had disregarded the agreements. The take-up of passage back to Africa was considerably less than planned even when boosted by a number of white women whose presence was used to fuel anti-abolitionist sentiment.

Of the 350 black emigrants who eventually set out for Sierra Leone on 23rd February 1787, 35 died during the voyage. The settlement proved to be disastrous. Many died and many others were sold to French slave traders. The agricultural exercise proved difficult to establish: seeds failed and the expected crops were a disappointment. During a conflict involving an American slave ship, a British man-of-war and a local ruler, the emigrants' town was burned down. After four years only 60 of the original group were left.

In 1791 Granville Sharp and Henry Thornton, the Chairman of the Sierra Leone Company, helped 1,100 black loyalists from Nova Scotia to settle in what is now Freetown. It is not known how many of these were maroons living in the remote area of Nanny Town, but it is likely that they would have been very interested in the prospect of returning to Africa. This initiative proved a much more successful operation and laid the foundations for modern Sierra Leone.

Developing an Informed Public Voice

The increasing use of an informed public voice was an act of resistance which not only satisfied the enslaved African's compulsion for engagement in struggles for liberation but also created allies better informed for having had access to information about slavery 'from the inside'.

Olaudah Equiano, known as Vassa during this stage of his life, never reached Sierra Leone. Instead he found himself in conflict with others involved in the expedition. He spoke out against fraudulent activities which inappropriately used up the Sierra Leone funds, thereby shortchanging the black people involved. Equiano protested and was dismissed from the project.

Equiano came to be known later as a writer and champion of the black cause. He emerged as one of the leaders of the black community in London in the second half of the 18th century. Like most forcibly transported Africans, Equiano harboured hope of being reunited with his homeland. Disappointed by the Sierra Leone experiment, he turned to writing and lecturing all over England on the subject of the black cause. His story will be treated more extensively in the next chapter.

Ignatius Sancho

The role determined for Africans once selected as slaves was that of cheap labour. They were considered unable to rise above the savage conditions from which they had been 'rescued' by whites. With a few notable exceptions, any literary or academic enterprise was severely discouraged.

Ignatius Sancho was born on a slaveship while crossing the Atlantic in 1729. The distressing situation of his

19. Ignatius Sancho, South East London's earliest black writer

birth can be surmised from what is known of conditions on board slave ships. Unlike men, women were generally not shackled. There were usually fewer women on board and they were stored separately from the men. Holed up in a severely cramped space used for eating, sleeping and crude toilet facilities, many African men and women died of dysentery and other contagious illnesses. Used to a more open air existence in tropical Africa, the slaves' experience of life in the dark slave quarters of a claustrophobic slave ship reeking like a cess pool would have been horrific. In these circumstances Ignatius Sancho was born, just another slave child entered as a number in the captain's log book.

It is hardly surprising that Sancho's mother died in childbirth. His young father, only a rough partition away from his wife but powerless to offer support of any kind, was one of a number of slaves who successfully resisted slavery through suicide. He seized a momentary opportunity to make the only bid he could for freedom, throwing himself overboard rather than further endure the destructions of slavery.

At about two years old Sancho was brought to Greenwich and became a servant to three young sisters. The Greenwich ladies were positively against the idea of his learning but Sancho ran away and successfully pleaded his cause with the Duchess of Montague, who employed him as a butler at Montague House in Blackheath. It is to the credit of the Duke and Duchess that they indulged what many would have seen as a bizarre tendency towards learning on the part of an African of indeterminate status. In the Montagues library, Sancho taught himself to read and write. That he envisaged such a possibility for himself and created the opportunity was a remarkable act of resistance to the narrowly prescribed routes mapped out for African slaves. Sancho's first publication *The Letters of Ignatius Sancho* captured the attention of the British public and became a bestseller. His was a stunning achievement not yet attained by other blacks.

The Duke of Montague had previously involved himself in the education of Francis Williams, a boy born to free blacks in Jamaica. Wishing to see if education would affect a black child in ways similar to a white, the duke had provided for the young Francis to be educated at a grammar school and then at Cambridge University. In 1722 Montague was granted some West Indian islands which included St Vincent. This suggests that the duke himself profited from the plantation system. The intriguing question is why Sancho went to the Montague household with his request for assistance. Could it be that this Blackheath personality was known by Sancho to have been involved in the education of another black person and therefore potentially sympathetic? It is likely that local black people would have seized any opportunity to exchange news and stories, particularly about sympathetic whites.

20. The Duke and Duchess of Montague who allowed Sancho access to their library at Montague House, Blackheath, where he fulfilled his ambition to learn to read.

Prior to the 18th century, there was an almost wholesale acceptance of slavery in Britain and there is little evidence that the closer proximity of slaves on British soil was itself enough to mobilise anti-slavery action among the white population. The act of running away and, particularly in the cases of those fortunate enough to have legal representation, the furore of the ensuing debates certainly stimulated the thoughts of observers. Moreover, the legal cases, whether for insurance claims or on humanitarian grounds, brought information about slavery to the attention of a wider public.

With the growing testimony of black voices such as Sancho's resistance was beginning to make an impact locally as well as nationally. It is true that Sancho's artistic interests were not always directed at presenting a case against slavery. Equiano was, in this respect, much more direct. However, what was significant in Sancho's case was that more people were getting used to the notion of a common humanity with black people, despite their overwhelming representation as slaves and servants.

5
THE STRUGGLE FOR EMANCIPATION

"...towards a total suppression of that infamous and iniquitous traffic of stealing, kidnapping, buying, selling and cruelly enslaving men!" Ottobah Cugoano, 1786

The groundswell that would so shake the foundations of Atlantic slavery as to finally dismantle it took several forms. In the Caribbean intermittent revolts gave expression to the fervour of local anti-slavery feelings. In London popular persuasion developed as the means to mobilise support that would lead to anti-slavery legislation and emancipation.

Until the mid 18th century the institution of slavery looked indomitable. Economic benefits to planters, merchants and the British national purse left it largely unchallenged in the metropolitan areas. It was only a matter of time, however, before the humanitarian contradictions integral to slavery became glaringly evident. One of the problems that would undo slavery lay among slaveholders themselves. There were planters and merchants from every social strata, including many who claimed the highest moral ground.

There is another argument, put by Eric Williams, that the demise of Atlantic slavery was due to it becoming economically out-moded. There is no attempt to argue against this here but rather to draw out the influences upon local action at the time. It is clear that the mobilisation of public opinion by committed individuals and groups played an important part in the anti-slavery movement. Where once there had been silence and acquiescence, many of those powerful enough to influence the public and to bring about changes in legislature did so out of a moral commitment which was freshly voiced and outspoken.

The Role of the Church in Slavery

In 1739 the Reverend John Wesley preached at Deptford in a place called Turner's Hall to an audience of some 2,000. With such a large turnout to see and hear the charismatic young preacher, the hall floor gave way. Wesley preached on regardless. He was a regular visitor to Deptford and had family connections with Dr Annesley, a member of the family resident in Lee in Tudor times. Wesley was not preaching against slavery. Like many Christian leaders of the time, he himself held slaves. His concern with slaves amounted to exhortation that they be good slaves and serve their masters well.

The Deptford Quaker Meeting House could not have held numbers to rival those attending John Wesley's sermon. It is ironical, however, that this Meeting House made its place in local history sources on account of William Penn's conversations with Peter the Great, Czar of Russia, who was a tenant at Sayes Court after Admiral Benbow. Later in the century the impact of Quaker information upon the wider world would impact upon the colonisation and slave practices that Penn had helped to put in place through his part in the conquest of Jamaica.

21. *Deptford Quaker Meeting House in the High Street, where Czar Peter the Great spoke with William Penn, the founder of Pennsylvania whose son conquered Jamaica for the English.*

18th century Britain boasted of its Christian principles yet it was reaping staggering profits from "stealing, kidnapping, buying, selling and cruelly enslaving men". Kentish London had its quota of both established and nonconformist churches.

Until the mid 18th century the church continued to defend the slavetrading practices of the state. With the expansion of trade went missionary expansion. Christianity was used as the ideological basis for moral and spiritual white superiority over enslaved people. The wealthy and influential condoned slavery. Members of different Christian groups held slaves. Individual Christians, though moved at times to charitable acts, did not seek to influence or change the practice of slavery. Yet, in London in 1757, dissent with the prevailing order came to the fore within the Quakers, a Christian sect as enriched by slave profit as any other.

In the Caribbean Quakers had been as involved with slavery as any other group, particularly in Barbados where, within 55 years of the first English settlers, 58 Quakers owned 1,626 slaves. Some of the Quaker slaveholders owned very large plantations and six of them owned more than 100 slaves each. However, it was not the planter Quakers in the Caribbean who pressed for change. Instead it was from the American group, preoccupied with issues of religious and secular liberty, that the call first came.

Quakers as Liberators

The quarrel which Quakers took with slavery lay precisely in the contradiction perceived between the spiritual concerns of the group for its members and slaveholding reality which negated the spiritual guidelines held dear by the group. The Quakers, or Friends as they were also known, were regarded in the wider society with a measure of suspicion. They were pacifists in a period of numerous wars and faced hostility on that score alone. For some members the integrity of the sect was at stake if, through slaveholding, they were undermining or eroding the very values upon which their dissenting existence was founded. In the 1750s Quakers were primarily concerned with the spiritual wellbeing of their members and for this reason, they sought to be kept informed about slaveholding among fellow Quakers.

Correspondence between Quakers in America and London drew attention to the material conditions of slavery. Pennsylvanian Quakers were in regular contact with the London group. The details they sent spoke of the horrors of plantation slavery. Such information gave rise to tremendous concern about the slave trade among the London Quakers. A visit to America was sanctioned so that London members could see for themselves some of the realities of slavery. The Yearly Meeting of Friends in 1757 warned members against involvement in slave trading and a year later Philadelphia Quakers ruled against slaveowners holding positions of responsibility in the church.

A century earlier the son of William Penn, ardent Quaker and founder of Pennsylvania, had played a key part in the English displacing of Spain in the Caribbean, directly increasing Britain's role as a slave trading nation. Yet in the mid 18th century Quaker areas such as Philadelphia were urging an end to the trade.

Following three years of intense debate, the tide turned in 1758. The London group committed itself not only to prayers and discussion but to anti-slavery action. Important though this action was, it did not immediately hinder slave trading even among Quakers themselves.

Olaudah Equiano

Little is known though much can be imagined of what went on in the minds of African men and women present locally as a direct result of their enslavement. Many lived out their lives in isolation. Most were denied access to a public voice and very few wrote of their experiences. One who did so was Olaudah Equiano and his story throws a great deal of light on the life of the enslaved in London. His story survives because, on purchasing his freedom and returning to England, Equiano worked at developing a public voice to speak out against slavery.

Born in Nigeria in 1745, Equiano was kidnapped by slave raiders around the age of 11. He was sold for 172 cowries, little white shells the size of finger nails. Enslaved and separated from his sister, whom he never saw again, he awaited transportation. He never forgot the smell of the slave ship packed with its human cargo of fellow Africans in the tropical heat.

Amid the rattle of leg irons that chained the adult slaves, the shrieks of the women and the groans of the dying, the young Equiano was transported across the Atlantic. In Barbados he was sold into the West Indian plantation system. For the slave nothing was certain and his stay in Barbados was short-lived. In a matter of weeks he was taken to North America. Boy slaves were in constant demand and Equiano was about 12 years old when he was sold to Michael Pascal, a naval captain whose ship was bound for England.

Equiano's first visit to Deptford was quite an occasion. His master, a naval officer, had been promoted to first lieutenant of the man-of-war, The Preston. At 1,044 tons, the ship was designed to carry 350 men. It was launched in 1757, the same year that London Quakers were beginning to agitate for change. The Preston still smelt of new paint when Equiano boarded her in Deptford.

On 10th December 1762 Equiano returned to Deptford where his master was due to be paid off at the King's Dockyard. At Deptford Equiano was bodily removed by his master who, reminding him of his position as a slave, promptly resold him to the captain of the next available ship awaiting the tide to sail back to the West Indies. The experience was shocking to Equiano, who had spent years on board ship taking his share of all that the sailor's life entailed. Equiano believed himself to be free as he had seen action alongside his master and had all but forgotten that he was property, that he was a slave. Equiano had lived the life of a seaman since having last been purchased. He had also taken the precaution of getting himself baptised in February 1759.

> *I have served him many years...and he has taken all my wages and prize money, for I had only got one sixpence during the war; besides this, I have been baptised: and by the laws of the land, no man has a right to sell me.*

Equiano's statement articulated the slave's understanding of baptism as conferring not just freedom of soul or spirit but a freedom which was legal and very much of this earth. Equiano confirmed his belief in this principle because he had heard, he stated, lawyers and others pronounce as much.

In 1763 Equiano was purchased in the tiny island of Monserrat in the Caribbean by a Quaker merchant, Robert King who came from Philadelphia. Equiano was given the duty of organising the sale of fellow slaves.

> *I used frequently to have different cargoes of fresh negroes in my care for sale; and it was almost a constant practice with our clerks and other whites, to commit violent depredations on the chastity of the female slaves...I have known them to gratify their brutal passions with females not yet ten years old.*

Whether having a Quaker owner made a difference to Equiano's life in Monserrat is debatable. In any event King was persuaded to allow Equiano to purchase his freedom for £40 after three years service. He returned to Britain in 1767 and became an apprentice hairdresser. Before long he was back on board ship travelling to many lands but this time he was legally free.

Equiano assumed a prominent part in the anti-slavery cause leading to Emancipation. As a political activist he publicly engaged in debate denouncing the condition of slavery. Writing was central to his political activity. His autobiography,

22. Olaudah Equiano, kidnapped into slavery as a young boy, was abandoned at Deptford by a master he had served for many years. Sold onwards, he eventually bought his freedom from a Quaker owner and dedicated his life to the anti-slavery cause.

The Interesting Narrative of the Life of Olaudah Equiano or Gustavus Vassa, was first published in 1789. He summed up his life experiences with a measure of irony.

...and did I consider myself an European, I might say my sufferings are great: but when I compare my lot with that of most of my countrymen, I regard myself as a particular favourite of heaven.

This "particular favourite of heaven" not only published what was to be a bestseller in its time but also took the responsibility of lecture tours to give personal testimony against slavery, including describing how at some times

I now wished for the last friend, death, to relieve me.

Equiano's record of the conditions of slave existence offers a wealth of invaluable detail. After capture in slave raids, trans-Atlantic transportation was the next traumatic stage for the African-born enslaved. Shackled and bound for most of the journey in the stinking and cramped slave holds, many, not surprisingly, lost appetite for both life and food. It was, however, in the captain's interest that they ate. Therefore, slaves were regularly whipped on board ship for not eating. The holds of the ships, accommodating great numbers of slaves in an inadequately small space, were insanitary and foul places. As Equiano put it:

The stench of the hold, while we were on the coast was so intolerably loathsome, that it was dangerous to remain there for any time.

Conditions on the plantations were as brutal as on the slave ships. Though Equiano's new master, the Quaker Robert King, was benevolent, the material circumstances for most slaves was both exploitative and punitive. The two pivots of plantation slavery – hard labour and punishment – went hand in hand.

The iron muzzle, thumb-screws, etc. are so well known as not to need description and were sometimes applied for the slightest faults. I have seen a negro beaten till some of his bones were broken, for only letting a pot boil over. I have often asked many of the men slaves who used to go several miles to their wives, and late in the night, after having been wearied with a hard day's labour, why they went so far for wives, and did not take them of their own master's negro-women, and particular those who lived together as household slaves. Their answers have ever been – because when the master or mistress choose to punish the women, they make the husbands flog their own wives and that they could not bear to do.

Not surprisingly, with such a catalogue of injustices against them, rebellions among slave populations in the colonies in the Caribbean were frequent, indicating the slaves' determination to be free. Since Venables and Penn encountered the first revolt on capturing Jamaica, African slave revolts had been a feature of Caribbean history.

The Black Community and Re-exportation

Black communities in South East London consisted not only of servants and sailors, some of whom had worked on ships involved in the Atlantic trade, but also freed persons and runaways. Such communities included enslaved people who had been re-exported many times over. In 1768 Sir John Fielding described a situation within the black community in London which the pro-slavery lobby had reason to fear.

A great number of black men and women who have made themselves so troublesome and dangerous to the Families who brought them over as to get themselves discharged...enter into Societies and make it their Business to corrupt and dissatisfy the Mind of every fresh black Servant that comes to England: first by getting them christened or married, which they inform them makes them free.

Again the shared belief in baptism is made explicit and it seems that black people encouraged each other in this. Mutual support was available to face the baptism ceremony. Fielding's statement also gives the impression of networking among black people agitating for better conditions. Here was useful action being taken by those 'in the know', for slaves arriving from the West Indies or Africa would not expect payment for their services or demand conditions on a par with local servants. Blacks living locally were in some instances 'voting with their feet' and leaving employment where they met with abusive or unfavourable conditions. Fielding also suggested in 1768 that runaways got the Mob on their side.

Doubtless the re-exportation of slaves from Jamaica helped, particularly with privateering activities, to spread the word of rebellions among slave populations and other forms of anti-slavery protest. Of 497,736 slaves imported into Jamaica from 1702 to 1775, some 28 per cent or 137,114 were re-exported.

Slaves brought back to British ports such as Deptford were anxious about resale into worse conditions. The horrors of plantation slavery, the long hours of labour characterised by the whip and the mean living conditions were feared by Equiano and others with experience of a different lifestyle. Conditions in England, even with adjustments for an unfamiliar climate and social isolation, remained preferable to the trauma of plantation existence. A response to this situation was the 'running away' described in the previous chapter. Many slaves, seeing the white master's religion as a form of salvation, became baptised. It is largely because of this practice that we have a record of their presence in parish registers locally.

Quaker Anti-Slavery Action

The year before Equiano took the step of getting himself baptised, the core group of London Quakers had begun the move against slavery that was to snowball into a powerful abolition campaign. The Society of Friends were not only among the first to speak out against the slave trade but the first group of whites to take action against it.

The 1758 Yearly Meeting described the slave trade as

a most unnatural traffic, whereby great numbers of mankind, free by nature are subjected to inextricable bondage.

The Quakers hoped that such a denouncement would discourage British Quakers from the practice of slaveholding and place the spotlight upon those engaging in the practice. American groups within the wider Friends movement were persistently urging action towards the abolition of the trade. They argued that if the British, leaders of the slave trade in that period, ceased making slaves available slaveholding itself would end. Action against slaveholding within the Friends' movement was stepped up during the following year when the London Yearly Meeting took the unprecedented action of

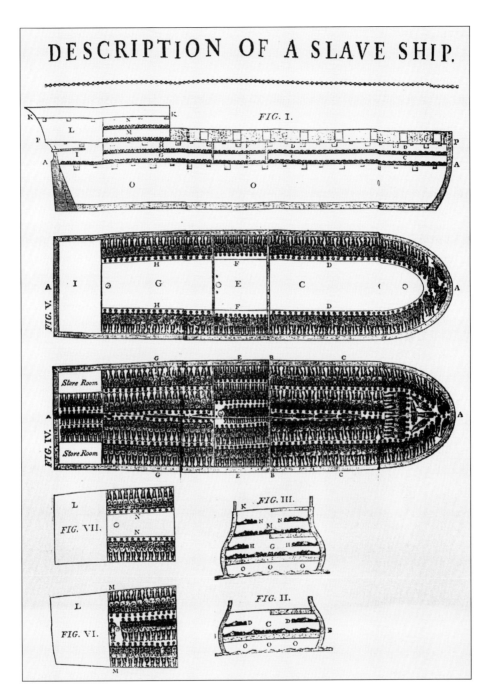

23. *This drawing was published by the Society of Friends (Quakers), in one of their anti-slavery pamphlets. The title page read: "The Case of our Fellow Creatures, the Oppressed Africans, Respectfully Recommended to the Serious Consideration of the Legislature of Great Britain, by the People Called Quakers. London: Printed 1783."*

making non-participation in the slave trade a condition of membership.

One argument suggests that it was the first hand accounts of two London Quakers, Christopher Wilson and John Hunt, representing London on a visit to America which made the critical difference. It is thought that their eyewitness accounts of slaveholding Quakers in Philadelphia and Virginia led to the call for Quakers not to hold slaves.

The first flurry of enthusiasm gave way to a period of inaction but then the unprecedented action of banning Friends from the slave trade came into effect. In 1762 Pennsylvanian Quakers wrote of their approval of the London action. On 29th May 1767 the Friend's Book Committee recommended that Benezet's tract arguing the anti-slavery cause be given to every member of both Houses of Parliament. The campaign had shifted from moral pressure on individuals within the Society to a determined bid to influence the Parliamentary process as well as the nation. Thousands of leaflets were distributed.

So, finally, the Quaker campaign for abolition came into being. This group, well acquainted with Parliamentary ways, began waging a tactical battle for the abolition of slavery.

The Quakers' leaflet campaign proved invaluable to the struggle. Benezet's anti-slavery works resulted in Thomas Clarkson's subsequent involvement in the abolition movement. Clarkson met frequently with Friends of the Committee.

24/25. *Activist Joseph Hardcastle and Hatcham House where the anti-slavery lobby met to discuss tactics.*

Joseph Hardcastle was resident at Hatcham House in New Cross from 1788 until his death in 1819. During that time Hardcastle was in business as a Russia merchant dealing with leather and tallow. Through his position within the non-conformist church Hardcastle became the first treasurer of the London Missionary Society which sent missionaries to foreign parts, including the Caribbean.

Hardcastle received in his home a number of distinguished guests involved in the Emancipation campaign, including Thomas Clarkson and Granville Sharp. We do not know whether any black activists of the period were among them. From the end of 1788 Clarkson and Sharp were regular visitors to Hatcham House, Clarkson using his time there to write some of his *History of the Abolition of the Slave Trade*. Discussion of the work in progress would have been lively and intense.

The Printed Word

The power of the printed word was much used in the fight for Emancipation. In London the debate continued in newspapers and pamphlets. In Jamaica a free black man, Edward Jordan, began publishing *The Watchman*, a twice weekly paper exposing the excesses of the planter class and their mistreatment of enslaved people.

Integral to the Quaker campaign against the slave trade was the use of published material to educate the reading public about the issues involved. The committee published and distributed key pamphlets, first among men of influence and later to the general populace. They also ensured that the press was kept informed. For example, the London and Middlesex branch of the Quakers distributed 2,000 copies of *The Case*, an anti-slavery pamphlet to key local figures. Similarly, in the spring of 1785, *The Caution*, another anti-slavery publication was sent into schools and universities.

In June 1783 the Parliamentary Committee of the London Friends had discovered that the House of Commons was to debate a bill forbidding employees of the Royal African Company from privately engaging in the slave trade. Friends drew up a petition asking that the clause referring to employees be extended to all persons. The petition was signed by 273 members.

Though literacy was far from widespread and despite the living conditions of black people, many former slaves took particular trouble to learn to read and write. Black literate individuals also took up the pen in order to espouse the cause of liberation for individuals as well as the enslaved masses denied a voice. A letter from Mungo, secretary of the Black Society, published in *The Public Ledger* on 23rd October 1772 expressed concern for the welfare of a black maidservant in London who had been declared a chattel. Her destination on resale would most likely be plantation slavery.

The Case of the Slaveship Zong

On 29th November 1781 the captain of the slaveship Zong had ordered the jettisoning of 113 slaves into the Atlantic. The ship's Atlantic crossing had been devastated by illness. Many of the crew and slaves had died and most of the surviving slaves looked unlikely to fetch a good price. The journey would represent a huge loss in profits, hence the order to throw the Africans overboard. With the slaves effectively murdered, the slaveholders set about using the English legal system to recoup the losses endured through having to throw their 'livestock' into the ocean. This shocking case moved an anonymous court spectator to write to the press where Equiano read of it.

In March 1783 Equiano called to see Granville Sharp. Sharp had already earned himself the reputation of being an influential ally of enslaved Africans, notably in the case of Jonathon Strong described above. On this occasion Equiano wished to discuss with him the case not of an individual slave but of more than a hundred thrown overboard mid-Atlantic. The case, known initially as Gregson v. Gilbert, came to be popularly referred to as 'the case of the slaveship Zong'. The case reached the courts initially as an insurance dispute between a slaveship owner and his insurers. Equiano told Sharp of this and he, in turn, set in motion legal action which drew public attention to the matter, not as an insurance claim but as an urgent humanitarian matter. No-one was prosecuted, however. The West Indian pro-slavery lobby was still powerful. This group was nicknamed 'the Oran Otang philosophers' by Equiano and other black activists because of their belief in black people's inferiority due to a biological closeness to orangutans.

New Arguments and the Backlash

When the moral argument seemed ineffective in bringing closer the desired goals of abolition, the Quakers sought to produce documentation highlighting the economic advantage of manumission. The abolitionist cause gained momentum when the Quakers proposed a boycott in 1791 of West Indian produce, especially sugar. At the start of the 18th century the average annual import of West Indian sugar was 34,800 hogsheads. The figures had increased steadily and in 1792 a staggering 153,000 hogsheads were imported. Of these, 105,000 were landed in London, along with 27,500 puncheons of rum. By the summer of 1791 Clarkson established that up to 300,000 were supporting the boycott of sugar. In May 1796 the London Yearly Meeting recorded this, and took credit for the fact that they had been foremost in taking positive anti-slavery action.

In the final decade of the 18th century the pro-slavery West Indian lobby was being eclipsed by the abolitionist argument. The abolition debate had so gained ascendancy that news of black-led Haiti's triumph over France in the West Indies in 1804 was greeted, in some quarters, with jubilation. The assumption was that the British people would be sympathetic to the victory of the black liberators in the Caribbean.

> *...a great point gained in to the cause of humanity that a Negro domination is in fact constituted and organised in the West Indies under the command of a Negro chief or king [of] the black race whom the Christian world to their infamy have been accustomed to degrade...Every liberal Briton will feel proud that this country brought about the happy revolution.* THE LONDON GAZETTE, 12/12/1798

Much of the information at the heart of the press debate on abolition was collected and disseminated by the Abolition Committee, many of whose members were active church men, so that the church, far from acquiescing with slavery had become one of its staunchest critics. The testimony of many witnesses to the evils of slavery was collated so that the British public could know the horrors of each stage of enslavement.

Defenders of the slave trade were quick to link slave revolts with the Abolition Campaign and stressed concern that unrest would spread to Jamaica with dire effects on English interests there. When news reached London of slave revolt in Barbados in February 1791 the backlash began. International forces were impacting on national concerns. There were fears about the spread of the revolutionary movement to Britain. The backlash meant there were no public campaigns for abolition between 1792 and 1804. By the time the political atmosphere was again right for reform the Quakers had stepped back from the campaign, partly because their pacifist opposition to the war in America and Europe made them vulnerable to criticism.

Equiano died in 1797, some four decades before slaves were emancipated. The work that he and countless others did to dismantle slavery would mesh with other voices taking up the cry. Most importantly, the Emancipation cause would come to be seen not only in terms of its adverse effects on black people in the Caribbean but as profoundly influencing the lives of all British people whose lifestyles slavery supported. Abolition was at last on Britain's political agenda.

6

BROTHERS AND EQUALS: BREAKING THE CHAINS

"I have felt what a slave feels, and I know what a slave knows; and I would have all good people in England to know it too, that they may break our chains and set us free." MARY PRINCE

Sugar came to be the symbol of slavery and planters pressed ahead with increased production in spite of widespead calls for change locally and in the Caribbean. There were plans for improved facilities for handling West Indian produce. One proposal, from wharfinger and shipbroker Mr Ogle suggested enlarging the existing quays and deepening the river down to Deptford as well as establishing a day and night service to prevent smuggling. The estimated cost of the project was £565,000.

Deptford was not selected as the site for the new West India dock which opened in 1802 and in the wider world the broad movement for political change locked into the single issue of the abolition of slavery. Middle class reformers, sections of the working class movement and the campaign for women's suffrage each drew upon the wider significance of slave emancipation.

At Home: Abolishing the Trade

Publications which helped in the abolitionists' cause included James Stephen's The Crisis of the Sugar Colonies in 1802 and Henry Brougham's Inquiry into the Colonial Policy of the European Powers in 1803. Both offered fresh critiques of the slave trade, analysing the contemporary crisis of war with France in the Caribbean and outlining the positive impact that abolition would bring to bear upon that danger. Britain had armed thousands of black people in the Caribbean to fight the French.

Both Stephen and Brougham became, in 1804, members of the renewed Abolition Committee with Thomas Clarkson. The new committee systematically gathered evidence against the slave trade, keeping the anti-slavery parliamentarians at least as well informed as their opponents, the West Indian planters and their representatives.

On the death of Pitt the Younger in 1806 a coalition government came into being which included Lord Grenville and Charles James Fox, two influential abolitionists. To keep the issue of abolition on the agenda beyond the forthcoming General Election, Grenville and Fox proposed a general resolution.

That this House, considering the African Slave Trade to be contrary to the principles of justice, humanity and sound policy, will, with all practical expedition, take effectual measures for the abolition of the said trade, in such manner, and at such period, as may be deemed advisable.

The resolution had no power in itself but it would ensure the party winning the election would begin its term with a documented obligation to act upon the principle outlined. The evidence and the arguments would have reached a wide middle class audience locally through the newspapers.

The general election brought the abolition issue to the forefront of national politics and the Abolition Committee intensified its public campaign, using the power of the media to bring concerns about the slave trade to the attention of the general public. One Liverpool anti-abolitionist complained:

Every measure that invention or art could devise to create a popular clamour was resorted to on this occasion. The church, the theatre, the press, had laboured to create a prejudice against the slave trade. It had even been maintained from the pulpit that England could never expect to be victorious in war while she persisted in such an abominable traffic...The attempts to make a popular clamour against the trade were never so conspicuous as during the last election, when the public newspapers had teemed with abuse of this trade, and when promises were required from different candidates that they would oppose its continuance. There had never been any question agitated since that of Parliamentary reform, in which so much industry had been exerted to raise a popular clamour. In every manufacturing town and borough in the kingdom all those arts had been tried.

In October 1806 Charles James Fox died and the abolitionist cause lost an important champion. He is reputed to have said on his deathbed

Two things I wish earnestly to see accomplished – peace with Europe and the abolition of the slave trade.

Lord Grenville decided that the bill to abolish the slave trade should be debated first in the House of Lords. He presented it to the House at the beginning of January 1807 and the ensuing debate lasted until nearly four o'clock in the morning when the count was taken and the first bill in England to end the slave trade was passed by 100 votes to 36. Passed in both Houses and receiving Royal Assent, the Foreign Slave Trade Act became law. From New Year's Day 1808 it would be illegal for British ships to take part in the Atlantic slave trade. In the enthusiasm and euphoria which followed, popular opinion underestimated the extent to which the Emancipation battle was yet to be won. While the 1807 Act banned the introduction of new slaves, inter-island trading was still legal, with slaves being re-exported on a wide scale.

1814 saw another upsurge in mass campaigning in the abolitionist cause when some 806 petitions with one and a half million signatories objected to a proposal to renew the rights of French slave merchants. Parliamentary abolitionists pressed for further legislation. They wanted a register of the slave population of the West Indies to monitor slave smuggling as a means of increasing the slave population. A bill was introduced in 1815 and a measure of agreement was reached about the maintaining of local records in the colonies. Wilberforce and his supporters, wary of the possibility of distortion in the record keeping, pressed for a central register.

Abroad: Rebellions and Retaliation

In 1802 the 4th West Indian Regiment mutinied on the island of Dominica. Easter 1816 brought news of the latest slave rebellion in the West Indies. The trouble spot was the island of Barbados. To the ruling plantocracy, fire was the first sign of trouble. It was approximately 8 pm on Sunday 14th April when the first fire was lit which was to set a third of the island ablaze within a matter of a few hours. One black and one white person were killed by the rebels. Despite this, the pro-slavery lobby drew attention to reporting which dwelt on the violence and bloodshed among the rebels. The uprising was put down with great loss of black life. The retaliatory action was such as to teach the slaves a lesson not to be hurriedly forgotten: over 250 people were killed and another 132 were deported to Belize. Their masters were compensated to the sum of £170,000.

Despite this lesson in terror, slave conditions were so unacceptable that uprisings continued, and were ferociously suppressed. The Rear Admiral in command of the squadron stationed in Barbados at the time commented

The Militia, who could not be restrained by the same discipline as the troops, put Many Men, Women and Children to Death, I fear without much discrimination.

In the light of such rebellion and the pro-slavery propaganda fed by it, Parliamentary abolitionists retreated. They feared accusations that the abolition debate itself had fuelled rebellion on the plantations. Abolitionist activity was lulled again but the campaign had developed a concept of freedom and rights which surfaced in other forms of political expression in Britain. Radical notions were being linked to anti-slavery sentiment and politically active black people were among those swept along by the appeal of such radicalism.

A Radical Working Class Movement

The radical movement out of which several black radicals emerged claimed the interests of local people as well. The London Democratic Assocation (LDA) met in sections all over London. One of these groups met at the Spotted Cow on the Old Kent Road, described as a 'ramshackle beer house'. It is not known whether any members were black. The better-known of London's black radicals such as Robert Wedderburn and William Davidson, were public figures because they faced trial for their political action.

The working class Society of Spencean Philanthropists advocated support for slave revolts and emancipation. The group included the ex-slave Robert Wedderburn, born in Jamaica in the 1760s the son of a slave woman, Rosanna. His father was a Scottish plantation owner who, like so many slave owners and their agents, sexually exploited women slaves on the plantations. Robert Wedderburn, outspoken in his condemnation of his father on several counts, wrote passionately of his mother's abuse.

By him my mother was made the object of his brutal lust, then insulted, abused and abandoned.

Wedderburn came to Britain at the age of about 17. He became a seaman and later a tailor. In later years Wedderburn met Thomas Spence whose ideas were to have an immense influence upon him. Wedderburn became very actively involved within the Society, finally assuming a leadership role. In 1818 his polemical work *The Axe Laid To The Root* was published and led to his being prosecuted for sedition and blasphemy. In a debate at a local meeting of the Spencean group, Wedderburn argued for the right of slaves to kill their masters, a particularly sensitive subject at any period during slavery. He was jailed for blasphemy.

Wedderburn found ways to get his printed words into the hands of slaves in Jamaica. Defying imprisonment he exhorted slaves to strike and urged rebellion, arguing against the degradation of petitioning the oppressors for emancipation.

William Davidson, a contemporary of Wedderburn, was born in Jamaica, also the son of a slave woman. Unlike Wedderburn, Davidson's father, the Attorney General of Jamaica, provided for his education and upbringing. After a chequered career which included being pressed into service as a seaman, Davidson set up business on Walworth Road. He was a cabinet maker by trade and he was also a literate individual strongly influenced by Thomas Paine's *The Rights of Man*. A member of the radical group, the Marylebone Union Reading Society, Davidson held meetings in his home and the group's banner featured a black flag with skull and crossbones. Their motto read: "Let us die like men and not be sold like slaves".

Davidson was tried for high treason with four others for his part in the Cato Street Conspiracy. Though he maintained that he did not take part in any plot, that he only happened to be in Cato Street at the time, all five were found guilty. Davidson was hanged and executed with the other co-defendants on 1st May 1820.

Robert Wedderburn and William Davidson are two black men who may be placed within the context of British radicalism. Perhaps grown bold by a greater public voice for and by black people, each acted out of radical beliefs. Davidson was hanged for his part; Wedderburn was imprisoned. While black individuals were politically active within radical groups, the abolitionist movement returned to the matter of slavery and the degraded lifestyle it continued to demand. The slave trade bill had not altered the conditions of slavery.

Gradual or Immediate Abolition

The Society for Mitigating and Gradually Abolishing the State of Slavery Throughout the British Dominions was set up in 1823. Its members included both Clarkson and Wilberforce. The idea of this society came into being as a means of appeasing the pro-slavery lobby in the wake of the passage of the 1807 Act. Not all abolitionists favoured the gradualist approach. Among those opposed to this stance were the radical women increasingly giving public voice to political ideas. In 1824 the pamphlet *Immediate Not Gradual Abolition* appeared. At first anonymous, it later became known that the author was one Elizabeth Heyricke.

In 1825 the society began publishing *The Anti-Slavery Reporter*. Between 1826 and 1832 there were 3,500 petitions submitted to the House of Lords. When the Anti-Slavery Society was re-formed in 1830, well over 3,000 supporters sought access to the first meeting. More than 1,000 were turned away. Immediate, not gradual, freedom was the focus of the group.

On 2nd November 1830 B C Challis addressed a local anti-slavery meeting at Reverend Barker's Chapel in Deptford High Street. The speech was printed as a pamphlet by Warcup in Deptford Broadway, Ellis in Lower Road and J Cole in London Street, Greenwich.

Several resolutions were then read and carried and a Petition praying the Total Extinction of Slavery adopted.

Women in the Fight

In 1831 the first autobiographical testimony from an enslaved African woman in the West Indies was published. This was *The History of Mary Prince, A West Indian Slave* and it was recorded at Mary's insistence by the editor of *The Anti-Slavery Reporter*. In many ways Mary's testimony reflected the direct involvement of women in the abolitionist movement.

> I am often vexed and I feel great sorrow when I hear some people in this country say, that the slaves do not need better usage, and do not want to be free...I say, Not so. How can slaves be happy when they have the halter round their neck and the whip upon their back? and are disgraced and thought no more of than beasts? and are separated from their mothers, and husbands, and children and sisters, just as cattle are sold and separated...There is no modesty or decency shown by the owner to his slaves: men, women and children are exposed alike. Since I have been here I have often wondered how English people can go out into the West Indies and act in such a beastly manner...They tie up slaves, like hogs – moor them up like cattle, and they lick them so as hogs, or cattle, or horses never were flogged; and yet they come home and say, and make some good people believe, that slaves don't want to get out of slavery.

The part played by women in the fight against slavery has been little documented. How many times did women take the small but significant steps in assisting slaves? The Guerin sisters in London, relatives of Equiano's master, taught Equiano to read and sent him to school. They also supported his being baptised. Often these gestures of support were isolated acts. However, through the anti-slavery movement many women found a public voice. In the years 1825-33 ladies' anti-slavery associations were established in Camberwell, Peckham and Southwark.

The women's anti-slavery movement became active in many large cities. The London Female Anti-Slavery Association undertook publications, fundraising and petitioning. They collected a total of 187,157 signatures in 10 days and presented this

26/27. *Mary Lloyd (left) and Anne Knight campaigned against slavery in the 1830s. Anne was later involved in the women's movement*

on 14th May 1833. Several anti-slavery women's groups had called for the immediate emancipation of women slaves.

A demonstration organised by the Union of the Working Classes in October 1831 drew 70,000 supporters. Women were also calling for the vote and Roman Catholics were 'emancipated' in 1829. Reform was in the air. Even key plantation owners were ready to stomach the emancipation of slaves provided they could be assured of compensation. The numbers of women attending anti-slavery meetings swelled.

Even the king's secretary commented upon the feelings aroused by the emancipation debate.

Of all the political feelings, and passions and such, this rage for emancipation is rather more than a matter of interest – it has always struck me as the most extraordinary and remarkable.

Apprenticeship: Slavery by Another Name

In May 1833 the Colonial Secretary introduced the Abolition of Slavery Bill. Modified and amended, it received Royal Assent in August 1833. Planters were to be pacified with compensation of £20 million pounds and slaves were to be apprenticed for a further 12 years. There remained yet another round in the fight to loosen the stranglehold of established patterns of domination and oppression of enslaved peoples.

Following the Emancipation Act abolitionists and the slaves themselves resisted the conditions of apprenticeship which required slaves to be bound to their masters without pay for three quarters of the working week at stipulated wages. The whip, an everlasting symbol of the wretchedness of Atlantic slavery, remained the prerogative of masters, as did the jail and the treadmill.

In 1836-7 Joseph Sturge made an inspection of the West Indies. In November 1837 he addressed a large rally at which a Central Emancipation Committee was set up. The text of his address *The Narrative of James Williams, An Apprentice* was written up and made available in a pamphlet. The new committee soon launched the journal *The Emancipator*. The campaign against apprenticeship was set for a final run.

Chartism: the Black Man and His Party

The Chartist movement started in the late 1830s as a mass political movement of the British working class. A key Chartist demand was the right to vote.

William Cuffay was a black Chartist active in London. There seems to have been some association with black people among the London Chartists for *The Times* referred to them as "the black man and his party". Cuffay represented the London Chartists at the National Convention in April 1848.

Cuffay was one of a group tried for planning an uprising in London. George Davis, who joined the Wat Tyler Brigade of the Greenwich Chartists to spy on them, gave evidence for the prosecution at Cuffay's trial. On 16th August 1848 Cuffay and his group were arrested and faced trial and later Cuffay was transported to Tasmania.

Deptford and Lewisham Chartists were among those in the working class movement which was to be influential in urban areas in the 1840s. Deptford Chartists started meeting in May 1841 and in the summer of that year they met together with the Greenwich group. The Lewisham Chartists met every Tuesday in the George and Dragon on Blackheath Hill. In July 1842 over 2,000 Chartists gathered on Deptford Broadway and even more turned up the next day on Blackheath. A Chartist meeting attended by around 700 people on 28th February 1846 was chaired by Mr Ellis, "an opulent tradesman of Deptford". On 15th March that year another mass Chartist rally was held by the Greenwich and Deptford Chartists on Blackheath.

> *The Chartists of Greenwich and Deptford being determined not to be behind hand with their chartist brethren in other parts of the country in demonstrating their respect to the patriotic people of France, and their firm adherence to the principles of the People's Charter, called an open air meeting to be held on Blackheath, on Wednesday afternoon last, March 15th. No sooner did the placards announcing the meeting make their appearance, than the minions in power set to work to destroy the meeting if possible. Hundreds of special constables were sworn in, and the whole of the police from the neighbouring stations were ordered to attend on the day of the meeting likewise the mounted police from London.* NORTHERN STAR, 18/3/1848

General Eyre and the Jamaica Revolt of 1865

Slavery had ended in the Caribbean but very few planters were willing to offer adequate wages and conditions to the local black population they had known as slaves. Many of the population took to peasant style smallholdings. The whites who were selling their plantations did so in large plots well beyond the reach of ex-slaves, a strategy to keep ex-slaves dependent on the meagre wages offered for labouring on post-slavery estates. One group, led by black Baptist preacher Paul Bogle, petitioned Queen Victoria for land in Jamaica. The Queen's response, displayed on 50,000 posters around Jamaica, exhorted the petitioners to labour for wages

> *steadily and continuously, at the times when their labour is wanted, and for as long as it is wanted.*

Petitioners attempted to meet with Governor Eyre but he refused to see them. Feelings ran high until the Morant Bay courthouse in Jamaica was attacked by a group determined to rescue one of their number being held there. There was an attempt to arrest Paul Bogle and a number of his followers but arresting officers were met with force. The following day when hundreds of black people marched on Morant Bay the militia met stone-throwing with gunfire and martial law was declared.

The ascendancy of the abolitionist movement is sometimes represented as liberal sentiment in England towards the descendants of Africans. In 1865 the uprising in Eastern Jamaica was to test British opinion. Military response to the rebellion involved the loss of 500 black lives and the severe punishment of yet more. Punitive action made free with the whip, an instrument symbolic of slavery itself, and at least 600 were flogged. Atrocities to children and pregnant women were on an unprecedented scale and over 1,000 homes were burned.

In the debate which followed, English opinion was sharply divided. General Eyre found himself supported by influential figures such as Charles Dickens, Charles Kingsley and the historian, Thomas Carlyle. His opponents included John Stuart Mill, Thomas Huxley and Charles Darwin, who set up the Jamaica Committee.

The City of London branch of the Radical Reform League which campaigned for the extension of the vote, held a demonstration against the excesses sanctioned by Eyre. There were League branches at Greenwich and Deptford and their members and supporters would have attended the demonstration.

The 1833 Emancipation Act and the end of the apprenticeship system brought a legal end to slavery. No more would black people find themselves the property of others, transported and abused at whim. The campaigners of the anti-slavery movement had whet their appetite for information in the movement. Local subscribers who would have received the Anti-Slavery Reporter in the 1820s and 1830s included William Mansfield of Camberwell, M Robinson of Dulwich, Peckham Ladies African and Anti-Slavery Association, Southwark Ladies Anti-Slavery Association and James Rice Williams of Lee, Kent.

The abolition of slavery had been the most important international event of the period and one that people locally were involved in whether or not they chose an active role. Influenced by it, if only in the use of the rhetoric of slavery and freedom, equality and brotherhood, a wider radical movement had developed.

28. "This Book tells man not to be cruel; Oh that Massa would read this book". From 'Scripture Evidence on the Sinfulness of Injustice and Oppression', 1828

PART THREE

Nkyin kyin:
'Changing oneself,
playing many roles'

To the motherland

7

TRAVELLERS WITH PASSPORTS

*"All that I would wish is
to answer the universal hunger
the universal thirst"* AIMÉ CESAIRE

In the late 19th and early 20th centuries, black people in Lewisham and South East London moved 'beyond the middle passage' though constantly in its shadow. It was a time of increasing visibility when black individuals faced a new struggle to realise personal and collective dreams and visions.

In the Lewisham area the black population was largely a settled one. There were few newcomers and those were mainly transitory from the recently acquired colonies in Africa and India.

In local south east communities at the turn of the century, there were black people who had only ever lived in Britain. But throughout the Empire there were many more black people who were British subject citizens. British rule had created global demands for commodities, services and the trappings of English culture. In the Caribbean English culture was promoted principally through education, itself promoted through the Christian churches established in the region. Those churches were largely led by the ecclesiastical dictates of the metropolitan areas.

Plantations Beyond the Seas

In the Caribbean, the work of the Christian churches continued to expand in the 20th century. Britain's missionary role represented an important part of this expansion. Public interest locally in missionary work was maintained through exhibitions such as the Lewisham Deanery Exhibition which opened at Ladywell Baths in January 1932. On the first day some 800 people attended. The object of the exhibition was the promotion of overseas missions. Each of the 27 parishes in Lewisham deanery as well as five mission churches were included.

The focus of the week-long exhibition was 'Plantations Beyond The Seas'. The exhibition paid tribute to Abraham Colfe, parish priest and local benefactor, who during Cromwell's protectorate, left a legacy with provisions for such plantations.

Colfe's 60-page will directed that £5 of lawful money should be paid yearly for ever to an ordained minister "who is a Protestant and an orthodox divine" to write a commentary on parts of the canonical scriptures for the benefit of those in English plantations beyond the seas.

> The story of the church in Lewisham was last summer presented in vivid and impressive pageantry in St Mary's vicarage garden. This week the modern story of the missionary work of the church is being effectively told at an exhibition at the halls nearby in Ladywell Road. The latter event, like the former, is drawing clergy and laymen from all parts of the deanery to the parish of the mother church...One of the great figures impersonated in last year's pageant was Abraham Colfe. Probably every Lewisham man and child is today familiar with what he did for the church...but less familiar with the provision he made for the teaching of the Gospel and the English Bible to the child of the heathen in English Plantations beyond the seas.

In January 1935 the Rev J C Calman from All Saints in Sydenham was one of the recruits taking up mission work abroad. He was destined for Nassau in the Bahamas, a diocese created in the post-slavery heyday in 1861.

The Education of Empire

Black people living and working locally continued, as in earlier periods, to be an invisible section of the population. Race continued to play a significant part in the way black residents were perceived and the opportunities they would be allowed. They continued to find in day-to-day relationships that, despite slavery's end and with imperialism the order of the day, concepts of race grounded in Atlantic slavery still thrived. Furthermore, in the period of Empire, notions of superiority of English culture were further institutionalised through educational material, popular reading, entertainment and the documentation of imperial ideology.

In schools in the south east, as indeed all over the British Empire, children were provided with learning material about themselves and other British subjects. From respected publishers 'Readers' for many areas of the curriculum found their way into schools. They contained material, posing as factual information, which was to form the basis of knowledge of different cultural, national and racial groups.

> 1. Negroes form half the population of the British West Indies. As a rule they are lazy, and that is one reason why the islands are less prosperous than formerly; but in Barbados, the most easterly of the islands of the archipelago, the blacks display exemplary industry.
>
> 2. The negroes in Barbados must either work or starve, because the island is so densely peopled that every spare inch is highly cultivated. On other islands a black family can always find a plot of land which will hold their hut, and will supply them with a sufficiency of fruit and vegetables at the cost of little labour.
> COLLINS' WIDE WORLD GEOGRAPHY READER

The Sun Never Sets

The Queen noted in her speech to open Parliament in January 1897 "the depressed condition of the sugar industry in our West Indian colonies" had seriously affected their prosperity.

The propaganda of the British Empire proved extremely effective in the hands of colonial agents and missionaries for another half century. The colonies produced raw material cheaply for transporting to Britain where it was manufactured into goods that were shipped again to the edges of Britain's vast Empire and readymade market. British subjects in the various corners of the Empire were then exhorted to 'Buy British'.

In the extended market place which the colonies became, children learned from educational fare similar to that of the mother country. The first decades of the 20th century saw black people travelling to Britain from the Caribbean, mainly from the newly educated élite. They represented a new wave of incoming African-Caribbean people challenging the stereotypes of the former era of slavery. They travelled to London with the specific intention of increasing the knowledge and skills which would consolidate their new status.

Black Politics and Professionalism

Possibly the first decisive episode in the Pan-African Movement was the one realised by Africans stepping on board ships docked in Deptford which had been prepared to return to Africa. The first group bound for Sierra Leone experienced insurmountable difficulties but the movement for Africans to be reunited with Africa was to take several turns. It involved Africans scattered by Atlantic slavery as well as those from the continental mainland.

Henry Sylvester Williams was born in Trinidad in 1869. At the age of 28 he enrolled at Gray's Inn as a law student, having passed an entrance examination which included Latin, History and English. As a young barrister in London he developed the idea of a convocation of African representatives from all parts of the world. As a result, the first Pan African Congress was held in Westminster Town Hall. Among the delegates were Frederick J Loudin, Manager of the Fisk Jubilee Singers, Dr Mandell Creighton, Bishop of London, Sir Thomas Fowell-Buxton and Samuel Coleridge Taylor.

In the period leading up to and after Emancipation there was likely to have been substantial networking among people of African descent throughout London.

Samuel Coleridge Taylor, the well known black composer who lived in Croydon, attended the first Pan African Congress. In 1911 he represented 'the African race' at the First Universal Races Congress in London. In 1912, following his early death, Lewisham Choral Society and St Peter's Church Brockley Chorus were among those to honour his contribution.

29. Samuel Coleridge Taylor. South London composer and black activist who died in 1912.

Among the group seeking top professional roles lauded by British society were the children of recently freed slaves as well as the sons, for they were mostly sons, of unions of black women and white men who had had the fortune to escape slavery. William Henry Strachan, eldest son of Colonel W H P F Strachan, was educated privately in Jamaica. He chose to study medicine in England and gained a place at Guy's Hospital. Strachan qualified as a GP and became a member of a variety of medical institutes including the Royal Sanitary Institute. In this period a black medical student needed ample proof of ability and achievement. Strachan satisfied the strictest demands. The Colonial Office list shows him as a medical professional in Jamaica from 1882. He became Principal Medical Officer of Lagos Colony in 1897 and was honoured in 1902 with the Companion of St Michael and St George. Who's Who 1918 gave his address as The Great House, Teak Pin, Chapeltown, Jamaica.

Strachan had made the pioneering journey to England in the century that slavery ended. Fifty years earlier, his role as a doctor and thus his claim to a well-respected profession, would have been unthinkable. Dr Strachan died in June 1921 at 56 Wickham Road, Brockley, after a long illness.

Another West Indian, Harold Moody, came to London from Jamaica in 1904 to study medicine at King's College. Having qualified in 1910, Dr Moody faced many difficulties in getting himself appointed to a medical post, so eventually he started his own practice in Peckham in 1913. He was not accepted for one post because the matron was not prepared to have a black doctor in the hospital. In Camberwell the Board of Guardians turned down his application down for the sake of 'the poor' who, it was decided, would be against having "a nigger to attend them". Gordon Martin recalls that Dr Moody also had a practice on New Cross Road.

A report from 1918 suggests that some 50-60 West Indian students were studying mostly in London and Scotland. Like Harold Moody they found it hard to gain lodgings as racial discrimination was so widespread. Moody's experience of racial prejudice led him to become actively involved on behalf of black people. In 1931 he founded the League of Coloured Peoples. The League's publication *The Keys* was issued quarterly.

Black Artists and Entertainers

The small number of black professionals such as the doctors who came to reside locally influenced perceptions of black people. But there was yet another group who were profoundly to shape early 20th century perceptions of black people. These were entertainers, principally from America.

In August 1886 the Fisk Jubilee Singers performed at Brookdale Hall in Catford. This group of black singers from Nashville in the southern United States was formed in 1871 to raise funds for the new Fisk University for black students. The singers made a number of visits to Britain, firstly in 1873 and later in 1875. By 1878 the original choir had splintered and some were no longer directly involved with the university but other entertainers were to follow and black people began to be seen and appreciated in this role. Large audiences applauded solo artists and groups at prime local venues. Groups like the Jubilee Singers set a trend for black entertainers that musicians such as Louis Armstrong would take up in the early 20th century. As more black people engaged in independent travel across the Atlantic, inevitably the public became aware of new roles being played by the group formerly thought of as slaves.

30. The Fisk Jubilee Singers who travelled the world raising money for Fisk University, played at the Brookdale Hall in Catford in August 1886

In Britain Turner Layton and Clarence Johnstone were popular African-American musicians of the 1920s and 1930s. On 23rd September 1932 they were billed to appear at the New Cross Empire. The duo were also stars of the popular gramophone culture of the period.

Layton and Johnstone, that inimitable pair who have been stars of the gramophone world as well as Vaudeville since they came to this country, will be at New Cross Empire next week at the head of a first rate bill.

A host of other black entertainers visited Britain. They found an enthusiastic reception in the music halls and large venues offering popular entertainment. The Versatile Three comprising musicians Haston, Luck and Mills were popular from around 1915. Not only did they enjoy success in the music hall, but radio and record companies also snapped them up. Scott and Whaley also became great favourites with enthusiastic reviews of their performance at New Cross.

Scott and Whaley kept the house in an uproar with their 'elegant' burlesque, and finished to a storm of applause with their dance. Several 'tab' calls left the audience still shouting for more. ENCORE, 19/2/1925

A few days later, Encore reviewed the Georgia Jubilee Singers.

The Georgia Jubilee Singers (Darkies) are John Lester's latest importation, and they justify their inclusion, although some of their songs might be improved by shortening slightly. We are surprised to learn that 'It Ain't Gonna Rain No Mo" is "a song of Slavery Days" but, as it is included in that category in the programme, it must be so

On August 11th 1933 the young Louis Armstrong, jazz musician and trumpeter, performed at the New Cross Empire. So popular did the image of the black entertainer become that, in some quarters, it began to replace the stereotyped slave image in the popular imagination. Instead 'blacking' began to become synonymous with entertainment. Thus white entertainers came under pressure to 'black up' as minstrels in a number of local venues in the 1930s, including police minstrels at the Lewisham Unitarian Hall and a children's party at the West Lewisham Labour Party.

The Martin Family

It is not known how many black people living locally were members of the League of Coloured People. In Deptford, Stephen Martin was a member. The Martin family lived at 5 Arklow Road. There were five children, all born in Deptford: three girls and two boys, Thomas and Gordon. One advantage of membership for League members with families was the summer outings to the seaside for children. Gordon Martin, the younger son of the family born in June 1922, recalls the charabancs.

I can still remember where we had to go and meet at a place called Spurgeon's Tabernacle in Croydon. There were six coaches. I thought to myself 'if this is all the coloured people from all over London, there's not that many'.

31. Stephen Martin

Mr Martin, originally from Jamaica, was remembered as a strict father insisting on high standards from his children. He had been a seaman but little is known of his career. It is known that in the post-1919 period there was great hostility to black seamen. By 1925, with the connivance of the National Union of Seamen, blacks were denied a seamen's career. The Aliens Order 1920 and finally the Coloured Alien Seamen of 1925 designated all black men aliens regardless of British nationality. Stephen Martin became a Deptford Borough Council employee and Mrs Martin combined her housewife duties with the local Labour Party of which she was secretary.

The Martin children attended Clifton Hill Infants, then Childeric Road Juniors and finally Stanley Street School. Each left at the age of 14. Thomas, the eldest, developed a passion for boxing and left home to travel the boxing booths with the fairs. The Martins' neighbour, Mr Webb, worked for a newspaper in London and it was decided that this would be a suitable career for the young Gordon. In the meantime Gordon found a job at Berry's, a local firm making water tanks. At the bottom of Arklow Road was the big Stones' foundry, famous for having made the propellers for the *Queen Mary*. It was there that Gordon got a new job when he tired of being burnt in the welding process which his old job involved. He earned 10 shillings per week. On Saturday mornings he made an extra shilling by helping out on the milk round.

Another Jamaican doctor, E C R Campbell, became associated with the Martins. In November 1940 the *Kentish Mercury* reported that Dr Campbell married Jestina, Tommy Martin's sister. The wedding ceremony took place at St Paul's Church, Deptford. Dr Campbell's family address was given as Montego Bay, Jamaica and the best man was Mr

32. Gordon Martin

Donald A R Campbell, a relative of the bridegroom.

The Martin family are remembered with affection by now-elderly white neighbours who are keen to point out that the Martins were accepted into the Deptford community with no trace of racist ill-feeling. Their importance to this history is that they are the earliest black family in the Lewisham area for which substantial details can be discovered. Nationally, too, they became well known, principally through the high profile of the eldest boy, Tommy Martin, who gained fame locally and in the sports pages of the national and local press as well as in sporting magazines as 'The Brown Bomber'. Tommy's fame was spread by his fight for equality with white boxers.

The Brown Bomber

Popular entertainment focused not only upon musical activities but also on sport. In 1910 Jack Johnson shattered delusions of white superiority in the USA by beating James J Jeffries, who had retired undefeated in 1905 and was attempting a comeback. Jack Johnson became the first black world champion boxer. Pictures of the triumphant Johnson sold newspapers on London streets the following day and when he visited Britain in 1911 he was feted by Fleet Street. His victory would impact upon the lives of struggling black boxers worldwide, including local black hopefuls.

33. Jack Johnson, the African-American boxer whose victory over James J Jeffries in 1910 encouraged black hopefuls around the world. This photograph shows his visit to Brooklands race trace in June 1911.

Tommy Martin emerged from the boxing booths of touring fairs as a rising young champion and his local community hailed his early sucesses. In local playgrounds the young Tommy was often the subject of conversation among youthful boxing fans. Len Smith, one of the Martins' neighbours, attended Clifton Hill School with Gordon Martin. Amateur boxer and enthusiast, Len recalls Sunday afternoon sparring between Tommy and his father in the Martins' garden in a scene appreciated by the entire street.

After his early fairground fights Tommy's boxing career formally began in November 1933. By Christmas he had fought four fights. In 1935, Jubilee Year, Tommy was back in Deptford after a season in the boxing booth. On 19th October 1936 the reorganised National Sporting Club opened to the public and Len Smith watched Tommy Martin box there on 17 occasions.

By the time he was 21 Tommy had been fighting for some five years. He stood just short of six feet and weighed just over 13 stone. He was already so much a champion that he sailed to the colonies in search of further promotional fights. He fought and the heavyweight champions of British Guiana and Jamaica. The trip was dubbed 'Tommy Martin's Caribbean Campaign'.

The *Kentish Mercury* referred to Tommy Martin in 1938 as "one of the fastest men in the country". The Martin family were an important source of support. His younger sister provided secretarial help answering fan mail from Trinidad and East Africa, while Gordon talked proudly of him at school. By this time Tommy had defeated Battersea's Frank Hough at Earl's Court and in 1938 he went to Australia to promote his boxing.

34. Tommy Martin, Deptford's 'Brown Bomber', training with his makeshift weights. Despite his success, Tommy's boxing career was blighted by the Colour Ban which prevented him from fighting against white boxers.

On Wednesday July 19th 1939 Tommy made the cover of *Boxing*, the threepenny weekly sporting publication. Tommy had a large following and a charabanc or coach regularly carried local fans to his fights at a range of venues. As well as his boxing, Tommy's gentlemanly demeanour contributed to his popularity. However, despite his skill and success, Tommy was having increasing difficulty in finding fights. Outside the boxing ring, and controlling it, was the toughest challenge he had to face.

The Boxing Board of Control had put in place regulations which would stop black boxers like Tommy Martin fighting really prestigious heavyweight championship bouts. The bare fist fighters of earlier days had been sponsored by the aristocracy and powerful businessmen. In the wake of Jack Johnson's triumph and the subsequent antagonism, a regulation which appeased American boxing counterparts and ensured white superiority in the boxing ring was put in place.

In the summer of 1940 Tommy visited the USA. There he had access to a number of black boxers. America was the home of Joe Louis and many black boxers who had gained national and international acclaim. On his return he campaigned against being denied access to fights on racial grounds within the UK. As demand for forces personnel grew for World War II, Tommy joined the RAF. His personal fight, however, was the struggle to be allowed the opportunity to realise his full potential as a boxer and he campaigned strenuously against 'the Colour Ban' which prevented him having top fights at home. In this fight Tommy found a few allies locally.

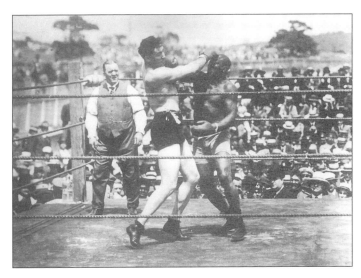

35. Jack Johnson, whose 'spectacular fights' against white boxers led to the ruling by the Boxing Board of Control against any fights between 'opponents of different colours'.

DEPTFORD BOXER'S FIGHT AGAINST COLOUR BAN

Mr W H Green, the Member of Parliament for Deptford, has taken an interest in the 'Tommy Martin case' which involves a question of colour ban, and is to put a question on this subject to the Home Secretary.

The case which Martin, Deptford's 'Brown Bomber', is fighting, concerns the British Boxing Board of Control rule that forbids all coloured boxers from participating in contests for the British heavyweight title. This confines Martin to Empire honours.

Mr Green's question in the House of Commons is as follows: "To ask the Secretary of State for the Home Department if he is aware that a British-Born subject, now serving in the Royal Air Force, has been barred by the British Boxing Board of Control from competing in British boxing competitions on the ground of colour; and, having regard to the harmful reactions on the war effort among our many coloured subjects such a decision will have, will he take steps to discourage such discrimination against British-born subjects solely on colour grounds. KENTISH MERCURY, 1/8/1941.

The Home Secretary's response to the Tommy Martin case highlighted British concern with 'spectacular fights' involving black and white fighters. Jack Johnson's earlier fight had been spectacular. In the wake of the fight, Johnson had further irked white majority America, especially by his open defiance about relationships with white women. The regulation effectively banning black boxers from the most prestig-ious fights was not lifted until after the war. By that time Tommy Martin was past his prime.

TOMMY MARTIN
CONTENDER FOR
BRITISH EMPIRE HEAVY TITLE.

36. The Brown Bomber. Restricted to Empire Honours by the colour ban

DEPTFORD BOXER AND THE COLOUR BAN

The Home Secret-ary's Explanation.

Tommy Martin, Deptford's 'Brown Bomber', who is a friend of the Mayor of Deptford (Lieut- Col. C. G. Blanchard, J.P), was the subject of a statement made by the Home Secretary in the House of Commons last Thursday.

The Home Secretary replied [to WH Green's question]: "While I am in entire sympathy with my hon. friend's view that there should be no discrimination against British subjects on colour grounds, I understand

that there are differences of opinion on the question whether spectacular fights between opponents of different colours ought to be encouraged; and that it is for this reason, and not from any prejudice against coloured boxers, that there is a rule of the British Boxing Board of Control applying."
KENTISH MERCURY 8/8/41

The colour ban or bar, a direct legacy of racial slavery in the Caribbean, would continue to impact upon future generations of people with African origin.

Finding Local Black Residents

Even during this period, when the black presence was becoming so much more visible and the subject of heated debate, it is often difficult to find out about local black residents. Sometimes a photograph or a snippet of information comes to light and the challenge of discovering more is both exciting and frustrating.

Some of the earlier black residents of South East London had, like the general population, moved to areas with better employment prospects. Others moved to communities where numerically they made a difference. Still others preferred to be assimilated in overwhelmingly white communities. The Salvation Army's 'Deptford Chums' photograph from around 1923 reveals at least one local black family other than the Martins. On July 22nd 1932 the *Lewisham Journal*'s picture of North Lewisham Scout Group exhibition shows two black boys among the group. No further information is given about them, suggesting that they are local.

A 75 year old woman, described as 'a native of Trinidad' was a victim of a Catford road accident. She died as a result of being struck by a motor coach, an incident reported in the *Lewisham Journal* of 8th March 1935.

The Port of Deptford

Deptford remained an important source of black visitors. Black seamen came to rely on the accommodation offered by Carrington House on Deptford Broadway. A common lodging house for men opened on 21st November 1903 by Countess Carrington, wife of the Chairman of the LCC Housing Committee, it housed 345 men in separate cubicles.

In April 1949, just one month after over 800 people packed Lewisham Town Hall to hear black singer Paul Robeson, Carrington House was the focus of a distrubance by 'coloured seamen' venting their frustrations about being denied social opportunities on the basis of colour. During the fracas a bottle was thrown at nearby Norfolk House and five black people were later charged with 'insulting behaviour'. In court Moses Ida Hosa complained of being banned from public houses and public dances and stated "I am brought to this court just because of my colour". The magistrate dismissed the plea of racism and found the group guilty, declaring "in this country no difference is made between black and white".

In mid-June more riotous scenes took place outside Carrington House. This time the black men furthered their protest by singing and dancing in the street. Thirty men were arrested and when they appeared before the magistrate seven West Africans were identified as 'troublemakers'. It is not recorded whether Moses was in this second protest but certainly his complaint was to remain a familiar problem for generations of Africans and African-Caribbeans in the area.

37. This photograph, like many of its kind, gives no detail about the life of the young black man selling ice cream. Its main purpose was to comment on the heat of the summer which brought so many people out on to Greenwich beach.

38. Many black characters, such as this Deptford roadsweeper, have been the focus of photographers' interest. But still we don't know his name....

8

ANSWERING THE CALL TO ARMS

"As is usual in times of national peril, Great Britain calls on her black colonial subjects in Africa, Asia and the West Indies – as much as on her white subjects."
AMOS A FORD

Church and newspapers were foremost among the recruiting agents in the Caribbean calling for men to commit themselves to the service of the motherland in the two world wars.

The Great War

Anglicans, Catholics, Baptists, Wesleyans – each of the major denominations of the Caribbean took on the role of moral persuader in the cause of battle. Grenadian would-be recruits were urged to be "missionaries of manhood" in the unrelenting campaign conducted in the name of the war effort.

The targeted men were labelled slackers, cowards or patriots, depending upon the nature of their response. When direct appeal to young men seemed not to be yielding the numbers required, mothers and wives were cajoled to encourage the recruitment of their young men. Many of those recruited enlisted as patriots in answer to the call to arms. The Archbishop of the West Indies delivered the following farewell speech to Jamaica's first war contigent which underlined the men's patriotic response.

You are going forth at the call of your king and country on a great enterprise and there you have the sympathy of the whole people of Jamaica and also our constant prayers. Quit you like men; be strong.

You have bravely undertaken to join these great armies of our Empire which are contending for right against might, for liberty against despotism, for peaceful growth and progress of nations against the domination by force of one great nation over the mental and material progress of the rest of mankind.

Yet the rhetoric did not match the reality. The black soldiers' experience of war consisted largely of special duties as non-combatants. They were stationed in areas such as Egypt or Mesopotamia, away from the main action. Nonetheless, thousands were recruited in the Caribbean.

The young Norman Manley, later Prime Minister of Jamaica, enlisted in Deptford. Born in 1893 at Roxburgh in Jamaica, Manley won a Rhodes Scholarship in 1914 and he and his brother Roy joined their sister, a teacher in England. Norman enrolled at Oxford but by the end of the year both brothers had decided to enlist. At first they tried the air force but they were expected to finance their own training at a cost of £150 each. Instead they joined the Field Artillery, after searching for four weeks for a suitable recruiting centre. The one they found was in East Deptford. Their fellow recruits, who included Yorkshire miners, slowly learnt to call Norman 'Bill' instead of 'Darkie'.

Within a year Norman Manley had become a Corporal. It soon became obvious that the rank and file disliked taking orders from a coloured NCO but Norman found their attitude mild in comparison to that of the fellow officers who were spiteful and conspired to get him into trouble. Roy died in Ypres in 1917. Norman was desolated at witnessing his brother's death.

I cannot speak of how I felt. We were good friends and I was to be lonely for the rest of the war – lonely and bitter.

39. Norman Washington Manley, who enlisted in Detpford in World War I, became Prime Minister of Jamaica after the country won its independence in 1962.

Norman himself returned to Jamaica in 1923 and after independence in 1962 he would be one of the country's most popular prime ministers. Manley documented his experience of racial prejudice within the army. So profoundly did that experience affect the light-skinned privileged member of the Caribbean elite that Manley opted to get himself demoted in order to be relieved of the unwelcome attention of his white brothers in arms.

Like most West Indians serving in the forces the Manleys had been ill-prepared for the difficulties they would encounter within British ranks even before meeting the enemy. It was not until manpower shortage made black recruiting, as distinct from the West Indian contingents, a necessity. Despite the rhetoric of persuasion, hurdles were erected at each step of the process. For the British West Indian contingents the initial medical selection itself proved a tough first hurdle. Many recruits were found to be medically unfit. For those who passed this stage there were anxieties about where service might take them. The prospect of service in the USA was worrying: it meant segregation and the harsh racial intolerance of which many had heard. There was concern, too, about Britain's reluctance to place black men as combat troops.

British awareness of the service of West Indians in the Great War remains patchy precisely because so many black servicemen were allocated labouring roles or given obscure duties in a variety of outposts of the Empire. At the 10th anniversary of the brotherhood movement held at the Congregational Church in Torridon Road, Rev. Ernest J Barson remarked

Perhaps the most striking characteristic of the present war, certainly from the Christian standpoint [is that] never before had men sunk all differences of class, creed and colour to attain a common end. THE LEWISHAM JOURNAL, 15/2/1918

Other than this, it is difficult to find much evidence in the local press of any awareness that the cause of national war was being served by black recruits.

There were many sources of bitterness for Caribbean recruits. They experienced discrimination in pay, allowances and conditions, housing, promotion and other related aspects of war service. For those with families allowances often proved inadequate. The absence of breadwinners caused homes for destitute children to be set up in the Caribbean. Matters came to a head following demobbing in 1919 when black soldiers rioted in a number of areas including London.

Many disgruntled black soldiers returned to the Caribbean after the First World War. They had been involved in war and perceived themselves to be men of action. Shabbily dismissed from service to the motherland, they were prepared to fight against similarly shabby conditions on their return home.

In British Honduras (now Belize) a Commission of Enquiry was sent from the UK to investigate a riot involving returning soldiers. On 5th July 1919 500 disbanded soldiers took to the streets of Belize City in protest. They had served in Mesopotamia (Iraq) and, like many black soldiers at the end of the war, had found themselves dismissed with no pay. Seeking to redress this grievance through colonial agents at home they had met with customary lack of respect and threat of force. In addition, they faced the prospect of lack of employment compounded by a huge increase in the cost of living. The result was riot.

In Grenada, Antigua, Jamaica and Trinidad strikes began to feature in the battle for better pay and conditions. In the period 1911-20 over 123,000 people migrated to the USA. The Great Depression of the early 1930s was indiscriminate in its impact.

Charles McLean was born in Jamaica in 1917. He left school at the age of 13. He recalls the 1930s as a period of numerous strikes which led into a movement for political change and indeed to agitation for independence for the colonies. Charles McLean later emigrated to Britain and settled in Lewisham.

In 1938 there were many marches [in Jamaica]. The whole country was on strike. If you said you were a Bustamante trade union man, you were locked up. There was no if or but about it. CHARLES McLEAN, SPECTRUM, WINTER 1981/2

The Second Call to Arms

In comparison to the lack of records pertaining to the First World War, there is substantially more evidence of the experiences of African-Caribbean and other black people during the Second World War.

It was not unusual for young men to be called up at the age of 18 but this was not the case for Gordon Martin, brother of Deptford's Brown Bomber. He so enjoyed his driving job that the firm managed to keep him out of the services until he was 19 and he was called up in 1941. Gordon opted for the RAF. It seemed the more attractive choice.

I didn't like swimming which implied the navy. I didn't like having a rifle put in my hands although I still had to have a rifle in the air force. When I first went in we were taught how to use them. I didn't much like the idea of the army. So...I didn't like flying but I knew I wouldn't be a pilot so the RAF was the option. I went into the Air Force.

Gordon became a driver in the air force. When a mechanics course became available, he took it and passed, qualifying as a driver and mechanic. He earned 1/6 a day. He volunteered for service overseas. More money was paid to those who worked with armoured cars. Gordon was not to know as he sailed away on the SS *Highland Brigade* that his first posting was South Africa. It was not until the ship sailed that they learnt from the crew where they were headed. The first stop was Sierra Leone and then Durban. When they landed in Durban, the ship was given an unexpected welcome.

She was known as the lady in white. She was an opera singer, a white South African lady. Every time a troop ship came to Durban or left, she went and sang at the quayside.

40. Gordon Martin joined the RAF in 1941. He was posted to the training school for pilots and crews at East London in South Africa where he expected to face racism but was spared "because of the uniform".

Gordon's posting was to the training school for pilots and crews at East London in South Africa. He had heard of the South African colour bar but, with his light complexion and British uniform, he did not suffer from it. He went into town, frequented bars and lived the usual servicemen's life. He was in South Africa for six months.

Obviously it was because of the uniform. I never got turned away from anywhere. That is one of the real things that surprised me.

After South Africa came the Middle East. Gordon started off in Egypt and moved later to Palestine. When the convoy crossing the desert stopped for their meal, Gordon wanted to know how they would make the tea. He watched as the more seasoned men dug a hole in the sand, positioned a few large stones strategically, poured petrol in and perched the billy can on the tripod of stones. Gordon's first Middle East station was in Romilly. Later they moved to Ikea, and then Liva.

The war in the desert by then had reached Tripoli. The western desert had all been captured by Montgomery. When the call came for volunteers for RAF armoured cars,

Gordon signed up. He passed out of the driving course as AC1 which meant a little bit more money. The air force had two squadrons using armoured cars: one in Palestine and one in Iraq. There was more money for the posting in Palestine where men were needed to guard the oil pipelines. Gordon was in Palestine for three years. From there he was suddenly moved to Iraq. It was the first time ever that he would go up in an aeroplane. He served in Iraq for a year, after which his overseas service of four years duration was complete. From Baghdad he returned home to Deptford.

War in the Caribbean

The impact of war was immediate and real in the Caribbean. The war effort was not a distant appeal. Take Trinidad, for example.

What, the unknowledgeable reader might ask, had Trinidad to do with a war that was being fought in Europe, some 5,000 miles distant? The fact is that Trinidad was the British Empire's biggest producer of oil and, as such, was making a vital contribution to keep the British Navy afloat. All this, of course, was well enough known to the Germans – who sank a large number of tankers and merchant ships carrying food in the Caribbean. COLIN WARD

Trinidad was not the only territory in immediate danger. In St Lucia, for example, war arrived spectacularly. In the inner harbour of Castries, the island's capital, the *Lady Drake* was sunk. Such sinking of ships in Caribbean waters made an undoubted impact on the lives of local people, especially when there were local passengers on board travelling between islands.

In Caribbean territories, parallel systems and organisations were set up through the colonial infrastructure to mirror the war response in Britain, including Civil Defence Forces, Air Raid Wardens and so on. When the call came for recruits to the forces overseas, it was not necessarily those already serving who answered most eagerly. All over the Caribbean, British subjects responded to the demands for recruits. Commodities, such as timber, much of which was imported, were in short supply in the mother country. In order to boost Britain's supply, a request was made for British Honduran mahogany foresters to travel to Britain. There was initial demand for 500 foresters to work as civilians in Scotland from 1941 as part of the war effort. A second contingent of 341 men left in 1942. Their story, of false hopes and sometimes despair for a group at the mercy of an uncaring host community was described as "involvement in that tragic phase in human mischief and pain".

Some of the civilian recruits did not get as far as Scotland. Perceived as troublemakers when they protested, they were sent back. Those who did arrive in Scotland worked in demanding conditions, far short of what was offered and returned home. Of those repatriated, some would later return. Of those who found jobs locally some went to centres like London and some found themselves in Lewisham, where they were later joined by other islanders in the post-war immigration.

In South East London, the colonies were barely of interest given the wartime sufferings at home. For a few, however, the colonies appeared to take on a heightened reality during that time of war. Henry Brooke, MP for West Lewisham, proposed more purposeful and dynamic links with the colonies once the war was over. His suggestions would have included a high profile for British MPs within the Caribbean to enhance personal knowledge of 'the Colonial Empire'.

EMPIRE TRAVEL FOR MPs

A closer personal link between Members of Parliament and the Colonies was advocated in the House of Commons on Thursday, by Mr Henry Brooke, the Member for West Lewisham, in a debate on colonial administration particularly bearing on problems of the West Indies.

"It is not for us as private Members", he said, "to dictate to the government on the question of how our personal knowledge of the Colonial Empire might be improved and enhanced but there should be joint thought between us and the Secretary of State on the plans that can be made when war is over and travelling becomes easier, to make certain that every group of colonies is in the ordinary way visited by six or eight Members of Parliament every year."

In reply to an observation by Earl Winterton, Mr Brooke said they had to consider how, by collective action, they could make certain that the growing knowledge of the West Indies should be developed until the House was "as closely in touch with all colonial territories as each of us aspires to be with his own constituency within this island". KENTISH MERCURY, 22/4/1943

Mr Brooke's thought-provoking suggestion was never tried. If it had been, would the experience of post-war immigrants have been different?

Natural-born Subjects

The West Indian populations in the first half of the 20th century were British subject peoples. Yet British military regulations consistently showed an ambivalence to black recruits. On the one hand, African-Caribbean people were responsive, as British subjects, to Britain's call for servicemen and women. On the other hand, they frequently came up against the hard edge of administrative duplicity in relation to black subjects. For the purposes of armed services, Britain seemed undecided as to whether her black subjects were 'aliens' or not. *The Manual of Military Law* includes this telling section.

...number of aliens in any corps is not to exceed the proportion of 1 to every 50 natural-born subjects...A relaxation in favour of Negroes and persons of colour was originally made in consequence of Negroes captured in slavers being taken into the service of the crown, and was continued to legalise the recruiting of natives on the West Coast of Africa for service in the West India Regiments (now disbanded).

In 1944, at the age of 17, Eric Ferron and a small band of friends enlisted in Kingston, Jamaica for the RAF. Until his call-up papers arrived, he kept the decision secret from his family. The *SS Cuba*, in which he journeyed for five weeks, was in a convoy of 30 troop ships bearing some 3,000 West Indian recruits.

As a young man, Eric wanted adventure and to experience a bigger world than he knew. The idea of England, nurtured by a missionary-colonial education system became an important focus of this motivation.

I had joined up because I had wanted to get away, do something new, something different. I did not tell my parents I had applied until after I had been accepted. They objected, of course, but by then it was too late. I wanted to get into the war. But most of all I wanted to see England. I never had any intention of staying away for any length of time. It would be more of a visit to do my service and then come back. I boarded the ship in great excitement. It was a childhood dream fulfilled. I was on my way to England.

It was to take 28 days. As we sailed away from the island everything seemed possible, from finding German submarines to seeing King George. We were excited. We did not know what we were going into. ERIC FERRON

On the SS *Cuba* and in the rest of the convoy were recruits from Jamaica, Trinidad, Barbados, Guyana and the rest of the West Indies. For security reasons the men were not told their destination. They had an indication that they might expect to see Canada. After their first stop in New York, they were well into the Atlantic crossing, before they were they told that they were heading for England.

During the journey the troops heard an announcement that they had been attacked and had drowned. This piece of German propaganda was partly true. The convoy had been attacked twice by enemy fire but the men were very much alive. Eric was certainly one of the youngest African-Caribbean recruits to see action. This is how he describes it.

The first attack...as far as you could see was all lights. The ship could have been hit. There was a tremendous light as if the whole ocean got lit up. And the explosion! We heard it, but don't forget there were 30 ships in the convoy. It was near! All the destroyers were sounding their horns! The panic! We were told to be prepared to take on casualties. There were about 100 people landing on our ship who were picked up at sea. And they were our people, black people.

41. Eric Ferron, who enlisted in Jamaica, became an army medical assistant.

Not all the recruits were sailing to England. Those going to the Far East parted company from the convoy. Meanwhile, the youngest members, three of them close friends of Eric, accommodated their romantic notions of their role in the war to the grimmer realities facing them. The UK contingent landed in Scotland, somewhat closer to realising their dreams. Eric hoped to be a gunner in the Anti Aircraft Regiment.

Eric Ferron never achieved his ambition to be a gunner. Because he had ambitions towards pharmacy and the most minimal experience at it, he became a medical assistant. When he was demobbed, this was the role he developed.

The Colonial Office ruled that those recruited abroad would be repatriated at the end of the war. However, an option allowed for training for civilian life, provided it was related to an occupation held within the forces. Although Eric was anxious to return home, he sought a qualification before his return. A great number of able West Indians took up the opportunity of further training. Eric wished to do pharmacy but the length of the course exceeded that allowed by the conditions of training laid down by the forces. The optimum course length was three years. Instead he was offered nursing. It was that or nothing so he accepted.

Eric's association with Lewisham came through his involvement in social work courses at Goldsmiths College in New Cross from 1970. He founded a panel of black social workers and negotiated with a number of London boroughs for an input to their courses. The arrangement with Goldsmiths has been the most enduring. After 25 years, Eric still gives occasional lectures there.

Black Women at War

The invisibility of black servicewomen is even more pronounced. Eric's biographical details indicate that, wherever armed forces personnel served, they could have found their way to the capital and to areas such as Lewisham. We have no information about women who served in the forces and subsequently lived or worked in the Lewisham area. However, it is likely that more information will be brought to the fore as this area is further documented.

42. A US Army postal unit "composed entirely of Negro members of the Women's Army Corps" arrived in the UK in February 1945 to assist with postal services.

Good Wishes From Chicago

One of the links between the two world wars was Mr Mills of The Versatile Three. When the *Kentish Mercury* launched its Smokes Fund, Mills' friend, Fred Coochey of Manor Lane, wrote to him in the USA. His response caused a nostalgic editorial in the *Mercury* the following week.

Do you remember 'The Versatile Three' who were a popular turn at New Cross Empire a few years ago? From far away Chicago one of them, Mills, has sent his contribution to the Smokes for the Troops Fund.
It comes through Mr Fred Coochey of Manor Lane, Lee, whose individual efforts have benefited the funds so considerably. Mr Coochey wrote to Mr Mills, a friend of long standing, recalling the happy New Cross Empire days and mentioning, incidentally, that the Mercury was running a successful fund for providing smokes for the members of the fighting services. Almost by return came the reply - a very welcoming two-dollar bill and with it a letter wishing good luck to the effort. KENTISH MERCURY, 5/4/1940

Together?

The service of West Indian personnel in the armed forces has raised a number of issues. Principal among these is their invisibility in the records of the two wars. The latest omission contributing to this continued invisibility was the decision in May 1995 to leave out Caribbean men and women as well as Africans from Government commemoration of the 50th anniversary of the end of the war. The selected focus for the commemoration was Europe and the disregard of black service is argued on the specious grounds of an insignificant presence in Europe.

43. The role of West Indian and other Empire regiments in the war effort was recognised in this poster. However, in practice most West Indian recruits were posted to non-combatant duties and their role has been largely ignored.

BANANA BOATS AND MIGRANTS

"I assumed that it was very easy. Providing you had the brain and the tenacity, the opportunity was there. I was sadly wrong." RONNIE GORDON

"When I came here, I thought I was only going to stay for five years. But it was easier to come here than to go back!" CHARLES MACLEAN

It was the middle of summer when HMS *Empire Windrush* docked at Tilbury in 1948 sending shock waves across Britain. The 492 West Indians who disembarked were unaware of the alarm that would ricochet across the motherland at sight of such a visible black presence.

Of the group, mostly Jamaicans, mostly men, many were returning to England having served in the war. For others this was a journey with elements of pilgrimage, adventure and potentially enhanced career prospects. The boat train taking them from Southampton to Victoria passed sights and place names made familiar through school textbooks as well as by the popular media, radio and cinema. All this had been as much part of their life as hot weather and sandy beaches.

These passengers on the first ship bearing post-war Caribbean immigrants to Britain were children of the West Indies of the 1930s who had had the benefit of increased education opportunities. At the same time, their knowledge of the world had been greatly extended through information about World War II and the benefits they had been told would come from victory. West Indians, like the British, had had their expectations of a better future heightened by wartime promises. In addition, large numbers had travelled beyond their home islands to Central America, the USA, Europe and other war postings in the Pacific or Africa.

Several of the passengers of the *Empire Windrush* gave destination addresses within the Lewisham area. Five mentioned Wickham Road, Brockley and two gave Tanner's

44. HMS Empire Windrush which brought 492 Jamaicans to Britain in 1948.

Hill in Deptford as their proposed address. Since most of the passengers had no accommodation arranged, 236 men sheltered in the deep air raid bunker on Clapham Common. When that was closed on 12th July, 20 were sent to Government reception centres in Camberwell and Deptford. Many more were to arrive in the Deptford and Lewisham area in their search for jobs and homes in London.

45. West Indian immigrants at Southampton dock.This photograph was the subject of a 1956 Picture Post article headlined 'Thirty Thousand Colour Problems'.

The men and women of the *Empire Windrush* had sailed to the motherland as British citizens exhorted to play their part in the rebuilding of post-war Britain. Newspapers, radio and the church continued to process the patriotic rhetoric that made the purchase of a passage to Britain seem a natural and glorious next step.

These were the first of the post-war wave of Caribbean immigrants to the south east and many more ships followed. Some migrants travelled on cruise ships. Others booked passages on liners that came to be known as 'banana boats', which combined the established business of the transportation of bananas with a new passenger service to Britain.

Immigrants of the Post-Windrush Decade

While information about West Indian arrivals appeared in British homes under headlines screaming 'PROBLEM', the new Caribbean migrants to South East London in the 1950s had taken a bold step into a hopeful future in Britain. They had hard-earned skills and they were prepared to work hard to develop both skills and qualifications and generally to improve their lot. Though they had been schooled about England, to the exclusion of much else, they were largely unprepared for what they would encounter.

Ronnie Gordon arrived in London from Grenada in May 1950. Only six months out of one of the most prestigious grammar schools his island offered, he had come to study, travelling with his brother. The two knew no-one else in London and had only the vaguest idea of how they would survive in London.

We just didn't know where we were going...I had heard of the Balmoral Hotel. At that time the Balmoral Hotel was a place run by and for colonial students: Africans, Nigerians, Ghanaians. All colonials who were students could go there. So that's where I ended up...The people who came up from Grenada were people who had scholarships. The Island Scholarship was a big thing. Those were the only people who were coming up at that time. Their funds were provided for and they went to the Balmoral Hotel. That was the only information I started with. RONNIE

The propaganda of imperialism had been deeply impressed upon black colonial subjects through a number of outmoded rituals which became the focus of specific

46. This young girl, stranded at Victoria station in 1956, was also due to appear in the Picture Post article . After the long journey, she must have been wondering what future awaited her in the new country.

holidays. These occasions involved almost the entire community since it was compulsory for all schoolchildren to attend. Military-style parades were the order of the day. Uniformed groups of schoolchildren, scouts, girl guides, cubs, cadets and so on paraded at length in the sweltering heat. The Red Cross was very much in evidence since numbers of schoolchildren would faint in the heat as they waited for the marching to be through. The Governor of the island, or occasionally the Governor-General, would be a special focus of the parades. The 24th May, Empire Day, saw just such ritual.

On the day after his arrival in England, despite having had only two hours sleep, Ronnie was up and dressed in his best suit ready for the Empire Day celebrations. He expected the celebrations to be all the more spectacular for being in the mother country. As he hurried out, expecting ritual on a grand scale, he encountered a colonial official who found his enthusiasm a source of some mirth.

> I said to him, 'I must hurry you know because I want to attend the May Day celebrations'. He said, 'my, my you're smart. Mayday celebrations? What sort of celebrations are you asking for?' I said, 'Well, it's Queen Victoria's birthday'. He said, 'Queen Victoria is dead'. Of course I knew she was dead but in Grenada we all paraded in the market square. There we would be in the sun, my fellow beings, sun pouring down, fainting...policemen, kids.

This was the first dent in Ronnie's perceptions of England, its values and customs and the realities of its existence. He was 17 years old and thoroughly schooled into believing that the practices highlighted in his own colonial education were those of all British citizens. Ronnie hoped to train as a chartered accountant.

Other men landed in Britain secure in their knowledge of a trade. George Rhone arrived in November 1953. Born in rural Jamaica, the young man had gained carpentry skills through sheer determination and, initially, against the wishes of his father, a subsistence farmer who wanted George's assistance with his livestock. Having seen a carpenter at work in the village, George longed to do that job when he grew up. He persuaded his mother to plead his cause to his father. This she did successfully. It was a five-year apprenticeship but the young George Rhone was only too pleased to be learning, not only a trade, but the trade of his choice.

> My daddy had lots of horses and mules and we had to help him out and I use to like to do carpenter work. I always see this man working, like them plane wood, they cut the wood. I said to my mum, "Could you let me learn that trade?"...And one day now, this man was building up this house, and I go down there and beg him and say, "Could I come? Will you take me to learn me what to do?". They chalk the line and line the board. I went down on my mum and she asked the man. The man say yes. When I started out I start to do cabinet making. My dad give this man £5 to buy some tools.

Beckett Turner arrived in London from Jamaica in August 1955, a month before Hurricane Janet devastated much of the West Indies. He was 37 years old when he flew into Heathrow. Beckett planned to continue his studies to qualify as a dentist. He intended to support himself financially through employment while he studied.

> It was a bit strange coming from little Kingston, Jamaica, to big London and the mother country, which I had always looked forward to...I was amazed at

the buildings and the helter skelter of the place, the traffic going hither and thither. It really was very busy.

Men were the majority among those early immigrants but women soon followed. Mostly, the women had friends or relatives whose journey had stimulated an interest in travelling. Relatives at home sometimes tried to dissuade interested family members. On the other hand, luxury goods sent over to the Caribbean by those working in England seemed to indicate a very profitable existence. These goods proved very persuasive.

> *In those days my cousin use to send us down barrels of pleated skirt, stockings and all, tights that we have never known about and bundles of curtains and all the rest of it. He didn't tell me he use to go down Petticoat Lane and buy them cheap. We thought that he was really doing so well for himself, because all my friends use to envy me in my pleated skirt and my this and that that he use to send me, and my elaborate curtains and so on. So I write back to him and said to him "You've been in England for the last five years and you going to America. Why don't you want me to come?"* SYBIL PHOENIX

The exotic packages and barrels arriving from London contradicted the letters which warned of difficulties to be found in employment and social conditions. Many, undeterred, booked their passages and set off for London.

In 1956 Sybil Phoenix arrived in London, a young woman in her late twenties. She planned to develop her Trubenising [shirt making] skills since she had a thriving family business to return to in British Guiana. She hoped to use her time in England to diversify the business into millinery and to have a holiday. With those objectives achieved, Sybil expected to return home. Her planning was so purposeful that she brought a sewing machine with her to London! The machine, a bulky foot pedal model, was a source of considerable amusement to the London cab driver at Victoria station. To Sybil the sewing machine was a practical and necessary piece of equipment. Since she had several in British Guiana, taking one to London seemed a sensible idea despite the £27 excess baggage charge.

England was not always the favoured destination of those who travelled in the post-Windrush decade. The USA had, however, placed severe restrictions on entry. The opportunities for travel, personal development and ready cash abroad were appreciated and England offered another option. Young adults saw in this situation an opportunity not to be missed. Annie George arrived in London in 1958. She had passed the screening procedures of personnel on her island and planned to study as a nurse.

> *It was just that all my friends were coming so I thought I might as well come too. Because a lot of the young people around the area was coming. England was never really my first choice. I never fancied coming to England, but everybody else was coming so I thought I'd come too.*

Expectations of the Motherland

Those arriving in London for the first time from 1948 onwards had high expectations, often based on faulty information. The source of the misinformation was largely the formal education from the established churches which idealised the British way of life through the printed material from which children were taught. The popular media confirmed these impressions. England, the West Indian population had been taught, was the land of opportunity, in direct contrast to the West Indies. Merit, knowledge and skills, it was believed, were the keys for colonial subjects to abundant opportunity.

Because I had gone to a good school and I acquired a Senior Cambridge, I wanted to do a course. I knew I wanted to do accountancy. We just knew that England was the motherland and we assumed it was better than everywhere else. Well, it was a complete fallacy. RONNIE GORDON

Education and further training were usually aims of the new migrants. Many ambitious students selected law; still others opted for medicine. Many years later the choice of articled accountant seemed preposterous for a young African-Caribbean man, given the difficulties.

The only people in my category in the first five years who really partly succeeded were guys who did law. It gave you a certain amount of independence. The big hurdle I found was that, of course, I had the wrong ideas completely. So brain-washed with the old secondary school image and all that, I chose what I wanted to do. I wanted not certified, but the highest one, chartered accountancy. That was completely out of reach, I found out. RONNIE

The student migrant group rarely had independent financial means of support. Progress in study depended upon regular employment to pay course fees and maintenance. To achieve their goals they took a variety of jobs. Beckett's first job was as a cook and housekeeper in the private residence of Sir Richard Winstead, former Director of Education in Malaya. In the mid 1950s Sir Richard and his wife retired and with minimal savings, Beckett's studies were set back.

Ronnie and his brother had exhausted their funds after three weeks at the Balmoral Hotel. It was difficult to find information about accountancy courses. Ronnie was required to register for employment with the Youth Employment Bureau. His certificates indicated to the career officers a future in clerical work but he had no experience. After six weeks he found his first job in London. The firm paid according to age and experience and assumed dependence on a family at least for housing. Although his employers took an interest in him, Ronnie found it hard to pay for accommodation and other necessary expenses as well as save towards his studies on £3 per week.

The brothers rented a room from a Scottish landlady. Even the most frugal existence left them unable to purchase the necessities to survive the winter. Ronnie walked to work. When his shoes wore out, he negotiated a rise of 10 shillings. He discovered that the accountant's career he had prized required 'articles' which would further delay his earning capacity. Ronnie was advised by a less-schooled acquaintance to apply for a job in a factory where he might earn £14 at shift work. Despairing of the immediate professional career he had dreamed of, Ronnie went in search of a factory job offering better pay and taking him slowly nearer to his goals.

Culture Shock

Black people in the colonies had always been presented with sanitised images of English life. A great number of profoundly shocking experiences awaited them and they rapidly formed more realistic impressions of 20th century inner city life.

I had my first shock horror when I drove into Victoria station and saw this white woman painted, what my minister at home use to call 'painted devils'. Those days they were wearing the beehive and her hair was up in this beehive and she had the green eyes and all of that and I see her sweeping the platform! ... I don't know what I was expecting but I certainly wasn't expecting to see her sweeping the platform!

White people, having always been the masters and in positions of authority in the Caribbean, had come to be associated in black people's minds with higher forms of behaviour. In the Caribbean this was reinforced by the fact that servants and menials were always black while those in the highest positions of authority – church leaders, government officials and so on – were invariably white.

So much was different: the lack of space, the housing, the prevailing social conditions, the essential expenditure on seaonal needs such as heating and winter clothing. One of the first hurdles was finding employment. The pay packet held the means to survive the difficulties of the new lifestyle. Ever present, too was the awareness that families and partners back home depended, in part, upon the income received.

Employment: Only the Dirty Jobs

Noel Alexander arrived from the Jamaican parish of St Ann's in 1953. This was his second major venture abroad. He had been employed in the USA as part of the 'manpower' programme which recruited large numbers to work in industries directly servicing the forces and to serve as a reserve labour army. On his return to Jamaica, Alexander invested his savings in a shop and he became self-employed.

He was 33 when he came to England, with 10 years experience as a self-employed shopkeeper. He recalls that times were hard in post-war Jamaica. Commodities, particularly imports, were difficult to purchase for his shop and goods were still being rationed. Fixed price lists were the order of the day. Profits were so tightly curbed that the sale of a dozen boxes of matches yielded only a penny profit. Noel's sister had emigrated to England earlier and she wrote to him of the possibilities for work. He had friends in England who also wrote suggesting that they fared much better there. He was encouraged to try his luck so he sold the shop and came to this country, at first to Reading, Berkshire. Reading, like Brixton in South London, had become established as one of a few areas where black people could find accommodation and where they would be less isolated.

The following year Noel tried London. Though willing to accept almost any job, he found job hunting in the capital extremely difficult. There were advertisements for jobs in the Thames Valley but it was impossible to find accommodation. He was employed almost immediately at Huntley and Palmer's biscuit factory and he stayed with friends until he could find a room. The take-home pay was around £5 a week which seemed reasonable enough. Rent for a bed was £1 and food was relatively cheap. He even managed to save but finding somewhere to live was still difficult.

Before long Noel heard that those on the night shift earned an extra pound so he requested night work. He discovered immediately that only white men did the night shift. They made it very clear that they did not want a black man working among them. One night the most overtly hostile of the men started a fight. He was due to work with Noel on 'the roller' which required the co-operative effort of two men.

The white co-worker refused Noel's partnership and attempted the task himself. He then complained to the foreman that Noel was shirking. Not satisfied with the foreman's response, he started a fist fight. The fight ended in a bloody face for the white worker who complained again to the foreman. This time he said he had been assaulted in a general attack upon the white staff by Noel. The foreman did not believe that one black man had attacked his 10 white co-workers without extreme provocation. Such was the rage of the complainant, however, that in great temper he accidentally dropped a 56 pound weight on his own foot and spent the rest of the night in hospital. Noel did not stay in the job.

He returned to Brixton where his intended wife lived. At this time a steady stream of West Indian immigrants were arriving. Part of the strategy of dealing with their search for employment was to disperse them by offering jobs far afield. Noel was offered a job in Dudley by the South London labour exchange. He refused.

He was finally offered a job as a machine operator in the Dunlop Rubber Company's warehouse at Greenwich, making cardboard boxes. It was a clean job and Sunday work was available. He worked there for about eight years. When the factory closed in about 1971, he was made redundant. Luckily there was a vacancy as a stoker and boilerman with the Department of the Environment in Kidbrooke where he worked until he retired in 1985.

Ruby Alexander lived with a cousin on Somerleyton Road in Brixton. In that part of London, if you went shopping on a Friday or Saturday, the chances were not only that you would meet fellow West Indians but that you would meet, if you were Jamaican, others from your own island.

John Stewart travelled to London in November 1955 by boat from Trinidad via the Canary Islands and Genoa and overland to London Victoria by train. He was 28 years old and went to live in his sister's home inhabited mainly by fellow Trinidadians and with some Irish neighbours on the top floor.

What was surprising to me was that it seemed so big, everything in a grandiose form. When I came out of the station I saw the murky atmosphere and that surprised me but then I saw where I was going to stay. I made the remark "that's a big house, you live there?". It was a terrace house. She just lived in one of the terrace houses but I was thinking it was all one house.

John planned to travel and to study electrical engineering. His search for a house brought him to Lewisham around 1957. He had tried the Holloway and Archway areas but the estate agents were not optimistic and he found himself losing his deposits. He began to appreciate that there was a 'credibility' problem. His sister heard that there was a West African selling his house in Doggett Road near Catford Police Station. Soon John was working, studying and paying a mortgage. Like so many others he was prepared to be flexible to earn an income but found it hard getting a first job. After a job cleaning lamps on railway stations, he tried electrical work but found working in blocks of flats too cold and went back to British Rail. He settled down in Lewisham.

Nursing

The girls use to complain about not getting promoted enough. I was quite happy to do my SEN job and that's it. I didn't want promotion because I had a few kids by then and I didn't have time to think about promotion...just get enough money to help run the house. There were a few girls promoted but they used to complain of not being promoted enough. RUBY ALEXANDER

Ruby Alexander came to England in 1953 as a young single woman, 22 years old. Her brother was already living in Reading and she felt ready to leave home. She recalls that the way in which colour prejudice or 'shadism' operated in Jamaica at the time meant that a young black woman who had done well at school had three main employment avenues open to her. These were teaching, nursing and post office work, a lower ranking civil service position. She recalls, too, the English post-war advertisements for skilled people. Yet one of the first lessons to be learnt by black workers was that "no matter how skilled you were, you weren't skilled enough for them".

In England Ruby went into nursing. As in Jamaica, this was one of the few positions open to her. When she married and had her first child she left work. At the time and in the circumstances, no practical alternative offered itself, particularly in the light of advice from a welfare worker who had very frankly warned of the difficulties in finding a childminder because of the social stigma attached to a white person looking after a black child while the mother went to work.

Mavis Stewart arrived in London from Jamaica in September 1954. She was 18 years old and had chosen a career in nursing. There were two methods of selection for nurse training: either direct application to a hospital in response to an advertisement or selection through interview by the Colonial Office. The Minister of Health responsible for such recruiting at the time was Enoch Powell. In his ministerial capacity he would have circulated information through the Colonial Office in Jamaica guiding the selection of student nurses such as Mavis. The screening procedure ensured that Mavis met the requirements of age, academic qualifications, social background and medical condition. Having passed all of these, she made her way to Queen Mary's hospital in West Ham Lane. Seven years later she moved to Lewisham as a qualified midwife.

Many of the skilled and those with qualifications and professional aspirations were forced to adjust their sights. They accepted jobs for which they were over-qualified. The pressure to earn was very real indeed as there was rent to be paid and numerous other financial responsibilities.

Guests Unwelcome

The housing experience of the early West Indian migrants was a barometer of their reception in the UK. Only those fortunate enough to be in tied accommodation such as student hostels or nurses' homes were spared. A whole range of undesirable situations represented the choices available in the early years of post-war immigration.

For those with sufficient income and who looked sufficiently respectable, there was bed and breakfast in desirable accommodation. The disadvantages were that on no account were 'guests' welcome during the day.

They use to take in ladies that go out to work at 6.30 in the morning and come back 6.30 to 8 o'clock in the evening. The places that were nice didn't give you a front door key, so you knocked or you ring the bell and they let you in. The house was nice and you had a nice bedroom but you had to go to the bathroom to get water. But at least they had a bathroom in the house! I got ill in the winter and I was doing my millinery then, and this woman I worked for rung up and ask for me to come home. The landlady said "No". She said that maybe if it was a day when she wasn't having friends in, but she's got some friends in this afternoon so I couldn't come in. She said "maybe about half past six, that's the earliest". Somebody went across the road to buy a blanket for me and I lie down in the cutting room, shivering with fever and everything else. SYBIL

Sometimes 'flats' were on offer. These, however, did not conform to the usual ideas of flats but were a variation of one-room accommodation.

I knew what a flat was. A flat was a bedroom, a sitting room and your kitchen, and you got toilet and bath. I didn't know a flat was one room. She showed me into his room. I ask her for the bathroom. She tell me to go down to the bottom, turn left and immediately right and across the road, go down the other side and I'll find the bath. I said "It's the bathroom I'm asking you for". She said "I am sending you to the bathroom". I said "Where is the kitchen?". She then showed me the ring that was on the washstand. He had a basin and two buckets. He had the washstand and basin, the mug full of water, and one of those jimmy jam bottle of water. That was his kitchen, that was his sitting room, his bedroom, his dining room, his toilet in the night, his washroom, the lot. SYBIL PHOENIX

More usually the only accommodation available or affordable to black people was shared rooms. Cooking and washing facilities were also shared with a number of occupants. The rooms offered were often in overcrowded houses.

They'd converted the downstairs bathroom. He put board over the bath tub and he put three cookers – this is the bathroom I'm telling you about – three cookers in the bathroom. It had a big sink and a bathroom sink. He'd left a board in the bath and so that was used as a table that you could put things on, or sit on it, and when everybody finished cooking and the night is done, that's the time you had baths. First thing in the morning or late at night. SYBIL

The landlords renting rooms to black people were often Polish or Ukranian and others who had themselves experienced difficulties in the UK. They knew the problems and appreciated the extra cash.

At times in the 1950s there were not even single rooms to be had for black people travelling around England in search of jobs. In many cases people began by renting a bed, especially single men. While one or two occupants were on night shift, day workers could, for a share of the rent, take their turn and have somewhere to sleep.

Given the limited choice the poor quality of housing offered to black clients, a number of determined newcomers set their sights on the purchasing their homes.

Having children presented families with more housing difficulties.

If you had children and you're in one bedroom, especially if you're on one of the floors above, that child couldn't walk on the floor cause people would complain that the child is making noise. RUBY ALEXANDER

Ruby found in the papers what looked a favourable housing deal in New Cross. With £200 deposit a part-vacant house could be secured. The couple saved and applied. It was an all-inclusive deal for around £15 per month. On moving in, they found that a mother with two children held tenant rights to the flat upstairs. There was no bathroom and the only washing facilities were in the kitchen where there was a boiler for hot water. They were thankful for all of this but they had wanted something better.

The Phoenixes purchased their first house in the 1950s. Their experience was, in essence, a variety of the story of vulnerability, racketeering and racism which was to be a common thread in much of the black experience in Britain.

We got totally robbed because this house was up for demolition and we didn't know that, and the solicitor didn't tell us. When the next solicitor wanted to fight, he said that coloureds isn't supposed to own houses here. SYBIL

Seven years after coming to London, the Rhones bought their first house in 1960. They were not party to whatever plans had been made for the area in which their house stood and it was compulsorily purchased by the Council in the 1970s. The Georges bought their first home in the mid 1960s. Like every other black person, their choice was limited. They soon came to appreciate the difficulties of sitting tenants.

They had the best part of the house and paid less. Their rent was next to nothing and then you have all this mortgage and all that to pay so that wasn't ideal for us. So we looked around for a next house. We got one on Fernbrook Road, Hither Green.

It is tempting to conclude that the eager new house buyers were simply making expensive mistakes in their purchases but the reality was that, whether renting or buying, they were denied access to sound housing stock and deliberately offered the worst by estate agents, solicitors and residents ready to exploit insecurity and inexperience.

Along with availability of accommodation, the most important factor in the settlement of West Indians in the post-Windrush period was proximity to place of employment, relative or friend resident in the vicinity. At least the new arrivals looked first for homes near the areas they came to know.

Growth of the De-skilled

Soon an army of black people found themselves the reserves of a labour market. Before long the situation was compounded by mortgages and young families to be fed, clothed and educated necessitating the setting aside of excess pride about types of work. Return home was postponed. Very few got the jobs they hoped for, the housing conditions they expected or the opportunity for study which they had planned. Like Noel Alexander and John Stewart, they rolled up their sleeves and 'made the best' of whatever options arose.

The arrival of West Indians as a direct response to demands for skilled labour was unhampered by entry restrictions because of the 1948 Nationality Act. But action to curb black immigration was already under discussion. Within days of the arrival of the *Empire Windrush*, 11 Labour MPs called for the control of black immigration in a letter to Clement Attlee and in 1950 the outgoing Labour government founded a Cabinet committee to consider restricting immigration of coloured people from the British colonial territories.

Word travelled that labour was needed and jobs were available whether for skilled or not. As the Alexanders point out, when black people found out the irrelevance of their skills to the job market they wrote home telling others that skill did not matter. Another wave of black adults prepared themselves to migrate, find jobs and better opportunities. They would be joined by wives and children in the 1960s.

PART FOUR

Mframa-dan
(wind-house)
'House built to
withstand hard
conditions'

Putting down roots

10

GROWING UP BLACK IN THE SOUTH EAST

"Douglas Way is dreary
Idonia Street is grey
need somewhere warmer, brighter,
make the pain go away" LENNIE ST. LUCE

As an eight year old in 1950, Thelma Perkins travelled from Chislehurst on the train to St John's station in Brockley every Saturday afternoon to visit her baby sister Jane. Although all the children lived in a children's home, Jane was in the 'babies' section in Brockley while the older three children were housed in Chislehurst. Their father, Ernest Nicholas McKenzie, born in Trinidad, explained the children's circumstances.

> *The following are the facts. My wife is a Jewess and I am a negro. The two races are classified as inferior by Hitler and my race is so classified by all other peoples in the world, including the English. Although I have produced a good home wherein I hoped to bring up my children in accordance with the Christian practice, I find that the home is on the verge of breaking through pressure put on my wife by her family members who are bitterly prejudiced against my complexion.*

In the days of Thelma's weekly visits Brockley was very quiet. Tressillian Road, which was beautifully tree-lined, seemed miles long. The houses looked affluent and there were big cars in the driveways. These were mainly one family homes and it was evidently a street where the well-heeled lived.

Wickham Road and Breakspears Road were even broader, more gracious streets and the houses were enormous. Some of the people in the big houses were elderly and to the young Thelma they looked very, very old. Thelma attracted the old ladies and, as she pushed her little sister in a pram up to Hilly Fields, they often stopped to touch her hair or gaze wonderingly at the brown baby asleep in the pram.

Apart from the children in her own family, Thelma saw no black children at all.

It was not until she was a young teenager that she noticed significant changes in the local population. In the late 1950s and early 1960s, she began to notice more black people living in houses locally. The formerly predominant pattern of owner occupiers was changing and in Tressilian Road there were now younger people, some black, looking out of windows and otherwise being very visible. Thelma became aware that upper floors were being sub-let.

Thelma was invited to clubs which had sprung up in the basements of people's houses. Before long she was regularly being taken to one on Breakspears Road. Mrs Abdul, the hostess of this particular night spot, drove a pink Vauxhall Cresta, known then as the 'black man's Rolls Royce'. When the Cresta was spotted, local young black youngsters knew it was Mrs Abdul who was a flamboyant local character very much appreciated by the black young. Young black men had few places they could go and she created the social setting that they needed. Food was available in the club, as well as the popular evening drinks, Cherry B and Babycham. It was here that Thelma was introduced to Blue Beat and Ska. Mrs Abdul provided a valuable social service, creating a venue where the young men could meet women or socialise with each other.

Someone else who provided an important service was Madam Hector, the hairdresser on Lewisham Way, between Malpas Road and Shardeloes Road. She displayed in the window the wigs that were so fashionable for the women of the period. Saturday mornings were busy times with much curling, dressing and pressing of hair as well as catching up on news and gossip so important in a hairdresser's.

In 1963 Thelma started work at Lewisham Hospital. The newly arrived trainee nurses and orderlies from the Caribean were always interested in her. Having been born in Birmingham, Thelma spoke differently to their ears and soon these new colleagues wanted to know where she was from. They would offer advice on her hair and skin in a time when few beauty products were widely available for young black women. Thelma noticed how on the wards the West Indian orderlies and nurses worked hard and cared for the patients in an exemplary fashion.

There was no doubt about how hard they worked, whatever they were doing, whether they were cleaning or being the tea lady. I can honestly say that for a very, very long time I never came across one who wasn't nice or kind to the patient, ever. Quite a few had obviously come over to be more than ward orderlies but that was where they had been directed. When I first started in the East End, me and a Kenyan Indian girl, we were the only two black nurses in the hospital. That must have been 1957 or '58.

Basil Morgan's family came to the UK in 1954. His father was a carpenter, his mother a dressmaker. They lived for a short time in Brixton. When Basil was five years old they moved to Ewart Road off Brockley Rise. In the late 1950s there were not many black families living locally, a few from Jamaica and a small community from Grenada. In these houses there were lots of single men.

Family life was typified by the cooker on the landing which everyone shared. The houses where West Indians lived were largely bare. There was a strong feeling of being in temporary accommodation. For most, there were no proper kitchens and in many cases, the landlord's family would have a kitchen while the tenants shared the makeshift facilities on the landing: a sink with only cold water. Bathroom and washing facilities were shared. For those lucky enough to have a single room to themseves, the trunk in the corner of the room collected purchases to be sent back home to the extended family. Many had short-term plans of staying for only three or five years so they gathered purchases for their return.

However, there were some who were better off than those in multiple occupied rooms. A number of Jamaican families and other nationals who were more established had their own houses. The Morgans and four or five other families around Forest Hill came to know each other very well. The social cohesion of the group was based on similar experiences back home, coming from the same extended family or having lived in the same district. The coming together also happened through social activities like the 'pardner hand'.

In each of the Caribbean territories a system of saving had developed. In Jamaica this was called 'pardner'. In Grenada it was called 'sou sou'. Essentially 'a pardner' was a group of people who agreed to save together. Each member of the group would 'throw a hand' by putting in the agreed weekly sum so that the same amount was saved by each member. It was decided how many weeks the saving would run for and when each member would get 'the draw' of the collective amount in any one week. If 10 people agreed to pay in £5 then a different member of the group would receive the total sum of £50 in each of the 10 weeks. This method of saving, elementary though it may seem, enabled members of the Caribbean community to make large purchases at a time when the banks would not accept them as creditworthy.

When Basil Morgan was old enough it was his job to collect the money from the families. It was an important responsibility for the young boy and it meant that he came to be well known by the growing local Caribbean community. He felt his responsibility keenly and worried from time to time what might happen if someone did not pay but he never had to face this unpleasant situation.

New arrivals to the area from the West Indies, especially those with families, sought out other established families such as the Morgans. They wanted advice on getting their children into good schools, finding accommodation, employment and suitable churches, so the Morgans became a kind of unofficial reception committee.

For young Basil growing up in Forest Hill, one shortcoming was the lack of black children his age. For a time there were no other black families living on the Morgans' street. He watched younger black children arrive in the area but it was not until he was at Dalmain Primary School that there was one other black pupil in his class and she was a girl. For his brother and sister, four and six years younger, school was different. There were more black peers. Even as a teenager, most of Basil's black friends were younger.

Another member of the group of black people in the area was a Jamaican who lived towards Brockley called Mr Good. He operated as a travelling salesman in those early days, taking his van around the houses of known West Indian families, selling brushes, dusters, cleaning material,

47. Basil Morgan

shirts, blouses, suits and candlewick bedspreads. The young Basil would have a new suit each summer from Mr Good.

Another supplier to the black people in the area was a Caribbean shop in Brockley. The shopkeeper also travelled to customers, many of whom worked during the day and were therefore unable to get to the shop. In the van each week, foodstuffs were brought to customers' doors. The Caribbean produce on offer included gungo or pigeon peas, yams, sweet potatoes, ackee and other familiar produce. These goods were all the more appreciated for not being available in the usual grocery shops and markets. The shop was just by Brockley Cross and although families grumbled that the Caribbean shops always charged a few pennies more than other grocers, they were satisfied to give their support by shopping there for at least some of their goods.

Basil's family belonged to the Church of England and attendance at church was, to all intents and purposes, compulsory. He became a member of the church choir of St Saviour's on Brockley Rise at his mother's insistence and he remained in the choir from the age of eight to 18. He was also a server in the church for a year and he taught in Sunday school for a year.

Tressillian Road was Paulene Grant's first Lewisham home. Her father came to London in 1954 and was later joined by his wife. Paulene was born in 1957. It was the height of the baby boom and there were no hospital beds available in Lewisham so Paulene's mother was admitted to St Andrew's hospital in Poplar. This caused acute difficulties for the family as Paulene's father, though working, had no transport. By the time he had travelled to Poplar, he would arrive very late at the hospital. Sometimes he would see his wife in the corridor outside the ward because it was so late and the other women had settled into bed.

Paulene was the new baby born across the water, the first English-born child of the family. Paulene's childminder, 'Auntie Katie', was white. She kept chickens in the back garden and Paulene remembers them coming into the house to roost underneath the sink. Paulene was very popular. Two big white girls called regularly at their house with requests to take her out in her blue pushchair. Paulene was also briefly minded by her aunt in Whitechapel but being a fair distance away, that was not very convenient.

Paulene's mother worked at Zenith Carburettor Factory on Deptford Creek. This factory employed many black people and it is interesting that one of the former employees has now returned to the site and specialises in carburettor repairs. Paulene's mother shared a work bench with another young Jamaican woman, Paulene's future mother-in-law. By the time Paulene was three years old the family were tenants at 3 Childeric Road. A white family lived above them and Paulene found herself a girl playmate upstairs. When the white family moved, they sold the house to Paulene's father and mother.

In the early 1960s Paulene's family owned two houses on Childeric Road. The double-fronted Victorian house where they lived was large so they sublet the downstairs part which had a separate front door. The Grants had tenants for many years and consequently they knew a lot of families who had passed through their house over the years.

Both parents were very hardworking and they had high moral standards which to the children at times seemed rather strict. Paulene's mother got a new job at St Alphege's hospital, now Greenwich District Hospital, where she worked until she retired. Her husband, a carpenter, was also hardworking but the houses in Childeric Road needed restoration so, although he was in paid employment during the day, he also worked on the houses, taking up floorboards, repairing joists and other jobs in his spare time.

Paulene attended Childeric Primary School. She was a bright pupil who spoke the language the teachers knew and so she did well. She had black and white friends and she attained high marks. She was also happy at school though she was aware that there were some teachers who hated the black children. One music teacher, in particular, was quite vicious with some of the children and on Wednesday mornings during singing practice, there was a great deal of pushing, hitting, dragging and even kicking of pupils. It was the black children who were frequently at the butt end of this teacher's anger and frustrations.

> *We all went to the local schools, people who lived locally. It was a very tight community and to a certain extent it still is. Anybody who lived down in New Cross at that time, whilst we don't have close links with each other, if you ever see anybody now and recognise them, you don't pass them. You stand and you chat and you catch up with news even if it is seven or eight years old. We all knew each other's parents and as people came over from the Caribbean, families grew and shared in the grief of deaths and things. It was a very close community.*

Paulene was minded from before she started school to the age of 11 by Rose Moore. Rose and her husband were white. 'Uncle Albert' served in the First World War and told many stories of it. In the winter, well wrapped up against the cold weather, Paulene would be taken to Deptford market in her push chair. She remembers the ironmongers on the corner near Stanley Street, the horse and cart outside the second-hand shop and the second-hand clothes stalls in rows in front of where the Albany now stands in Douglas Way.

It was at Sunday School that Paulene became very racially aware. She attended a thriving Sunday School in New Cross where productions were put on by the children at Easter and Christmas but the black children were given very peripheral parts. Many of the other children also attended the Boys' Brigade or Girls' Brigade and the vicar only seemed to recognise these children. Paulene and her sister felt uncomfortable there and very much outsiders. The two sisters stopped going and instead, they sat in the alley behind Woolworths, soon joined by two other black girls equally alienated.

> *One of my first experiences of being 'uncomfortable' – I think that is the first thing you feel when you start to become racially aware – was going to Sunday School at St James' church in New Cross. I remember feeling outside of it. So, with another couple of black girls, we stopped going. We actually spent the collection money on the way back. It was because we felt so totally alienated from the people there.*

Paulene followed her sister into secondary school. Like many local children, she had no aspirations to go to the local grammar school which was attended as far as they knew by a good many snobs. Her parents trusted the education system but at secondary level Paulene changed radically. The 1960s black power movement gained media attention and Paulene read widely all the books available, borrowing from her older brothers. She watched Mohammed Ali and researched her hero, Pele, the

Brazilian footballer.

Meanwhile, as one of only very few black children in primary school, Basil grew up identifying with the white images presented to him in books, yet at times he yearned for a black friend. His primary school days are remembered fondly with the exception of two minor incidents. One involved a supply teacher. Finishing off a lesson on 'The Empire', she asked that the children stand if they were proud to be born in Britain. Though only a baby on arrival in London, the young Basil had been born in Jamaica. He put his hand up to state this. The ignorant teacher told him sharply to sit down. Forty-five pairs of eyes turned to stare at him as he sat while they stood. The only other incident was when Basil was in the top Junior class. Another pupil, who had just been involved in a fight, swore at Basil and called him 'wog'. He was unsure what the word meant but the intention to hurt was both clear and effective.

Certain differences remained between Basil's experience and that of his peers. One of these was that his white peers took regular holidays with their families. This was not the norm in West Indian families of the period. Work-orientated West Indians like his father spent holiday periods completing tasks that could not be done at other times.

Basil's primary school was streamed and he was placed in the middle stream. At the end of the year the children were tested. Those who came first, second or third in the test always moved up a class. In the third year juniors Basil came second. His family was thrilled and they expected that he would go into the top class. In that year, for the first time, the top three children were not taken into the top class. The top class worked intensively as they were being groomed for the '11 plus' exams and they finished the syllabus in good time for this. Basil's class did not finish the syllabus. While the top class were revising for the exams, Basil's class was still sloughing through the syllabus. Basil worried about the exam. Passing it was important to him and as the ordeal came closer he became a bundle of nerves. He failed the exam and was devastated as he had wanted so badly to go to the grammar school.

Basil was the first black child in the local cubs pack. Though he hated cubs, his mother insisted that he went every Wednesday as it was 'good for him'. At secondary level he became a boy scout but he was never allowed to go to camps. Each year the scout master pleaded that he be allowed. When Basil asked his parents why they would not let him go with the rest of the scouts, they explained their fears for his safety as a black child. In the final year of primary school there was a school journey to Swanage and, though Basil pleaded with his parents to go, it finally took his mother's intervention before his father consented. It was the first and only time that he ever went away from home as a child.

The secondary modern school which Basil attended also streamed the children. Basil was placed in the top stream and in his final year he became 'head boy'. The school took particular pride in the fact that he was their first black head boy. At secondary school Basil's fight to be allowed to go on school journeys continued but as the children were inevitably taken abroad, it was further afield than the Morgan family were prepared to consider.

Another black family lived nearby, the Lindsays. The Lindsay children thought Basil 'spoke posh'. This was because in the Morgans' home standard English was the mother tongue and Jamaican Patois was frowned upon. It was a language the adolescent Basil felt a compulsion to learn later when he was 17 or 18. The values held by the Morgan family were middle class although, like many black migrants, they were skilled working class people. The family was respected in their community and Basil was constantly encouraged to be a model child in a model family, polite, well spoken. He caused no trouble.

Basil Morgan grew up between two worlds. All his friends were white, so was his church; the cubs, scouts, and his youth club were all white. His house was painted each year and he had nice clothes to wear. Yet, next door lived a white family of 13 in four rooms. The Morgans had to leave their house when it was compulsorily purchased for demolition. The end of the street where they lived gave way to a block of flats.

In the late 1950s Thelma trained as a nurse and she would regularly return to Brockley when she was off duty. She began to notice young black men in the area, or more accurately, they noticed her. They whistled and called across the road to her.

The first black family that Thelma remembers noticing was an African family who lived in The Crescent. Working with children as she did as a young nurse, she became aware of the Sierra Leonean children in the West African family and the family who lived upstairs from the Sierra Leoneans were from the Caribbean. Thelma got to know the families through the children. First she would meet the mothers and later the fathers and it was not long before she was introduced to their friends, most of them single.

48. Thelma Perkins in Tressillian Road, Brockley

We use to go to the pictures in Deptford High Street, the Deptford Bug Hutch I think it was known as...right on the corner of Edward Street where the traffic lights are now. We used to go down to Deptford City Mission Church, which I think is still on Tanners Hill, on a Sunday evening, but I use to go with a crowd of young boys, all white boys, apart from one who was mixed race like me. I think we just use to go in search of company.

Avril Augustine was born in Grenada in 1957 and she came to London wither her mother the following year. Her early years at Lee Manor School were difficult. Unlike Basil Morgan, she experienced hostility from her first teachers. She was also intimidated by the white boys who demanded her dinner money which she would hide in her socks. They called her names like 'wog' and she remembers feeling uneasy and unhappy until she went to the Juniors. When her younger brother started at school, she watched the same pattern begin again but knew that she had to assume a role which protected and supported him. Through this her confidence grew. Avril was the oldest of a large family and by the time she went to secondary school, there were eight children at home.

Avril's grandmother helped with the shopping and the children accompanied her to the market. Each market provided something different and the children helped to carry the bags home from Lewisham or Deptford market. Sometimes food parcels arrived straight from Grenada. Someone coming to England would be given a food parcel of Grenadian delicacies to bring from back home. In the box were guavas, cheese, spices, fresh cocoa, cornfish and dasheen. The parcels generated a great deal of excitement. Fom time to time a van would bring local groceries to the house.

Although Avril has always lived in Lewisham, she expresses a duality about the notion of Lewisham as home.

I have ambivalent feelings because I know that I was born in Grenada and because of that birthright I don't really see England as my home. Judging from the conversations with my family, I seem to have more of an affinity with there even though I've not actually lived there especially during my formative years.

At the end of primary school, selection was in the form of an 11 plus examination. West Indian parents knew of this. They knew less how to influence the results and Avril did not gain the grades for entry to grammar school. Prendergast School seemed a possibility on the family list but there were difficulties. Few black children got into Prendergast. Though her parents were invited to go into the school, she did not get a place. Two years later this was successfully challenged by a black parent and more black girls began to gain entry. Addey & Stanhope School offered Avril a place but because of her preference for a single-sex school, she was recommended Catford Girls which Avril went to and enjoyed because she was placed in a high stream.

At the end of secondary schooling, Avril's foremost concern was to contribute financially to her family. She took a job as a clerical officer within the DHSS. Five years later she took up studying again utilising the Access route back into education. Avril is now a teacher in Southwark.

Margaret Andrews came to Lewisham at the age of eight. She arrived from Carriacou on a cruise liner which to the two child passengers was a fun adventure. They had a three-week passage, being reunited with their mother on board ship, and it was summer when they arrived in Southampton. Lewisham seemed so much enclosed, grey concrete to the young Margaret, used to open spaces and green fields. Having arrived in the summer, Magaret had just enough time to become acclimatised before entry into primary school and the English school system.

Margaret went straight to St Saviour's school where there were very few black children and most of the teachers were Irish Catholics. She was put in a class with children a year younger than she was. She was bewildered and did not know that she had been put in the wrong class until in the playground someone asked how old she was and she told them. The children reacted to this asking whether she was there because she could not read.

Jacinth Browne first came to Britain from St Kitts in 1965. She was 12 and came to join the rest of her family already resident in London. She recalls the period as one of keen loss for home in the West Indies. In her selective school in St Kitts she had been seen as an achieving pupil of importance to the school community. In contrast, in London she was placed in one of the lowest streams in her new secondary school. Jacinthe's experience of boredom and disruption remains an integral memory of English education. The choices available for a black woman at the end of schooling appeared to her severely limited. Although she was one of those with most O-levels, she recalls in explorative discussions with a teacher, being directed to go and work in Woolworth's. It was not lost on her that white peers with similar qualifications were being encouraged to go on to try 'bigger and better things'.

I was one of the pupils with the most O-levels and I was being directed to go and work in Woolworths. Whereas girls with less qualifications than myself I noticed were being pushed and urged to do bigger and better things. I suppose that I was pretty bloody minded. The thought of working in a factory never crossed my mind, the thought of working in a shop never crossed my mind. Lots of my family had been teachers in the West Indies so I just automatically went into it.

Jacinth studied part-time for a psychology degree at Goldsmiths College from 1976 and taught in a Lewisham school from January 1987.

Shana Stroud came to London from Clarendon in Jamaica in the autumn of 1963 when she was nine years old. She travelled with her older sister to join her parents in London. The greyness of London and the houses joined together instead of the familiar bungalows struck her as very strange. She lived on Elswick Road, off Loampit Hill. A week after arrival she started at St Stephen's school.

There were a few black children at school and on the surface she seemed to settle in. In the first couple of years she was consistently called racist names such as 'nigger'. She had no allies at home or at school and the teachers had little academic expectations of her, expecting the children to get on with their playground relationships. She went to the same secondary school as her sister. To her, secondary school was boring. The two sisters left King Alfred School when the headteacher refused to let her older sister take the GCE exams she wanted to sit. The school had decided that she could take the less academic CSE route. They moved to Catford Girls. The issue of race came up a lot and the black children were constantly referred to as having a chip on their shoulders.

Shana's brothers began to be interested in black consciousness issues and they went to local meetings of groups such as the Black Unity and Freedom Party which had begun to meet in each other's homes. Unlike the boys in her family, Shana did not have the freedom of movement to attend these events. Her choices and work patterns at school led to CSE choices. She recalls that they were not expected to do well but Shana stayed on until the sixth form. When she left, she searched for jobs but first she had to learn about unemployment.

In 1968, the year of the Mexican Olympics, two black athletes stood together on the podium to collect gold and bronze awards for the 200 metres sprint. The winner was Tommie Smith who ran in black socks as a symbol of black power. John Carlos, wearing the same socks, took the bronze. Smith and Carlos came out for the victory ceremonies wearing one black glove each. When they were introduced they held their arms high, raising clenched fists in defiance to a world which represented white power. When the US anthem was played they turned to face the flag but, with their eyes staring at the ground, they held the gloves high. There were some boos from the crowd though not many but later the two were ordered to leave the Olympic village and divested of their credentials as members of the US team. These events took place far from Lewisham but at the flick of a switch they came instantaneously into the homes of thousands of young black people living under the strain of daily racism. Harry Powell watched them and he recognised the black power salute from his Lewisham home.

> *It changed my life. When I saw them and I felt what I felt from the clenched fist of 1968 given by those Americans, my life changed. I started to run with those that I could run with and walk with those that I had to walk with. My perception in terms of culture, religion, just simply sharpened up. There were things like Martin Luther King...and what had happened to Malcolm X. It was as if we had just been put in a meat grinder, ground up, and told we could reform ourselves. Rasta movement became suddenly triggered up in the country.*

Harry came to London to live at Upper Brockley Road in 1967 when he was nearly 13 years old. He went to Roger Manwood School at Forest Hill. The transition from Jamaica to London was hard enough because Harry had to get used to a family he hardly knew. Also, the English way of life was unfamiliar, even that of British blacks. He felt the pressure to transform into a British person almost overnight. Harry soon made friends in school because he was a stunning athlete. Still he felt the expectations and the demands to speak the language 'properly'.

> *We had a completely different way of thinking so it meant that we could inject change and challenge, challenge and change aspects that they couldn't, wouldn't, didn't know how to.*

Harry recalls that in the late 1960s and throughout the 1970s young black men were regularly stopped individually or in groups by policemen with the power to arrest them under the 'sus' law. This required only that the police suspected a person of being likely to commit a crime. The result was constant harassment of young black men, some of whom, like Harry, found ways to be active but keep off the streets and avoid the 'men in blue'.

> *You had to be smart by involving yourself in politics or things which didn't leave you on the streets too much. I got involved in the boy scouts because I saw where there were opportunities to actually gain knowledge.*

Harry took up canoeing and such outward bound type activities in his spare time because his dream was to become a professional sportsman. He had always been enthusiastic for sport and at school he was unbeatable over 100-400 metres. He won athletics championships at Crystal Palace and White City and he was captain of the school sprinting team. He competed in football, athletics and cricket skills in two age ranges, his own and the next one up. His father, a keen cricketer himself, dreamed of the young Harry becoming a professional cricketer so he got him a place on the ground staff at Kent. Before long Harry was offered a scholarship to go to the States as an athlete but having fairly recently been reunited with his family, he was reluctant to be separated again so he did not take up the place. Also, he was torn between athletics and football. He took up football and it kept him in England. In those days, first class cricketers still earned small sums of money compared to footballers. Besides, it also seemed to Harry that he could get rich quicker through professional football so stayed in London. Sporting injury would deny him that chance.

49. Harry Powell with one of his championship trophies

Regardless of individual background, the young people encountered racial prejudice which attempted to deny them life skills and opportunities. While the rhetoric of the educational literature claimed an interest in 'assimilation' of new migrants, the young people's experiences served to bond the black community in a common struggle. At the same time, schooled together, they grew to demand equal access to opportunities in common with white peers.

Each of these seven young black people, whose personal histories offer insights into growing up in the South East London of the 1960s and 1970s, became as adults particularly committed to the black community. As they grew up, often unaware of the legislation shaping their lives, the Immigration Bills of 1962, 1965 and 1968 became law, making it difficult to bring further family members from the Caribbean.

11

UP AGAINST THE COLOUR BAR: RACISM AND RESISTANCE

"I think society must recognise and realise human worth. Blackness does not demean that human worth."
ASQUITH GIBBES

The 'colour bar', a term given to restrictions imposed upon black people as a result of deeply embedded notions of white superiority served to limit the life chances of many, whether they were migrants or black people long resident in Britain. This factor became significant for large numbers of black people during the post-*Windrush* years. No area of life escaped the impact of this explicit racism. Housing, education, employment, leisure, religious worship, all were affected. The 'colour bar' determined the kind of jobs available, which clubs or pubs were frequented, what type of accommodation would be offered to a black person and in which areas, and so on. The incoming African-Caribbean migrants had been educated and socialised into the knowledge that they were British. The information on their passports stating "BRITISH SUBJECT CITIZEN OF THE UNITED KINGDOM AND COLONIES" was held to be a true indicator of a basic right to fair and equal treatment with other British citizens. Parity of treatment as citizen was not, however, the experience of British citizens who were also African-Caribbean people. The prevailing pattern was of discriminatory practice based on a racialized perception of black people rather than citizens.

'30.000 Colour Problems'

In 1956 the Picture Post ran an article headlined 'Thirty Thousand Colour Problems', a reference to the number of West Indians expected to arrive in Britain that year. Thus, even from the first arrivals of 'citizens of the New Commonwealth', they were received as 'problems', despite the ongoing recruitment drive in the Caribbean and the immigrants' own view of themselves as skilled and hardworking people come to help rebuild post-war Britain. While 312,000 European post-war immigrants were given refugee status as European Volunteer Workers, it was quickly forgotten that "the influx of West Indians was no refugee flight for which the immigrants should be grateful but was designed to meet British labour demands".

In 1962 the Conservative Government announced its intention to restrict immigration and the Commonwealth Immigrants Act brought the tangle of 'race' and 'immigration' into legislation, restricting entry into Britain for subject citizens born in the Commonwealth. The imminent ban encouraged larger numbers of Caribbean people already in Britain to gather together and send the necessary funds required to purchase passages and warm clothes to bring relatives and dependents to London. A decade later the debate was still raging. Edward Heath's government brought in the 1971 Immigration Act which, in turn, became central to the Nationality Act of 1981. The 1971 Act was seen as punitive by many black people and there were demands for its repeal. It required immigrants already 'settled' who wished to send for dependents to apply for an Entry Certificate. Once this was received in the country of origin a preliminary interview was followed by an average waiting period of 12 months in the case of the West Indies (and even longer for people in India and Pakistan). If refused the appeal procedure could take a further six to 12 months, so that years could elapse between application and a successful outcome. For children this was a particularly difficult situation.

In 1971 Vanda Marshall applied to bring her son Desmond to Lewisham from St Vincent. Vanda had left him with his granny as a baby when she emigrated as a recruit for J Lyons the caterers in the mid-1960s. She later trained as a nurse and saved up to send for her son. Years passed and even when Desmond's grandmother became bedridden with diabetes the immigration application remained unresolved. It was not until after the death of Desmond's grandmother in 1978 when Bob Ovuede of LCCR dealt with the case that mother and son were reunited.

In St Vincent we all hold British passports so I don't know why it's so hard
VANDA MARSHALL IN SPECTRUM, APRIL 1978

The 1971 Immigration Act also widened the powers of the Government to deport Commonwealth citizens on the same bases as 'aliens'.

Making the Best of a Bad Job

Employment, a central factor directly influencing the standard of living for black employees and their families, became a burning issue within black communities. The patterns of underemployment, insecure conditions of work and predominance in the lowest-paid sectors emerged in the early post-*Windrush* years and became a common core of the black experience.

Wrote a lovely letter and there was a job coming up for a storeman. I kept checking the post. In those days, the storeman's work wasn't sophisticated. No computers or anything, plain documentation. I got back a letter saying that I was selected, amongst the first six and would I like an appointment. I was very happy. I think they wanted three people, so three out of six I thought, well, they were impressed...I turned up at the office. You should have seen that poor young boy's face. He said, "Hold on, wait a moment. Mr G, is it? I have to go and consult with Mr so-and-so." You know they never filled that job for four months, and I waited, waited, waited, waited. I rang them up and they said, "Well, um, we haven't made a decision yet." Four months. RONNIE GORDON

A number of practices emerged which barred black employees at times from jobs, equal pay or even equal conditions of labour. Many skilled black workers found themselves denied the option of jobs in Britain to match previous experience or qualifications. Desirable jobs suddenly ceased to be available when black people applied or appeared for interview. A 1967 report 'Racial Discrimination in Britain' confirmed oral accounts by black employees of employers using Ministry of Labour employment exchanges who discriminated against blacks.

Black employees, particularly in employment situations with small firms found themselves regularly in the 'last to come, first to go' scenario.

I think I worked there about three weeks. The foreman came up and said to me they have to 'lay me off' because I'm the last to come and first to go. GERSHAN RHONE

House and Home

Adequate income from employment and the ability to pay for suitable housing worked in tandem. The lifestyles of African-Caribbean immigrants of the 1950s and 1960s show how racist responses to the black presence were met in large measure by strength of purpose as well as individual and community flexibility to resist at times intolerable difficulties. While employment was often a question of 'take it or leave it', housing shortages could be addressed, although usually only temporarily, with resources from within the community.

In the first instance, when black people met with blanket rejection in the form of 'No Blacks, No Irish, No Children, No Dogs', a system of sharing evolved. This system was heavily reliant on the goodwill of relatives and friends.

50. Racist grafitti has been a feature of life in inner city Deptford and Lewisham

In those days, after searching long hours you maybe might get a room some place. Nobody could afford to get houses in those days, and the white people didn't use to take you into their homes if you're black...So, it was rooms and now and then you might eventually get to meet those people who'd rent you a room or maybe one black person would get a house and everybody rent rooms from that person. ANNIE GEORGE

Mrs George, now retired, made her first marital home in her brother-in-law's house in Hither Green. Sybil Phoenix lived in her cousin's room before she married. Both were fortunate to have such relatively easy access to accommodation. Others had to spend many hours after work and at weekends visiting potential landlords only to be turned away. Alternatively, they would be offered rooms on the understanding that there were a number of conditions to be met. These often entailed very basic restrictions affecting the availability of cooking and washing facilities.

In Deptford the threat of major racial clashes loomed large. Flames of discontent were fanned by dire housing difficulties. An area dubbed the 'Caribbean Quarter' grew on the New Cross Estate around Childeric Road. The small, substandard houses had been offered to sitting tenants for £595. By 1960 they were being sold for £2,250-£2,750, many to Caribbean families desperate for housing. 'Sitting tenants' were up in arms. The new migrant homeowners were dissatisfied. They had been financially exploited but remained in a position of having bought less space than had been appreciated in the struggle to make the first purchase. Buying an old house was itself an idea which needed some getting used to since houses in the Caribbean were built to the buyer's specification. In London black people found for the first time that not only was it usual to buy old, rundown houses but, in some cases, there were privileged tenants already occupying a large part of the property.

Keenly aware of racial tension in the Notting Hill area which had led to the murder of black resident Kelso Cochrane in 1959 and prolonged strife in the multi-racial community of Kensington, local MPs Sir Leslie Plummer of Deptford and Richard Marsh of Greenwich brought the matter to the attention of the House of Commons in one of the longest sittings of Parliament. At the core of the issue was the practice of a £250 inducement system, approved by Housing Minister Henry Brooke. By this means, one of two white families of sitting tenants, whoever first accepted the inducement, would vacate the property. The property would then be sold at inflated prices to new purchasers, often black but more willing to pay the higher rate. Tension within individual houses frequently escalated when the new landlords were black. Such tensions spilt onto the streets.

The two MPs voiced concerns over the growth of the black population locally and the financial burden placed upon them by an exploitative housing system. In order to raise funds for the purchase of such essentially poor housing stock, black buyers were at times charged 25% to 30% interest rates. Bearing in mind that these house buyers were rarely in highly paid jobs, the inflated mortgages created a spiral of financial effects. One houseowner in Childeric Road purchased his property for £2,000. His weekly earnings were £12 for a household which included a wife and two children. Landlords in such situations were pressurised into renting out single rooms offering the very basic facilities so familiar to post-*Windrush* Caribbean migrants.

> *The system, which is perfectly legal, works this way: houses occupied by two white families have received most offers. Once one family accepts it, it is withdrawn from the other family. Then the house is sold to a coloured family...The general trend after the sale is that relations between the two factions begin to crumble through clashes over different ways of life. Result is that the white family move out.* KENTISH MERCURY, 5/8/1960

The inducement system was not restricted to Deptford but was widespread throughout the area now covered by Lewisham borough. The practice was temporarily halted in the wake of publicity following the debate on the subject in the House of Commons. In the meantime, racial tension built up locally. White tenants discussed the possibility of forming a white tenants' association as the community looked set to become openly polarised on the grounds of race.

It is perhaps surprising that, despite relatively low income, despite sending money back home and setting up new homes, a number of new settlers were able to purchase houses within five or so years. Those, like the Phoenixes, who were in a position to raise funds abroad to purchase housing locally did so. But these were individuals with rare resources. A more usual source of funding was the 'pardner' method of saving. One major expense was the sending for dependents whether spouse, children or relatives. Another was house buying, a burden sometimes shared between a number of relatives. In a period when access to loans was particularly limited for black people, each large expenditure would be assisted by the 'pardner hand' (see Ch.10).

The 'pardner hand' was a regular source of deposit for the purchase of houses. It was a method of saving familiar to all Caribbean peoples. 'Partners' did not require any proof of creditworthiness and the system did not involve any payment of interest. The concept of 'partner' was, in some instances, developed further into a Credit Union. This was the case in the Notting Hill area following the mobilisation of the black community in the wake of the Kelso Cochrane murder.

Black Men, White Women

As in earlier times, protests around fears of closer proximity with black lifestyle also focused upon real or potential relationships between black men and white women. The early migrant black population was male-dominated. Old myths resurfaced which emphasised that only certain vulnerable or outcast social groups of white women sought or maintained relationships with black men. As in the earlier Sierra Leone resettlement period, so in the post-*Windrush* years, the women were labelled 'prostitutes'. The Caribbean Quarter story, therefore, was suitably spiced by residents' alleged concern with black violence and white girls using rented rooms in the area as brothels. For some residents this was the real site of the tension.

White girls and this money offer cause the trouble. Take them away and the tension will go. KENTISH MERCURY, 5/8/1960

51. In London's Coloured Clubs, 1944

The Dartmouth Arms

As in housing, so socially, West Indians found themselves largely segregated. Certain hotels, clubs, restaurants and pubs operated a policy of refusal on the grounds of colour. This was the case at the Dartmouth Arms in Forest Hill where black people were refused service. The Dartmouth Arms colour bar was challenged in December 1964 when the Brockley International League of Friendship (BILF) organised a picket at the pub. Community activists demonstrated against the licensee. The picket included Joan Lestor who had stood as Labour's candidate for Lewisham West in the General Election earlier that year. Lewisham's mayor Tom Bradley tested the ban in January 1965 by going there with Melbourne Good, Vice-Chair of the BILF and local black resident. They were refused a drink.

West Indian Protection

On Saturday 23rd January 1965 the Deptford Union Movement held a public meeting. The repatriation of black people was central to their agenda. These Mosleyites had good reason to believe they were supported locally. Four years earlier in the LCC elections, the BNP had polled nearly 10 per cent of the local vote. An 'independent' politician canvassing on the repatriation ticket in the Deptford by-election of 1963 polled 8.5 per cent. The Deptford Union Movement offered a similar call to the people of Deptford.

1965 had begun dramatically and it was to be an interesting year. The Labour Government put into practice the White Paper to restrict immigration from the Commonwealth. The doors were beginning to close on black British citizens. In September the Race Relations Act came into force and the Race Relations Board was established. Using the powers of the Act, Michael X, known also as Michael Abdul Malik or Michael de Freitas, a black separatist converted to Islam, was prosecuted for inciting racial hatred.

Threats from the Ku Klux Klan and other extreme right wing groups such as the Union Movement were persistent enough to lead to a call for a protection group for black people living locally. The formation of a West Indian Residents Protection Society had been debated at a conference in Birmingham in August 1965. Roy MacFarlane, a member of the BILF, defended the need for such an organisation. So did Vernon Laidlaw, chairman of the London Standing Conference of West Indian Organisations and of the Brockley International League of Friendship.

We want to give our nationals confidence and assure them that they are not alone and that we have leaders who are prepared to stand by them and protect them from intimidation.

He added that the new group was in no way extremist and was not planning to arm itself to fight anybody.

But it is hoped that, once the national body has been formed, we shall be able to advise and warn our people if the Ku Klux Klan carry out any of their threats.

Another concern voiced by Caribbean representatives of the Brockley International League of Friendship was police handling of black people and resulting miscarriages of justice. The recruiting and appointment of black JPs was placed on the agenda for urgent action in order to ameliorate difficulties already visible in police relations with black residents in the community.

Pauline Crabbe was born in Jamaica in 1914, one of four children in the Henriques family. She came to London as a young girl in 1919 and was educated privately. In 1967 she was living in Hither Green and working as a welfare secretary when she was appointed as London's first black woman JP. She worked the Inner London circuit, served many years in Hampstead and was awarded the OBE before she retired on 24th February 1984, aged 70.

Rising Black Militancy

Racial discrimination whether institutionalised or individual was widespread. Young people with first hand experience of the education system had known racism. Adults in the workplace came face to face with it. Families ignored it at their peril on the streets. Yet black people learned to live with daily racism. From within a generation of young black adults, schooled at least partly in Britain, an articulate minority confronted the issues. It was now the era of black power. Rejecting the imposed identity of the label 'coloured', many reclaimed the term 'black' as a political-racial description.

Malcolm X visited the UK from the USA in 1965, watched carefully by British security personnel. His visit was of particular interest to young black activists. He spoke of a radical concept which caught their imagination: 'black power'.

Black power meetings and study groups were held locally as well as nationally. The general aim was to raise the level of black consciousness, to politicise the black community into understanding the nature of racism and its impact on the lives of black people. Of particular importance was the crucial understanding of how Britain kept black people powerless and the development of strategies to counteract that entrenched historical reality. Political mobilisation would ensure action on a number of fronts.

Before long radical black groups of politically differentiated persuasion emerged. The Black Unity and Freedom Party (BUFP) became established in the Lewisham area. Known colloquially as the 'black and white unite and fight' group, BUFP assumed a class perspective on the black struggle, emphasising the radical alliance of working class activists. The Fasimbas, in comparison, were closer to Pan Africanists. The North London based Black Liberation Front (BLF) assumed a culturalist/nationalist stance while the Black Panther Movement, with branches in South and West London, was largely modelled on the highly publicised original in the USA. These were perceived as young Marxists, class warriors verging on the militarised.

Each group organised meetings, social programmes and a published voice. Publications such as *Grassroots*, *Black Voice*, and *The Liberator* became the voice of the new black organisations and were made available to the wider black community whether they were out shopping or had been invited to hear a popular speaker. Membership of the organisations was not simply local. Young people travelled across London and further afield to attend and take up leadership roles in political activities which for many had ousted the ritual churchgoing of their parents' generation. These new activists radically challenged the role of the church in keeping black people passive or complacent in the promotion of their rights. They also willingly suspended the petty inter-island rivalries characteristic of the older group. The common identity of diasporic black experience was the rallying force. Black identity was reclaimed and forcibly asserted.

This was, by and large, a movement led by young adults more outspoken, more widely read, more confident and less passive in the wider world than their parents. They sought, if anything, to politicise their parents as well as their brothers and sisters. Furthermore, they were prepared to 'seize the time'. Each event was analysed politically and its significance to the black cause made explicit. Whether dockers were marching in support of Enoch Powell or another racist Immigration Bill was being debated or indeed another local young man was arrested under the 'sus' laws, the opportunity was taken to recruit other black people to the cause.

The young activists read and debated black history and the ideas of other black thinkers, perhaps for the first time in the recent history of black people. Pan-Africanism occupied a central place on the agenda. Published material from the USA was accessible and popular. Books by authors such as Frantz Fanon, Bobby Seale, Aime Cesaire, George Jackson, Huey Newton, Angela Davis and Kwame Nkrumah were foremost on the programme of self-education drawn up by these young activists. Young people were prominent in the black power movement of the 1960s and 1970s and black American activists were powerful role models.

Young women were by the sides of the men, equally visible, drawing up social and educational programmes, giving out leaflets, selling newspapers, attending rallies and organising programmes for the education of young black people who were being 'short-changed' by the education system.

> *We had a Saturday school. During that Saturday school, the parents had a chance to do other things. They were very happy to have us. We were so idealistic. We'd go and collect the children and take them off their parents' hands all day. We would feed them. I still see some of the parents of those children. They were very grateful for that. I don't know how supportive they were of us but they certainly tolerated us. I think they understood what we were trying to do. I think those were the first supplementary schools. After that they became increasingly institutionalised.* BEVERLEY BRYAN

The Black Panther Movement was the group of most immediate concern to the authorities. It attracted hard-core activists as well as idealists among the young adults and the educated in the black community. It demanded commitment measured in terms of personal learning and developing political analysis as well as community involvement.

> *I was working in primary school. I was active in black politics. I was in the Black Panther Movement. I was in the black Arts Workshop in the West Indian student centre. We did a lot of drama. There was a kind of cultural awakening. It was probably the most important and powerful period in my life and certainly formed my consciousness since then.*
>
> *The black panthers just took up all your time. You had to be out there door to door, selling the papers on the street, going to study groups, getting people to join the organisation, going on demonstrations, everything, every night. I think we had one night free.* BEVERLEY BRYAN

The main focus of the Black Panther Movement in London was police brutality. 'State racism' was the familiar term but it was mainly about what the police were doing to black people in the streets of South London. Police brutality in the black community was a common cry that could not be ignored. At the time the official response was an accusation of exaggeration.

The police took a keen interest in the radical organisations. Individuals and groups were tied up in legal action. By the mid-1970s most of the groups had been infiltrated or disintegrated. Beverley remembers that

> *it was like a meteor. It just rose and then by 1973 it had just fallen apart. Some people went to prison. At those demonstrations some people were picked out by the police and there were trials. We had big trials, publicity trials, which we attended. There were also smaller cases where people would get nine months. So people were getting records out of that period and people were beginning to ask questions.*

Radical groups had mobilised themselves against a backdrop of, and in response to, aggressive racism expressed not only by individuals on the street but by politicians in power and the police. It was not only radicals who were moved to act. Enoch Powell's "rivers of blood" speech on April 20th 1968 came a few weeks before the local elections in May. Black citizens reeled at the onslaught. Many involved with black people within their local communities sought to take action. It was in this period that Mike Steele, an Australian who had lived in South East London for some four years, had the idea of setting up an organisation aimed at developing community relations in a useful way locally.

Ladywell Action Centre: Allies in the Community

The Ladywell Action Centre, established in February 1969, developed out of a relationship between Mike Steele, then National Press Officer of the Liberal Party, and Frank Jeremiah. The connection followed the publication in the *Lewisham Borough News* of a joint letter written by Mike Steele and Liberal Research Officer, Ian Senior, attacking the paper's recent handling of a particular race issue.

Sylvia Jeremiah, wife of Trinidadian Frank Jeremiah, responded to the letter. After the telephone conversation, Mike visited the couple and subsequently got to know Frank Jeremiah very well. Mike was active in the North Lewisham Liberal Party where there were regular meetings with invited speakers. In September 1967 Frank Jeremiah was invited to speak to a meeting in the Albion pub, in the centre of Lewisham near Albion Way. Frank's talk focused on black issues.

In the Lewisham Council elections of May 1968 Frank was one of three Liberal Party candidates. Through canvassing the West Indian community as Frank's agent, particularly in and around Halesworth Road, Mike came to know three or four black families, including those of Faith Gayle, Lannie Fairman and Leattie Crooks.

The inaugural meeting of the Ladywell Action Centre was held on 30th January 1969 at Algernon Road congregational church. The group aimed to provide advice, information and help to individuals with problems around race relations, social welfare and housingand to foster good relationships between people of all races, creeds and nationalities in the Ladywell and Brockley area. The centre opened on Mondays and leaflets were put out to inform the public. It was self-financed and ran on a rota basis.

By October the Ladywell Action Centre planned to develop its programme by providing play group facilities for 20 children. The advisory role was extended. Perhaps the most effective role of the Ladywell Action Centre, however, was in taking up particular cases of black people discriminated against by the police.

An instance of this was when Faith Gayle, a mother of five, became involved in a row at Lewisham railway station which led to her being arrested by Lewisham police. In the fracas, she refused to be searched. The police insisted. Faith said afterwards that eight police held her down and searched her and she claimed that two constables were responsible for knocking out three of her teeth. She had objected to being referred to as a 'jungle bunny'. At that time, Faith worked as a seamstress and she gave this as the explanation for the pair of scissors found by the police. Faith was remanded and subsequently appeared at Greenwich Magistrate's Court. Bill Clark, first secretary of the Ladywell Action Centre, attended the hearing with Mike. They found that the police were either unwilling or unable to try to understand black people's fears and attitudes and ways of expressing themselves which resulted in Faith being taken to court. Faith was bound over to keep the peace. Other LAC cases, which will be described in the next chapter, resulted in acquittals or conditional discharges.

Humus 'Amos' Hurst came to Britain when he was about 20 years old from St Mary in Jamaica to Shell Road, Ladywell. In January 1972 he was introduced to Mike Steele by Faith Gayle's husband, Ken Brown, who explained that in 1966 Amos had been at the rough end of an encournter in his own home with Lewisham police. The two became firm friends and allies in fighting the black cause. Amos joined the Ladywell Action Centre and introduced Mike to the Lewisham Way Centre where he became a committee member. They were both active in the Liberal Party which they together refounded in Deptford at the time of the 1973 GLC election.

Amos suggested that Mike stand for the forthcoming General Election. In the two General Elections in February and October 1974 Amos was Mike's agent in Deptford, appealing for black people's support. Mike polled 8,181 votes but the area remained overwhelmingly Labour and John Silkin was returned as MP. For the Lewisham Council elections in the same year the two reversed roles when Amos stood as one of three Liberal candidates in Ladywell ward.

For the next 12 years Amos and Mike worked together as a team. In November 1976 Henry Moore, a respected black man living on Algernon Road, saw a group of white men grappling with two young black women. A concerned citizen, he approached and tapped one of them on the shoulder to ask what was happening. They were five plain clothes policemen. They set upon him and when they were through he had to be treated at Lewisham Hospital. Henry Moore was charged with assaulting the police. Amos and Nina Hurst were called to Lewisham police station under the Help on Arrest scheme and Ladywell Action Centre took up the case. On three consecutive Fridays members handed out leaflets at the busy Riverdale shopping centre requesting witnesses of the incident to come forward. Finally five witness emerged, four white and one black. Henry Moore was acquitted. He threw a party at the Albion pub to show his gratitude and he soon became an active member of the LAC.

During 1978 Amos, Mike and others, including Ladywell councillor Nicholas Taylor, met to refine plans for a new organisation. It was agreed that the group should approach the Manpower Services Commission for funds to establish the Black Leadership Project which would encourage and train black people to take on responsiblities within public life.

> *The project aims to encourage and equip people from the ethnic minorities to take part in public affairs by giving them: self confidence, self-assertiveness, management skills, raising consciousness issues, perserverance and determination.* 'TRAINING ETHNIC MINORITIES FOR LEADERSHIP', 1987

After a pilot course in 1979 the project was formally established on 2nd January 1980 with the help of a grant from the Commission for Racial Equality. After interview by the committee Amos was appointed the first paid Field Worker to recruit students to the courses, operating from 48 Lewisham High Street, the LCCR premises. Mike Steele, who had been chairman of the LAC since its foundation in January 1969 became the chairman of the new Black Leadership Project. At the end of 1980 he handed over both posts to Ken Small.

After four attempts the project persuaded Lewisham Council to provide Urban Aid grant to fund two workers. From September 1982 the project used a room in the new Albany Institute in Douglas Way, Deptford. Later they held classes in part of Goldsmiths College before settling into 1 Loampit Hill, provided by the Council on a peppercorn rent basis. For the first three years the project was run as a sub-committee of the Ladywell Acton Centre but in 1982 the two bodies separated and the Black Leadership Project became eligible for charitable status, although this involved a change of name to 'Ethnic Minorities Leadership Project' to concur with the Race Relations Act 1976. The LAC continued to serve its political function, critical of the police in their relations with the black community, while the new EMLP provided training.

With this digression to follow the story of the LAC and its child project the EMLP, we have moved into a period when the 'colour bar' had been transformed into an all-pervasive racism.

12

THE NIGHTMARE YEARS

"It is the hope of the black man that he should have power over his own destinies. This is not incompatible with a multi-racial society where each individual counts equally." WALTER RODNEY

A community can only put down roots if its members have a degree of control over their own destinies. It is this dream of self-fulfilment which brought so many people from the Caribbean and the same dream has pushed community leaders to fight discrimination and seek to succour all ages and needs within the community.

Over and over again the vision has been destroyed as the terrifying forces of racism have crushed lives and undermined the growing sense of belonging. On every occasion black people have fought back against the nightmare, often finding allies equally clear about the evils of racism and the importance of peace in a diverse community.

·Community Relations·

The Lewisham Council for Community Relations was set up in August 1969. Among its members was Tory Councillor Richard Wells who was at the centre of a local controversy surrounding "an error in Lewisham's immigrant birth figures". In March 1968 Enoch Powell had called for statistics verifying the birth rate of 'immigrant children' in comparison to 'British children'. This was a cue to bring into public view the maternity rate of black women recently resident in areas such as Lewisham. Most of the women under scrutiny, those from the West Indies, were British and giving birth to British children. They had been legally British all their lives and their parents and generations of foreparents had always been British, as Enoch Powell was only too well aware. Thus, the distinction between the two categories, 'immigrant' and 'British', at least in the case of migrant workers from the Caribbean, was largely a spurious one.

Eight per cent of Lewisham's total births for March and April were said to relate to the birth of black children. Subsequent calculations put the figure at 19.5 per cent. The statistical comparability of the two groups, black and white, was not at issue. The raw data was all that mattered. Councillor Wells of Lewisham urged an enquiry into the 'misleading' figures.

Wells occupied a strange position. On the one hand, his membership of the LCCR seemed to verify his interest in community relations; on the other hand, he denounced the Race Relations Act as 'odious' and responsible for worsening race relations. He was keen to make clear, also, that he had 'considerable support' locally. Views like his, from members of the Council, left local black residents with clear impressions of hostility. On the question of repatriation Wells was clear. He stated that he would like to see much more done to overcome the problems faced by the borough and for him that meant even tighter controls over immigration and the encouragement of voluntary repatriation.

Other members of the Council for Community Relations responded readily, distancing themselves from the views of Richard Wells. Frank Jeremiah, then Liberal candidate for Ladywell ward, spoke on behalf of the Brockley International League of Friendship. On the question of repatriation, he pointed to the movement back to the Caribbean of those already clear about not wanting to stay. The Ladywell Action Centre demanded Wells' resignation.

The Race Relations Act of 1965 allowed for the provision of Community Relations Officers (CROs) within local boroughs. Asquith Gibbes was appointed CRO for Lewisham in 1970 and the LCCR began a new era. A central role facing Asquith and the LCCR was improving community relations and furthering racial harmony.

To the black population of Lewisham the LCCR now offered a much-needed bridge to realising urgent needs. Prior to Asquith's appointment most Community Relations Councils had been basically white organisations with an interest in black welfare. However the CRO role was interpreted, Asquith's appointment signalled greater potential for black people to operate within the system and influence practice directly impacting upon their lives. In the early years black people needed to be persuaded that the system could be made to respond to their needs. Early copies of *Spectrum*, the LCCR's in-house newspaper, advertised its services and explained its relevance. In his 1972 Annual Report Asquith expressed his deep concern "about the inadequate response from black residents".

However, a range of issues began to be brought to the LCCR as trust grew. An extract from Asquith's first report gives an indication of the various strands of community work his post involved.

We have dealt with a large amount of personal problems during the past 12 months. The problems vary – housing, conciliation outside the Race Relations Act, immigration, employment, family conflicts and so on. We have also had quite a few referrals from statutory and voluntary agencies. We accept in principle that we are not a casework agency and wherever possible we do help people to make better use of existing services. However, we also find that in some of the situations which confronted us there are no established agencies to deal with them and in these circumstances we find it easier to deal with these problems ourselves. LCCR ANNUAL REPORT, 1970-71

Housing Again

Housing was a hot issue and one which the Ladywell Action Centre had picked up. Within six months of Asquith's appointment, he met with the borough's housing department to discuss 'the Allocation of Accommodation to Non-Indigenous Families'. Housing concerns were so high on the agenda that Lewisham became one of seven boroughs requested by the Select Committee on Race Relations and Immigration to give evidence on housing.

At this time the majority of black people knew little about access to council housing. Nonetheless, the properties made available to many black house buyers had been poor quality, frequently short-life housing stock. Given this situation and that of multiple occupation with several families renting accommodation at any one address, each compulsory purchase or resale of housing created difficulties for a number of occupants, many of them families with chronic housing needs.

Patsy Steele arrived from Grenada in the early 1960s when she was 22 years old. Her destination was Lewisham where she already had relatives and she moved in with an aunt. Before long she became a nurse, entering at the auxiliary level at the Brooke Hospital at Shooters Hill. Years later, married and with three children, her housing situation in rented accommodation was chronic. To make matters worse, her landlord was selling his house. She had returned to work since the birth of her second son. Her husband worked day shifts while she worked at night. The family was in no position to purchase property themselves.

When advised that her family would be served a court order to move to allow the sale of the house to go ahead, Patsy finally got herself on the Council list. The accommodation needed by the family could not be found at an affordable rate within the private sector. When the court order came, the family was distraught. The black landlord had been very supportive but the Council appeared to be dragging its feet and the family became increasingly desperate. After what seemed like an endless wait with no offers of housing, the frantic and angry mother took her youngest child to the housing office and left her there. The family was found accommodation shortly after. They have lived in the same flat ever since.

The desperation of black families was brought to the Community Relations Office. Housing authorities pleaded the 'Five Year Rule' which required that families be resident in the borough for a minimum of five years before they could be placed on the housing list. Once this hurdle was leaped a priority system operated. It was hard to find out who qualified and on what grounds. Because new residents were unaware of the procedures, even when they qualified they did not attempt to register. In any event, black families were not encouraged to do so. In the face of a racist reception into Britain, black families expected to pay their way and to be unsupported at all levels.

Many young families, however, had been caught in the short term housing trap, the only choice available to them. Responding to queries on behalf of those families, Lewisham Council pointed to a shortage of three and four-bedroom accommodation. Most black families were left in their chronic housing situations regardless of the high priorities of particular cases.

The 1975-6 Annual Report gave a breakdown of cases dealt with by caseworkers at LCCR such as the Nigerian, Bob Ovuede. Housing (360 cases) represented the largest single category. In comparison there were 145 immigration and 70 police cases.

> *From the number of inquiries coming to the office it is obvious that [housing] is a major problem for the black community. Many of these families live in large Victorian houses which have been divided up for multi-occupation under the 1961 and 1969 Housing Acts. There is a shortage of four-bedroom accommodation on the one hand and of accommodation for one-parent families at the other end of the scale.* LCCR ANNUAL REPORT, 1972-3

Deteriorating Relations

In February 1971 the Tory party which controlled Lewisham Council from May 1968 to May 1971 was again facing revolt in its ranks. Another extreme right wing councillor was about to be removed from the approved list of councillors. The touch paper was once again 'immigration'. Again bigoted views were said to be supported nationally, this time "by 90 per cent of the people".

While the black community struggled with racist housing rules, Asquith Gibbes' leadership wihin community relations was, in April 1971, under attack. Another Tory councillor took the offensive. Writing to the *Lewisham Borough News*, he recommended close scrutiny of Asquith's "pro-communist activities". Right wing locals were fuelled by these allegations. The letters section slammed Race Relations generally and Asquith specifically. One letter even scrutinised the activities of Dr David Pitt, also black though working in North London, and suggested that he had infringed the Race Relations Act. Assertions that key institutions such as housing and education departments, employers, the media and the police were acting against black people had angered sections of the local community. Pitt's views were described as a "monstrous assertion". Locals such as Mike Steele and Rex Andrews wrote letters of support. The *Lewisham Borough News'* "notorious views on the question of coloured people" were highlighted. Asquith Gibbes responded deriding the accusations.

Nowhere to Play

A borough-wide LCCR survey conducted in the early-1970s identified an acute need for playgroup facilities, particularly in the Deptford and Brockley area. Access to all services for black people was limited with a knock-on effect, particularly on black families since young black children were most likely to be growing up in cramped housing conditions. The LCCR set up a Playgroup Sub-Committee early in its programme.

Whatever 'race relations' came to mean in the wider world, to the black community it was important that children were a specific focus of community relations work in the borough at the outset. A playgroup was seen as a valuable contribution to the well-being of local children, regardless of race.

A hall was found to accommodate the group at the Brockley Baptist church in Rokeby Road. Planning permission followed and the necessary health and safety requirements were met. Twenty-five members of Task Force, a local community group, voluntarily gave their time during the Easter holidays to decorate the hall for its new purpose. Grants were secured from Lewisham Council, the Pre-school Playgroup, a national body concerned with play provision for under-fives, and LCCR. A series of fundraising events were organised to secure further funds for playgroup equipment. A qualified nursery assistant was appointed. The opening date was set for 7th June 1971 and a team of Goldsmiths students visited local homes to assess the needs of individual families.

The Battle for Education

Set against the social reality of poor and frequently over-crowded homes, which was the norm of the early-1970s for African-Caribbean families, such intervention was very welcome. But the black family was under attack on a number of fronts. Perhaps in the longer term the battle for education has proved the most insidious.

During the 1970s the site of that battle was ESN ('educationally sub-normal') schools. The single most compelling problem within education for black families was the disproportionate representation of black children in ESN schools.

Ricky Cambridge, leader of the BUFP, estimated early in 1971 that in the Lewisham area 40 per cent of the children in the three types of special schools were West Indian. The umbrella term 'special schools' covered a variety of provision for children deemed best catered for outside mainstream schools. Among the special schools were those for the 'delicate' and 'maladjusted' as well as educationally sub-normal. It was to the last category that many black children were misdirected. Like many other boroughs, Lewisham was placing a "fairly high percentage" of West Indian children in these schools to the dismay of families and the black community. The 1971-72 LCCR report commented on the situation.

A rather depressing aspect of this situation is the basic fact of the social stigma, its psychological effect, and the personal inadequacy being suffered by these children. And this is being encouraged by the Authority concerned, in the sense that the rate of these children's return to normal school appears to be slowed down. This process is causing the parents of these children a genuine anxiety with regard to their children's future.

It might be a consolation to note that the ILEA is now giving the question of ESN a serious study, but whether or not one should expect the parents to gratify themselves with this consolation is a question of individual opinion.

The conferring of ESN status upon individual children would have been sufficiently problematic but, in practice, schools designated entire families ESN. Mrs George describes the impact of this upon her family. She and her husband found themselves locked in an inexplicable fight with the education authority. Their five year old son, Nathan was deemed ESN and they were told to send him to a specific school.

They actually sent him to that school. We just got the notice that he'll be going to that school because the classes are smaller and they'll be able to pay him more personal attention.

The Georges believed the school to be pursuing the best interests of their child so they did as they were instructed by the authorities. Their observation, in the wake of their child's transfer to the 'special' school, was that his behaviour was deteriorating.

You could watch. The child was learning nothing. I mean a well-behaved child you send out to school and he is coming back disruptive and the way he's carrying on, it wasn't on. And then you seem to have no control over the situation. You can't just take him and send him to a next school, you know, because the Government send him to that school. The authorities send him to the Meeting House school. He's under the council care like that.

As if this was not enough, Nathan's brother, a year younger, on being accepted into school, was also placed in the same 'special' school on the grounds that he should "keep his brother company". These decisions were not arrived at by discussion and mutual agreement. Parents were informed and decisions formalised in writing. Black parents, unfamiliar with the system and therefore vulnerable, were at the mercy of teacher perceptions of their children, however little objective foundation there was in support of the teacher's informal assessment.

In the case of the Georges there followed a five-year dispute with the authority. Finally, the two boys were withdrawn from their 'special' school. Mr George made the firm decision to take them away and, although the authority threatened to take legal action, it was agreed that the child would be formally assessed. The assessment showed Nathan to have a very high IQ. His brother was 'normal'. The two boys were transferred to a mainstream secondary school. For all its unusual features, cases such as this were only too common in the West Indian community.

Sunderland Road

On January 3rd 1971 a large seasonal party was in full swing at 47 Sunderland Road, Forest Hill. Without warning three firebombs were thrown into the party, injuring 22 people, several with second and third degree burns. Some were in hospital for nearly four weeks. After police questioning four white suspects, all of whom had attended the party, were arrested. Cases against two of the suspects were dropped at the magistrate's court on the grounds of insufficient evidence. The other two were tried at the Old Bailey on charges under the Malicious Damages Act. On June 8th 1971 Pamela Holman was sent to Borstal. The following day Derek Reynolds was sentenced to five years imprisonment. As *Time Out* put it in a report they admitted was six months too late: "The outrage felt by the black community at the bombing was compounded by the fact that the national press gave it a grand total of 8 column inches.

Policing Against Black People

The Sunday after the Sunderland Road bombing seven black men and one black woman, all members of BUFP, were travelling home after visiting the hospital where victims were being treated. Outside the hospital they had been jostled by white youths, one of whom produced a knife. The BUFP members hailed a passing police car but the police refused to search the knife-wielding white youth. When the black people boarded the bus they were pursued by the police and subsequently arrested.

The Ladywell Action Centre held a meeting with members of BUFP several days later and were disturbed by the details which emerged. They issued a press statement

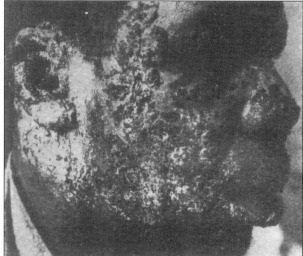

52. James Fuller and Renford Carty - two of the victims at Sunderland Road

deploring the deteriorating relations between the police and the black community.

We are extremely disturbed by evidence of deterioration of relations between police in Lewisham generally and Ladywell in particular and the coloured community with whom they come in contact. We feel that action must be taken by the responsible authorities, particularly the police, to see that this trend is reversed if serious and damaging incidents and an atmosphere of mutual distrust and dislike is to be avoided. We have evidence from more than one source which demonstrates the growing sense of injustice felt by the local coloured community against certain local policemen. SOUTH EAST LONDON MERCURY, 21/1/71

A meeting called by BUFP on the Sunday following the arrests was addressed by Ricky Cambridge and Treveor Sinclair. 150 people marched to Ladywell police station in protest against police brutality. The police denied any conflict with the black community. Chief Inspector Douglas Merry issued an invitation to LAC to meet with him at Deptford police station to discuss the issue. The LAC publicly welcomed the Inspector's invitation.

Guyanese-born barrister Rudy Naryan defended the eight BUFP members.
They were charged with threatening behaviour a month after the incident. It seems a bright afterthought.

The case was heard at Lambeth where seven of the BUFP members were found guilty, including George Joseph who received a three-year suspended sentence. He had restrained the officer from using his baton on the one young woman in the group. The court was told of the police message sent to nearby patrol cars which read:
Serious disturbance outside Lewisham Hospital, coloured youths involved. Knives being used.

Fights and confrontations with hostile police had become part of everyday reality for many young black people, particularly men. Black youths found themselves in a no-win situation. Whether they were 'subversive' or not, there was a strong likelihood of criminal charges following such confrontations. At the Peckham Fair in 1973 a fight flared up between black youths and white stallholders after a young black person had been beaten up. Approximately 14 arrests were made, all of them black youths. They were charged variously with obstruction or assault.

The Community Relations Officer's role was premised on the promotion of racial harmony. Relations between black people, particularly young black males, and the police were far from harmonious. Before long the issue was forced upon the attention of the LCCR. Its second report highlighted the tensions within the situation.

Police/Immigrant relations in this borough leaves much to be desired. I have dealt and am still dealing with cases of alleged police brutality in this borough. As a CRO I recognise my function as attempting to bring about mutual tolerance, understanding and peaceful co-existence between the various members of the community. As a result it is not part of my policy to allow complaints on police brutality to get out of hand...Unfortunately, in the majority of cases, I have had to reluctantly refer the client to see a solicitor.
LCCR REPORT, 8/6/1972

Asquith Gibbes noted 44 cases involving complaints about the police with which he had been involved in the year from May 1971. Early in 1972 the Greenwich and Lewisham Case-Con group gave details of six cases involving black people. They were concerned to point out that these were not isolated cases.

In July 1972 the South East London Council for Civil Liberties echoed the concerns expressed by the LCCR. Their submissions to the Parliamentary Committee on Race

Relations described a "total breakdown of communication between black people and the police". Claims were made that black people were harassed by the police on patrol, that arrests were made with undue force, that details of legal rights were not given to black suspects and that cannabis was at times planted on suspects. The CCL called for a full scale public enquiry under the Police Act 1964.

The immediate response through a press conference held by Scotland Yard was that the police "will not be provoked by West Indians". Locally, Chief Superintendent Morgan Thomas of Lewisham police denied the allegations. Instead he affirmed that relationships were good between police and immigrants. In the meantime, the cases continued. Two, successfully taken up by the Ladywell Action Centre, involved respectable, employed, married, middle-aged men who, one suspects, would never have been taken to court had they been white.

John Pinto had been stopped with a workmate and questioned. After searching, he was charged with possession of cannabis but acquitted at court because evidence from his workmate conflicted with the police description of which of them had been searched first. This case was one of the clearest examples of drug planting. Lanny Fairman became entangled in police activities outside his house when officers decided to investigate a possible theft of a neighbour's van. In the process, Mr Fairman, a grandfather known affectionately as 'Daddy', was beaten and then charged with obstruction. He was acquitted of assault charges by three lay magistrates at Greenwich and conditionally discharged for obstruction. The crucial difficulty for the Ladywell Action Centre was in convincing witnesses to attend court since the local black community had little faith in the legal system.

The Council Makes Waves

These cases alarmed Lewisham Council. In October 1972 Mike Steele and Deptford solicitor Jim McGoldrick of NCCL were invited by Leader Andy Hawkins to brief him and the Leader of the Tory opposition, Councillor Herbert Eames. Next day the Council responded with unprecedented concern. In a move suggested by Councillor Chris Eve, they called for an independent enquiry into police relations with black people. Councillor Ted Walker, who worked with young people in the Ladywell area, reported his experience of police harassment of black youths. The motion was debated and adopted.

> This Council is disturbed that the 1972 report of the LCCR officer and the evidence of the South East London Group of the NCCL to the Select Committee on Race Relations and Immigration contain serious allegations of certain attitudes and actions towards black residents on the part of local police officers which must, if true, exacerbate racial tensions. Facts within the knowledge of members of this Council and other responsible people in the Borough, particularly those engaged in community work, support the evidence of the bodies referred to above. The Council considers that an independent public enquiry into relations between police and black residents in the Borough is now essential to restore the confidence of black and white residents, to diminish racial tensions and to restore police morale.

The resolution was passed by the Labour majority. The Tories were against this move. The Home Secretary Robert Carr rejected the Council's request. The Home Office reply in November countered the need for such an inquiry.

i. The Home Secretary is satisfied that the Commissioner of Police does all he can to improve relations between the police and coloured people;
ii. The dialogue which the police maintain with coloured people is the most likely way in which effective and practicable suggestions for improving relations will emerge;
iii. A special Inquiry set up by the Home Secretary on the problems of a particular area would be justified only if there appeared to be major defects of police organisation which were causing grave and widespread public concern and which had not been clearly identified by ordinary methods of investigation.
iv. The Home Secretary has no evidence which leads him to believe that such defects exist in Lewisham.

The Council expressed its disappointment. In any event, Lewisham had signalled its distaste for the existing situation. In December 1972 Chief Inspector Merry was transferred and Ladywell acquired a new Commander, Douglas Randall. Eight days later Andy Hawkins called a meeting to consider the Borough's next step. The meeting was attended by about 140 leaders and representatives of local community groups, political parties and other organisations as well as senior police officers. The debate was heated. Commander Randall attended the meeting but did not speak.

Police/Immigrant Sub-Committee, 1972-1975

Against the backdrop of troubled black-police relations and the steady number of complaints, particularly against Ladywell Police, a Police/Immigrant Sub-Committee was formed by the LCCR. The group met on 5th September 1972 to prepare draft terms of reference. At the following meeting a 12-point programme was agreed, ranging from dealing with complaints to promoting racial harmony through talks and projects. They also nominated four liaison officers. Out of the final terms of reference, agreed by the police and the committee, came the 'Lewisham Scheme'.

The Lewisham Scheme began operation in May 1973 after a great deal of thought and goodwill. The voluntary police liaison officers were Miranda Hetherington, Bob Ovuede, Morris Pollack and Amos Hurst. They could be called out day or night to mediate in police/immigrant matters. The scheme aimed to provide liaison officers whom both the police and arrested black people would have reason to trust.

The creation of trust, mutual understanding and good community and race relations are thus the objectives of the scheme, apart from its practical advantages to the arrested person. LCCR LEAFLET, 'THE LEWISHAM SCHEME', 7/1/1975

Douglas Randall responded to the difficult situation he had taken on by initiating immediate discussions with those who had put forward criticisms of the police. Relations with the new police leadership led to plans for what came to be popularly known as 'help on arrest'. The idea had been tried before in areas such as Brixton.

Muggings

In June 1974 senior police officers attending the meeting of the Police/Immigrant Sub-Committee revealed statistics related to 'black mugging' within the borough from 1st January to 3rd March 1974. They gave total muggings as 125. Breaking down the figures, those committed by black youths were said to be 119 with only six by white youths. The police promoted the idea of bringing an outside patrol group into the borough. It was also agreed at the meeting that preventative action would be taken by visits and talks given on the subject in black youth clubs at the Moonshot and the Lewisham Way Centre.

The sub-committee was not informed when the police released figures for the period up to September. The total muggings for January 1st – September 30th 1974 were given as 203. Of these 172 were said to be committed by black youths compared to 18 by white youths. When the *South East London Mercury* published Randall's figures, LCCR chairman Rev Malcolm Johnson and Asquith Gibbes issued a joint statement condemning the figures and their publication. They argued that a breakdown of indictable offences rather than the isolation of one type of offence, 'mugging', would have been seen to be fairer.

We further question why he chose to publicise the figures in this way and deny any suggestion of a general joint operation to stamp out crime.

The Police/Immigrant Sub-Committee was trapped. Black people were sceptical of its role which was seen as largely tokenistic. The police treatment of the committee was poor and the Council's own police liaison committee issued press statements defending the police and condemning anyone "indulging in this kind of crime".

In October 1975 an all-day seminar on race and the media was organised jointly by the National Union of Journalists and the CRC. 'Mugging' was the subject of such heated debate that the chairman postponed the item until later in the day. Sam Uba, a delegate at the seminar, was vociferous in his condemnation of journalistic practices detrimental to the black community such as the use of the term, 'muggers' as synonymous with young black men.

In November 1977 another row over muggings statistics surfaced. Mike Steele, member of the Police/Immigrant committee, pointed out that the figures related to reported incidents, not convictions in the courts. He indicated the significant difference between the two concepts. The issue is far from dead as shown by Sir Paul Condon's highly-publicised statements of 1995 that street robbery remains a largely 'black crime'.

The Growing Threat

In the early 1970s Enoch Powell and the National Front held the public gaze. It was in his constituency that the NF and NP (National Party) racist candidates polled 44.5 per cent of the votes. 'Immigration', the new code word for 'black people', was highlighted in political debate. Through public meetings and marches the National Front made a bid for power in the hard right niche which seemed to be wide open.

In the General Election of October 1974 the Deptford NF candidate won 1,731 votes. Against this background the All Lewisham Campaign against Racism and Fascism (ALCARAF) came into being from a meeting of the Deptford and Lewisham Trades Council. As early as August 1976 John Silkin MP had called a meeting to consider action on the rise of racism in the borough. ALCARAF was a campaign to allow the voices of ordinary, non-extremist members of the community to come to the fore, in opposition to the fascism and racism visible on the street and in the media. Rev Wilfred Wood, curate of St Laurence Catford, played a key part in bringing together members of the local churches to take part in the campaign. Churches, trade unions, Black and Asian organisations, political parties and community groups were all represented. ALCARAF was launched on Saturday 22nd January 1977. Rev Wood was one of the two speakers at the Town Hall that day when 160 delegates listened to the opening address.

> *Our presence here today suggests that we have passed the stage where we personally need to be convinced that racism and fascism are evils which should have no place in our society. People have certain inalienable rights – such as the the right to life, liberty and the pursuit of happiness, and since the last-named includes such things as employment as a means of caring for themselves, shelter, and education – the denial to some people or curtailment of these rights is a way of saying that such people are not people. Racialism and Fascism would deny and curtail these rights.*

> *But why such a campaign, and why in Lewisham? Every now and again something takes place in some corner of the world and the world can never be the same again, because the effects of that occurrence will remain for as long as the world remains. We generally call these events 'discoveries' or 'inventions', of the atomic bomb, or the 'invention' of the gas chambers in which Hitler murdered millions of people in order to prove a political theory. But there are other kinds of discoveries and among these is one very important one of our day. It is this: a minority of the world's people whom we call white have seized force, laws, conventions, and trade-agreements have, for a long time, maintained this monopoly even though it meant that Black and Asian people existed in poverty in rich countries, died unnecessarily from diseases that could be cured by medicines and were denied the education which would have enabled them to help themselves. This is racialism, the use of a man's racial origin to determine his worth, and a system of awards and punishments based on the colour of his skin.*

The Lewisham 24 Affair

In April 1977 police in Lewisham began filming suspects of street crime such as pick-pocketing and purse-snatching outside the Lewisham Odeon and in New Cross Road. The video recording and still camera photography was to be used as 'back up' for a team of officers appointed to make strategic observations in the operation against pick-pocketting and purse-snatching. Over 96 addresses were obtained of suspects. About 60 homes were raided at dawn on May 30th and 21 young black men were arrested. Others were arrested at a later date. A range of charges were laid but none of theft from the person. The decision to undertake high technology surveillance had not been discussed nor the implications for police powers.

The Times reported the following day that community workers had prior knowledge of the raid. In anger at the betrayal Moonshot members occupied the centre. A defence committee was set up, involving parents of those arrested. Sybil Phoenix and Asquith Gibbes issued press statements and took measures to defuse the situation. During the summer and autumn the police dropped conspiracy charges against five people. The other 19 were tried for 'sus' and 'handling' and the case became known as the 'Lewisham 19 Affair'. All were found guilty and, through their convictions, became conspiracy defendants. The prosecution presented the accused in four groups. Each faced charges of conspiring both within the smaller group and with those in other groups to steal from shoppers at bus stops.

The 'affair' stimulated calls for the abolition of the general offence of 'conspiracy'. Fears were expressed about details of addresses not raided but held by the police and about the racialising of crime despite Metropolitan Police figures which showed that 88 per cent of all crime was undertaken by whites.

> *If no theft charges were brought against 16 of the Lewisham 19 and if the existence of a conspiracy could only be inferred then did the nature of the evidence differ substantially from that used in cases where Section 4 of the Vagrancy Act 1824 (Sus) is used?* LCCR 'CONSPIRACY AND COMMUNITY REPORT'

Bloody Saturday

The National Front used the case of the Lewisham 24 to promote the racial interpretation of 'mugging'. NF leader John Tyndall's speech at New Cross poured contempt on the Bishop of Southwark and the Church as a whole.

> *They're more interested in the rights of 24...Black muggers than in the rights of the native people of Lewisham to be able to walk the streets after dark.*

In planning their march through New Cross, Deptford and Lewisham, the NF were making a territorial bid. They had recruited aggressively and were displaying their power to black people and left-wing activists. Banners declaring the group's racist intentions were paraded and the message of hate was compounded by printed invitations to join the organisation. Their supporters included at least one 70 year old woman.

The immediate area around Clifton Rise where the NF march was to begin housed very many black people. Members of the black community awaited the event with

53. Bloody Saturday, 13th August 1977. The NF march at New Cross Road.

mixed feelings of rage, resentment and resignation.

Racism was a bad thing in Lewisham for many, many years. The National Front got away with more than they should. I was involved in the action against the National Front when it looked like whites were allowing the NF to march through Lewisham which we were hoping was one of the better boroughs in terms of how it was managed. We did things in that context. HARRY POWELL

The proposed march had mobilised the borough of Lewisham and a 'march for peace' set out from Hilly Fields. It was not only the NF and anti-Front demonstrators who showed their colours. Deptford Town Hall was festooned in a banner declaring the area to be against racism. Separated from the battles the churches marched for peace, led by the Bishop of Southwark. The Mayor's presence beside him signalled civic and person concern. Barbadian-born Rev Wilfred Wood from St Lawrence Catford also marched behind the ALCARAF banner, along with "councillors, Liberals, Socialists,

54. The ALCARAF 'march for peace' passes Ladywell Playtower, led by Mayor Roger Godsiff and Bishop of Southwark Mervyn Stockwood. These figures of the white establishment proved useful allies against racism.

Communists and the widest spectrum of community and trade union activists."

At the junction of Lewisham Way and Algernon Road the marchers were stopped by solid ranks of police whose priority appeared to be to ease the movements of the NF. Police power and civic power faced each other as the Mayor Councillor Roger Godsiff appealed to Commander Randall to let the march continue on its planned route. Police power prevailed and the march was re-routed away from Deptford. Many of the demonstrators took the option to disband and some made it to New Cross to take a part in the developing battle.

Meanwhile members of the Socialist Workers Party and many local residents had gathered in Clifton Rise to meet the fascists. Around 2,000 people listened to speeches made from the top of the men's toilets at the junction of Clifton Rise and New Cross Road.

The police arrived and it was clear that they had been given orders to break up that meeting, disperse everybody. The situation changed very dramatically. The next 15 minutes were very chaotic...violence...arrests...confusion. PAUL TREVOR, PHOTOGRAPHER IN CLIFTON RISE

The confrontation was bloody and a great many injuries were sustained. The first casualities arrived at Lewisham Hospital about 2.30pm. Shops and pubs were extensively damaged.

Sticks and stones were flying everywhere. You couldn't tell who was throwing what. SOUTH EAST LONDON MERCURY, 18/8/1977

In the mid-afternoon the police escorted the 1,000 NF supporters along Pagnell Street to New Cross Road. The role of the police in protecting the racists was clearly

55. Clifton Rise on Bloody Saturday. The police broke up the crowd listening to the speakers. The National Front were meanwhile gathering unseen in Achilles Street. – just off Clifton Rise to the left of this picture

appreciated. Both John Tyndall and national NF organiser Martin Webster thanked the police for their "splendid job" and suggested that they should have been allowed to "go in with tear gas, with rubber bullets and the whole works of crowd control."

And let me make this promise to the police, that when we get in [power] the police are not going to go unarmed into these affrays. We will give the police all the necessary equipment, we'll give them the money they deserve, the backing they deserve and the authority to sort the Red mob out. JOHN TYNDALL, NEW CROSS ROAD, 13/8/1977

The march moved towards Lewisham. On Lewisham Way 50 or 60 people linked arms across the road to stop the NF march which was still some way back. A police car rushed up from Lewisham, stopping inches away from the group in the road. Photographer Ray Rising saw a man ran up to it and smash at the bonnet with a piece of wood.

It might have made a small dent, but it made a very loud noise. Immediately the police car reversed some 50 yards back at very high speed. He said something over his little microphone and suddenly the SPG, helmets and all, with trunchions out came darting up the road...I thought everybody who was in front of them was going to get it...People were being thrown across the railings, out of the road. They were just clearing the road completely.

56. *The New Cross Fire – a tragedy of immense proporotions*

With the road cleared the NF march was free to move onwards towards Lewisham with police protection to catch coaches and trains at the end of a 'successful' day. With the fascists gone the Lewisham clocktower was the site of another confrontation, this time between the Left and the police. For the first time in England, the police were equipped with riot shields.

The New Cross Fire

Sunday 18th January 1981 marks a solemn date in the history of the black experience in Lewisham. Fourteen young black people between the ages of 14 and 22 were, in the final count, killed in a tragic fire the origin of which still remains uncertain. As the fire struck in the early hours of the morning, the birthday party of two teenage friends, Yvonne Ruddock and Angela Jackson, was still in swing. The fire transformed 439 New Cross Road into a raging inferno, scene of death, disfigurement and injury. Every black family's nightmare, anticipated by a history of racist threats and actual attacks such as the Sunderland fire bombing a decade earlier, materialised in news of the the dead and injured. One party-goer reported the suspicious behaviour of a man who drove off in a white Austin. Early media and eye witness accounts pointed to an arson attack. The tragedy devastated the families of the dead and injured, shocked the south east and touched the lives of black families up and down the country. Families of the fire victims came together in a Parents Committee.

In rage and grief, the local black community mobilised around a number of support groups. Prominent among these was the New Cross Massacre Action Committee (MAC) formed within days of the tragedy. The Massacre Committee made clear from the outset its belief that the fire was a racist attack. The view, consistent with early evidence and black community expectations and experience, became the cornerstone of an organising force.

57. Deptford Fire victims remembered

In the wake of the New Cross Fire we took a decision very early in the first meeting that it was a massacre politically. We decided that the protest would be Black-led and we decided that we would mobilise the whole country from a central co-ordinating gruop. I can remember very vividly being part of the debate. It was clear that we didn't want it to be part of a commission or whatever because those bodies are not political bodies. If we were to wage any struggle, it had to be a political struggle, purely based on the resources of the community. You don't apply for grants to take political action! TREVOR SINCLAIR

On the afternoon of the Sunday following the fire, around 400 black people marched from Pagnell Street Centre to New Cross Road and gathered outside 439. They faced the smoke-stained brickwork, charred window frames and galvanised doorway in a rare public expression of black grief.

Twenty year old Chris Foster of Childeric Road, whose brotheer had been the victim of a random racist attack in 1979, articulated the gulf that was rapidly growing between the black community and the police in charge of investigating the fire.

Go back to your communities and organise. Then come back to us with your information and we will decide what to do. CHRIS FOSTER, 25/1/1981

Messages of hate were sent to at least 12 family members. The contents sickened the black families and their well-wishers. In a determined bid to find the arsonist a £5,000 reward was put up by the newspaper West Indian World. The reward was announced at a press conference at Pagnell Street Centre where black councillor Russell Profitt, in whose ward the tragedy took place, stressed the importance of finding the killer.

We are angry that not enough is being done by police and others to find this twisted individual or organisation or those who planned this monstrous thing.

Though media attention concentrated on the question of who started the fire, contention surfaced. Newspaper reports, based on statements from the police, played down the possibility of a racist arson attack. Statements by the police suggested instead that they sought the culprit within the black community. Many in the black community voiced dissatisfaction with police handling of the inquiry.

MAC set up a fact-finding commission. This group made available information which, though agreeing with police information in many respects, nonetheless varied at crucial points. Critical to the different perspectives was police dismissal of the evidence of an incendiary device, the lack of suspects and a history of racial attacks which the police had been unable to solve.

One important function of MAC was to provide information which dispelled the rumours and distortions in the national newspaper coverage of the Fire. The Daily Mirror's account of the demonstration on the Sunday following the fire carried the headline 'One Cool Cop Calms A Mob', effectively reducing 400 grieving black people to 'a mob' and making the single white policeman the hero of an imagined drama.

The Black People's Day of Action

The Black People's Day of Action, the largest black demonstration in Britain took place on Monday March 2nd 1981. The day was organised by the Massacre Committee, led by John La Rose and Darcus Howe. An estimated 15,000 people attended.

They came to tell the rest of the country how they felt - not just about the terrible loss the community has suffered. But about the discrimination, the fruitless search jobless youngsters face, the problems so many children face in schools. SOUTH EAST LONDON MERCURY, 5/3/1981

Essentially this was a day of solidarity, the central focus of which was the victims of the fire and their families. Marchers came to London from many parts of Britain to join the demonstration.

We sent the message across everywhere. People travelled all over the country to black communities. We did that. The credit for it was in Lewisham because Lewisham happened to have a history of black political activity and a core of conscious political activists. There was a range of other people, not necessarily political but black. TREVOR SINCLAIR

The march began at New Cross, filed past 439 New Cross Road, moved onwards via the Houses of Parliament, Fleet Street and ended in Hyde Park. A delegation delivered letters to the Prime Minister, Scotland Yard and the Metropolitan Commissioner.

This was an historic event. The decision to hold it came from the NCMAC on 27th January. The decision was to show the determination of the black population that they will not be killed, maimed or injured with impunity and that if the state would not protect its citizens then the black population and its allies in the country would. JOHN LA ROSE

58. The Day of Action to remember the New Cross Fire was described by the South East London Mercury as a 'Day of Dignity' while the national press sensationalised the minority looting.

When MAC had announced plans for the Black People's Day of Action in early February the only press coverage was a brief mention in one Sunday newspaper. At local meetings the black community criticised the concerted silence of the national press which followed on from "sensationalist, inaccurate and inconsistent" reporting of the fire. After the Day of Action the press were criticised for distortion, inaccuracy and sensationalism. *The Sun* headlines included:

Black Day At Blackfriars; Riots and Looting as Marchers Run Wild; Day the Blacks Ran Riot in London.

The LCCR's complaint to *The Sun* was dismissed as 'claptrap' so an official complaint was made to the Press Council on 21st April 1981. Six months later the Press Council ruled against *The Sun's* article, finding it "damaging to good race relations", the first such ruling against a Fleet Street newspaper. In contrast *Time Out's* reporting was commended for maintaining a balanced viewpoint yet commenting on the troublesome behaviour of a minority of young people. The *South East London' Mercury's* lead article DAY OF DIGNITY was praised for catching the local mood after the fire, capturing both the sadness and the concerns for black people in this society. The 'Opinion' column condemnned the distorted coverage by the national press.

The Aftermath

At the first anniversary memorial meeting held in Deptford Town Hall, MAC chairman John La Rose described the tragedy as

an unparalleled act of barbaric violence against the black community in this country.

The inquest into the deaths of the youngsters lasted 13 days but police evidence was inconclusive and the coroner returned an open verdict which was rejected by the parents. In the light of the revelation that a "highly amateurish" incendiary device had been found outside the house, a fact only disclosed at the inquest, the committee lodged an appeal and parents requested a new inquest. The request was granted but the High Court turned down the application to have the open verdict quashed. Four and half years later in August 1985 the police file on the New Cross Fire was officially closed.

The Policy Studies Institute survey of Police in London released in 1983 contained damning and very rarely publicised evidence of how the fire "had the efect of focusing racialist attitudes within the Met". A series of racist jokes about the renaming of Deptford to 'Blackfriars' spread through the police force and officers were heard to describe the march as "hundreds of rampaging niggers" who were considered 'animals' and 'should be shot'.

Donald McTernan, whose parents came from Jamaica, remembers the threats of the late 1970s and early 1980s very clearly.

The NF demo was embedded in the psyche of black people in the borough. It was the first major publicised confrontation. It was unsettling because we had thought it can't happen here and it was happening. We didn't feel better afterwards becuase, although people had stood up to them, it had ended up with looting and fighting. It got taken over by left wing agitators or whatever you want to call them, rent a mob, thieves and others. It wasn't in our control anymore.

The march after the Deptford Fire was similar. Although for the people on ther march it had an impact because they knew it was a day of solidarity for black people from all over the country, when you saw the news afterwards all they showed was kids out looting. It showed again how little control we had over our own destiny.

The dream of self-determination had been beaten to the ground over and over again by the State, the police and the forces of neo-fascism. There were allies and there were triumphs but the longest journey was far from over. Just as the black community felt itself gaining in confidence and visibility, the 'nightmare years' showed racism in Lewisham, and the fear of racism, at its most disturbing. Those years showed also the very real possibilities for mobilising community support to resist that evil.

13

BUILDING A COMMUNITY: SHAPING LEWISHAM

"We are setting out to create a society in which a black person does not have to abdicate his blackness, vindicate his blackness or exaggerate his blackness in order to live a full life in it." REV. WILFRED WOOD, 22/1/1977

The West Indian community found itself having to adjust rapidly to the norms of the host community and to realign its expectations in the light of these realities. It was, at the same time, meeting the internal needs of its own community through a variety of responses. The late 1960s to mid 1970s were heady but tough years.

The period I'm aware of was that wonderful period between late '68 and about '74, when Lewisham and the surrounding South East was an absolutely rich and invigorating place of black activity, in terms of cultural activity, intellectual activity, people writing books and doing plays. Lots of projects were being set up: community projects, youth projects, lots of action being taken and the most enriching thing was that it was self help in the truest sense.

Social Responses

Young people had been a focus of concern for the black community since the beginning of the 1970s because of lack of employment opportunities, cramped housing conditions and poor leisure facilities.

THE MOONSHOT

The Pagnell Street Centre and the Moonshot Club came from the Telegraph Hill Neighbourhood Council which was formed in 1968 to develop social provison responsive to neighbourhood needs. The Moonshot, named because it was the time of the much publicised and exciting first moon probes, was part of the Neighbourhood Council's plans for young people in the area. Although some 200 young black people met regularly, they had no fixed base. After negotiations with Lewisham Council a Victorian mission hall, disused for five years except for one Christmas Post Office sorting room, was leased to the Neighbourhood Council. When the youth and community workers moved in, the initial job was clearing out. Rewiring, plastering, painting; all had to be done before the young people could come in. The warden of the centre from 1970 was Sybil Phoenix, who was awarded the MBE for services to the community two years later.

I became associated with Sybil Phoenix and the Moonshot Club and when I saw the dump that was given to young blacks, I found it appalling. There was a stalwart in Sybil Phoenix, a very conscious woman, very caring, known to the community as 'auntie'. She was trying to give the young people something to live up to, but once again a dump. Sybil set about it with the help of the church and the local authority. ASQUITH GIBBES

Sybil herself described the clearing process as "nauseating as well as strenuous". She worked closely with Rev Malcolm Johnson, one of the founders of the Neighbourhood Council. Together they determined the way the Centre developed.

If Mrs Phoenix was the fairy godmother, Rev Johnson was the fairy godfather.
GUS JOHN

By 1971 there were 340 members, mostly of West Indian origin, on the youth club registers. The club offered a wide range of activities from candlemaking to disco. One of the successes of the Moonshot was its football club which won trophies locally and nationally. By 1972 the Moonshot Club was meeting five nights a week. Princess Margaret visited the following year. During 1974 a one year experimental training scheme was set up to offer young people trainging in basic skills with a view to enhancing their employment prospects. While the project was well attended it was noted that it attracted largely those already taking up college courses rather than the truly unemployed.

59. One of the successes of the Moonshot was its football team which won trophies locally and nationally.

The Moonshot suffered a series of attacks. In May 1975 young people and organisers alike bemoaned the vandalism and damage to the Shaka sound system at the heart of Moonshot activities. An estimated £1,500 worth of damage was done to the music equipment. Roger Norman, editor of the *Mercury* until 1994, gave his usual sympathetic response.

Many of us could not stand it [Shaka Sound] or even understand it – but it must be accepted that the sound is of vital importance to hundreds of youngsters. And its destruction has been a severe blow to their morale. SOUTH EAST LONDON MERCURY, 8/5/1975

Worse was to come. In November 1977 a newspaper article stated that an NF meeting had included talk of burning down the Moonshot. On December 18th at four o'clock in the morning the Pagnell Street Centre was ablaze from an incendiary bomb thrown at the door. This was the time of the firemen's strike and the building was completely gutted. Sybil ignored the warnings of the police, entering the burning building to rescue the club's accounts. The roof was damaged, windows blown out and records ruined. Initially sickened, community workers rallied to give renewed support. In the wake of this attack Sybil made her intentions clear in a radio interview:

My name is Phoenix and, so help me God, out of the ashes I will rebuild Moonshot.

Over £50,000 was raised to rebuild the new centre. In 1978 Lord Pitt of Hampstead laid the foundation stone of the new Pagnell Street Centre and Moonshot Club.

99 BURNT ASH HILL

We are gravely concerned by the lack of appreciation of the sources of frustration experienced by many young black people living in the Borough – appreciation of the hard experience of living in overcrowded conditions, being unable to 'succeed' at school, of getting unfulfilling jobs or no jobs at all, of finding police and authority figures hostile which is producing serious alienation, disillusionment and embitterment. REV MALCOLM JOHNSON IN 1973-74 REPORT

A persistent concern within the black community was the over-crowded living conditions of many black families which drove young people onto the streets and into trouble arising from unsupervised activities. Unlike the unemployment problem, however, the housing needs of young black people could, in some measure, be met by community initiatives. Such an initiative was Burnt Ash Hill Hostel.

60. A hostel was set up at 99 Burnt Ash Hill in 1974 to provide accommodation in a stable environment for homeless black males aged 16-21.

In 1974 LCCR leased 99 Burnt Ash Hill from Lewisham Council for five years to provide accommodation for homeless black males aged 16-21. In the first six months,

14 young men took up residence. In its second year of work as a hostel, all the places had been filled. Seven of the residents were in full-time employment. The rest were students at school or awaiting employment.

We set out to provide a stable environment and to assist in inducing motivation, improving self-image and esteem as well as helping in the search for work and further education. In those days it was possible to obtain employment, access to training course was comparatively easy and a meaningful future was still conceivable. RAY MOORE, WARDEN

Often these young people were in trouble with their families as well as the police. The hostel therefore played important roles other than housing. It helped support the young men into further education or to get jobs and become independent. A major problem was finding suitable and affordable accommodation after the young people were ready to leave the hostel. Ray Moore, warden of the hostel, remained alert to the difficulties of accommodation after leaving Burnt Ash Hill.

Sometimes they just can't get accommodation and have to come back here temporarily. During the day most are out at work or college. Hostel is home base in the evening where there's friends and support in the constant battle to come to terms with discrimination and disadvantage.

Finance for the hostel came from Urban Aid (75% Home Office and 25% Lewisham Council). After five years a total of 78 young men had been resident there. In 1987 Lewisham Council took on the full grant responsibility for the hostel. By the end of the long, hot summer of 1989 the hostel showed signs of structural damage and the deteriorating structure brought a move to temporary accommodation. Despite the increasing homelessness of young black people and worsening employment prospects, this unique project closed in February 1992.

PLAY PROVISION

In the early 1970s black parents in the New Cross and Brockley area were contacted by community workers and some 15 families began to meet to discuss

61. Sybil Phoenix (left) at an early playscheme at the Pagnell Street Centre.

common problems. The isolation of many black families with young children was registered as a practical issue. Ros Howells was appointed as full-time development worker in the summer of 1974 to a project housed at the Pagnell Street Centre supporting young unmarried mothers.

Lack of play provision also gave rise to new demands. It was agreed to set up a nursery at the Moonshot, already attended by many young mothers. In November 1973 the Lewisham ILEA representative met with young mothers, playgroup workers and other community workers at Ladywell Baths to discuss needs identified by Lewisham Campaign for the Under Fives. By 1974 the LCCR operated multi-racial playgroups at Lewisham Way, Rokeby Road, Brockley Rise and Hither Green Lane.

The first summer playscheme project catering to the needs of young black children was held at Childeric Primary School in 1972. It was a scheme which welcomed black and white children alike. The playscheme continued into the late 1980s when funds could no longer be found to support it.

We recognised the need for young people to interact socially with other young people during the summer holidays. We recognised that black people didn't have the money to send their children out on tours and trips and so on and there was a need to have these summer playschemes. ASQUITH GIBBES

Trips were arranged to many places of interest. The Commonwealth Institute, Chessington Zoo and the seaside were favourites of children and parents. A day at the seaside exchanging the traffic of New Cross Road for buckets, spades and sandy sandwiches was always popular.

CALABASH

The Calabash Club grew out of the work of Cecile Murray, a community development worker who had compiled a list of 50 black pensioners around the borough but discovered a serious lack of provision for black elders who found the Council day centres unwelcoming. At first around 20 of the elders met in the LCCR meeting room where they had use of a kettle, a second-hand fridge and an old television set. The opportunity to meet was appreciated and soon games of dominoes and art and craft sessions became regular activities. Day outings were added to the social calender. These included day trips to Margate, Brighton and other seaside resorts. A number of those taking part had not been to the English seaside before, indicating something of the scarcity of leisure opportunities.

It was clear to Cecile that these black elders were largely uninformed about provision for the elderly and a leaflet called 'We Didn't Know They Existed' was produced. This was used in negotiations with Lewisham's Social Services department and, despite some opposition from councillors to avoid 'apartheid in reverse', provision for black elders was agreed in principle. A steering group was set up in 1981, including two LCCR officers, Leader of the Council Andy Hawkins and representatives from Pensioners' Link, Age Concern and Social Services.

A vacant lot was found in George Lane, Catford and the recommendation to build a centre was agreed in February 1983. Against a background of racist opposition from local residents, who seemed to believe that a club for black elders would be a focus for drug-dealing and all-night parties, the building was completed in January 1985 and opened in May by Les Eytle, Lewisham's first black mayor. The name Calabash, chosen by the black elders, is taken from the calabash tree familiar to West Indians.

LEWISHAM WAY CENTRE PROJECT

The Lewisham Way Centre was set up following the recommendation that a building be found where most of the young West Indians in the area could

come together to do responsible things in their environment with a view to helping them to increase their sense of identity and confidence in themselves.
ASQUITH GIBBES

The centre opened on 8th January 1973 at 138 Lewisham Way. Mervyn Henry, described by Asquith as "a lovely Trinidadian", was the leading force behind the project. Harry Powell, a professional sportsman interested in youth work, met Mervyn in early 1974. Mervyn offered him every support in setting up a programme involving young black boys and girls in sporting activities at the Centre. In 1980 Harry was persuaded to apply for the positon as Senior Youth Worker, developing, co-ordinating and leading the Centre's programme in the community. Under Harry's leadership, the direction of the centre changed. It was no longer a youth centre alone but a youth and community centre. He started to develop educational programmes addressing the needs of young boys, young girls and young mothers and fathers. He also embarked on providing a service for the older group without access to the provision they needed. School-based work was a focus and exclusion from schools began to be addressed.

Lewisham could have exploded into a massive situation like the Brixtons, the Toxteths, the Tottenhams. I think everyone's been very lucky because there have been some quality people working in Lewisham as community workers.
HARRY POWELL

Harry trained at Avery Hill College. There were six black students in the group of 24. They supported each other as vigorously as they challenged the content of the course. Another route into youth and community work which has been invaluable to black students has been Turning Point led by Trevor Sinclair. The Lewisham Way Youth and Community Centre has had many student placements from Turning Point.

LEWISHAM COMMUNITY RELATIONS

Many of the early local social initiatives had the support of the Lewisham Community Relations office. When the office was first established the emphasis on 'harmony'. This was a peculiarly slippery aim, its achievement made all the more difficult by the many forms of racism and hardship experienced by the black community. Nonetheless, yearly reports indicated a systematic tackling of social as well as economic issues which benefitted the wider community.

Individuals like Asquith Gibbes assumed a prominent role in the first instance, precisely because a feature of his appointment as Community Relations Officer was about making visible the routes available to the black community for the expression of their needs. He has served in that role for 25 years.

Asquith was born in the mid 1930s in Grenada. He had a distinguished school career and was prominent among the bright young hopefuls attending the prestigious Grenada Boys' Secondary School. Debating was one of Asquith's favourite pastimes. The West Indies familiar to the young Asquith was one in which anti-colonialism and demands for independence were burning issues particularly dear to the hearts of ambitious young men. Asquith came to London in 1960. A law graduate, he was appointed to the GLC's Legal Department before his post at Lewisham. In such a central position, Asquith worked alongside many other leaders in their own sphere.

If I've done anything good for the black community it is to ensure that the policy of Lewisham Council was operating sensitively. That is one good thing.

In 1985 the Commission for Racial Equality asked researchers to consider how to create more uniformity of practice among community relations councils. There followed changes in both name and, more significantly, in focus. Race equality became the central drive, representing a major shift in the perspective of the office of community relations.

I thought that was the best thing that could happen to us. Our functions, therefore, derive from the 1976 Act as does the Commission, i.e. the elimination of discrimination and the furtherance of equal opportunity...It's tied us down to issues of race equality. Therefore, we raise equality in housing, exclusion of black kids and so on. Asquith Gibbes

Economic Responses

The longer the African-Caribbean community settled in Lewisham, as in the UK generally, the more evident was the need for an increasingly diverse response to income generation. Two trends may be discerned. The first is a greater thrust into the professions and the second is a slow but steady establishment of black groups and individuals in the business sector.

REACHING FOR A PROFESSION

Young black people completing schooling in the late 1960s or early 1970s found themselves, by and large, able to secure places within higher education despite an education system determined to steer them towards more menial positions. Nonetheless, by the 1970s black teachers began to appear increasingly in isolated positions in local schools. Apart from those who had taken the route straight from school to colleges or universities, there were still others who gravitated from quite different experiences towards youth work, social work or teaching. Eric Ferron, a Jamaican who arrived in the UK as a war recruit, has been associated with social work teaching for 30 years. Elaine Burke, also Jamaican, did a variety of jobs before gaining qualifications as a youth worker and finally as a social worker. A sense of commitment has sent individuals like these back into the black community in support services. Gilbert Browne, born in Trinidad, started his working life in London as a community worker and moved on to teach and influence many young people into community work.

BLACK BUSINESSES

Black businesses, from hairdressers to grocery shops, developed initially as services to the black community. It was not long before the racism of the host community drove black clients in search of services provided by other black people. Though experiences varied, black houseowners soon learned to seek out black builders, plumbers and electricians in the hope that they would either be less exploited or at least have the satisfaction of feeling that they had dealt with the devil they knew.

As unemployment escalated in the 1980s black people increasingly investigated the possibility of self employment. Organisations such as the Deptford Enterprise Agency showed their interest in targeting black businesses for support. In 1986 Enterprise Lewisham, self-styled as 'the small business friend', moved to Aitken Road, Catford. It was important to the black community that the staff of these organisations included very visible black people at senior level, such as Joe Greenland who headed the Deptford Enterprise Agency until it was disbanded when Section 11 funding ceased in 1994.

Educational Responses

The educational response by African-Caribbean people to the British situation developed many tentacles.

SUPPLEMENTARY SCHOOLS

The concern with 'supplementary' support for those in compulsory education remained a priority. An important initiative in the area of supplementary education was taken by 'black power' activists of the late 1960s and early 1970s. Supplementary schools or Saturday schools became part of the community's resource for supporting the education of young people. Before long, they were organised by churches as well as secular groups. Cultural input was seen as equally important to curriculum content.

Black people were certainly at pains to get rid of the pathological model which saw them as low achievers in the educational results league because parents 'didn't care too much' or 'didn't get to know the system'. There were therefore many supplementary schools or Saturday schools organised by black people as a result of what they saw as insitutional racism, the low expectations of teachers and a racist curriculum acting together to marginalise black folk.
GILBERT BROWNE

A minority of the better-off turned from the distrusted state sector to the independent. At the same time, as larger numbers of African-Caribbean children completed schooling, familiar difficulties arose concerning access into higher education.

A CENTRE FOR CARIBBEAN STUDIES

The Caribbean community turned to its local university, Goldsmiths College. The idea of a Caribbean Studies Centre began to crystallise in 1979 when a working party was established to redress the lack of provision within higher education. In 1980 the working party submitted two reports to Goldsmiths' Academic Planning Committee to develop the academic study of the Caribbean and its diaspora. At that time there was no such centre in any British university.

The location of the college in New Cross was seen as an advantage and the focus of the new centre was both academic and rooted in the community. In 1981 a formal steering group was set up with wider black community membership including Trevor Sinclair, Buddy Larrier and Beverley Campbell.

Beverley came to South London in the 1950s when she was four years old. She trained as a teacher and began her teaching career in secondary schools. In 1975 she started working as a part-time tutor in the Frobisher Institute (now Southwark Institute) teaching English O-level one evening a week. The Institute at that time did a great deal of community outreach work. With a full-time community worker co-ordinating programmes across Southwark and Lewisham, the Institute had links with black organisations, including Sybil Phoenix at the Moonshot. In 1979 Beverley moved into community education to work with Afro-Caribbean groups. The bulk of Beverley's work was at Catford Institute. By this route Beverley came to be in Lewisham, based at Deptford Green school where she stayed for many years. Beverley eventually left the Ravensbourne Institute in 1987.

> *I have a long history in terms of Lewisham. It's really important to walk the patch and I've walked Lewisham. I got to know most of the nooks and crannies and all sorts of people, organisations and groups.*

When Beverley came to Goldsmiths in 1980 a Saturday conference was held to discuss the need for a Centre for Caribbean Studies at the college. Among those attending were many staff at Goldsmiths who had long felt this need and wished to respond to the issues being brought up by black students, black academics and black people in the local community. From the platform a number of speakers addressed the need for a Centre for Caribbean Studies. Out of that conference a group started to meet regularly to consider how the idea could be moved forward. The conference had brought together people from all over the country, black and white academics as well as a number of interested groups. A large committee of interested individuals was formed, guided by a core group. Beverley was a central figure in the negotiations and battles to set up the Centre for Caribbean Studies at Goldsmiths College. She trekked around seeking out potential funding agencies, convening meetings and dealing with the numerous issues.

> *One of the things that is fascinating is the notion of the black community. The Caribbean community is actually a real hotchpotch, an incredible mix of people. If you were to take us physically, yes...but within that there are people who are academics, operating on an intellectual level that was just absolutely amazing and those who were barely literate but were interested and wanted to talk, to discuss things, to relate to other people.*
>
> *I have a problem with the idea of 'the voice of the black community' because I don't think there is only one voice. What we did have was an incredible mix of black people from all walks of life who were all saying the same thing which was, there is a need to be able to study the Caribbean and get a qualification in it. There is also a need to be able to have access to those who are studying the Caribbean from a Caribbean perspective, to get access to the books that have been written. People couldn't get hold of the books.* BEVERLEY CAMPBELL

In 1982 Peter Fraser attended meetings of the informal steering group. Born in Guyana, Peter completed his academic qualifications as a historian in Britain. He believes the initiative for the centre came partly from local black councillor Russell Profitt.

> *Goldsmiths seemed to be an interesting place because it had lots of community education and adult education programmes as well as the higher education side. It seemed to be in a position to promote Caribbean Studies at that higher level which was comparatively unknown at that time, except for a few individual courses at universities. It also seemed to be in a position to do something about the failings of the British education system in meeting the needs of black people.* PETER FRASER

Financial support for a feasibility study into a Centre for Caribbean Studies came from Goldsmiths. The attendance of Professor Alan Little at a conference on Caribbean Studies was seen by delegates like Peter Fraser to indicate a more serious commitment on the part of the College. In 1983 grant applications for the centre were successful. The GLC's Ethnic Minorities Committee funded two salaries from December 1983 to 1985. David Dabydeen and Winston James were appointed as co-ordinators. Their posts sought to combine experience in community education, research and academic work, race relations, fundraising and development work. From the beginning there were tensions in the creation of these posts and the Caribbean academics involved in the debate pointed out the dilemmas and pitfalls in the dual focus on community and academic research.

Open access events organised by the centre included discussion forums which were very popular with black academics and all kinds of people. Two conferences were held in the first year, a major history conference and a major literature conference, both packed to capacity. People from all over the country began to see who the black academics were and what they were doing. A directory identified the kinds of books the Centre for Caribbean Studies ought to have. Preparatory documents for negotiations with Goldsmiths were drafted.

> There was a lot of argument and debate but, I think, a lot of agreement that what we wanted was a centre for two clear purposes. One was a centre which offered the opportunity to study the Caribbean at academic level and to attain the relevant qualifications. The second purpose was a centre which accessed black community to the resources, whether books, people or whatever, so it had a community brief in it. The idea of community was difficult for Goldsmiths to accommodate. We were always very clear that the black community is actually a whole range of people of different skills and abilities and achievements who might need to dip in from time to time, who might find it difficult to go straight into academic study but would buzz from being exposed to it. We wanted black academics to be able to go out and work in the local community and organisations.
>
> Black community is a weird notion. In my work as a community education worker I had booked leading black academics to come and do a session with black youths on Rasta or a whole range of different things. They did it because of their commitment to black people and the education of young black people. So it was to formalise that and make it part and parcel of the work of the Cenre for Caribbean Studies so that we would never end up with a situation where black people in academia totally disassociated themselves from the reality. Mind you, I think it is difficult for them to do that anyway. BEVERELY CAMPBELL

By 1985 the Centre for Caribbean Studies had two part-time members of staff. The abolition of the GLC directly affected the centre's funding and, although the London Residuary Body kept it going for a while, eventually that funding ceased and negotiations were held with Goldsmiths to take on the staffing responsibility. It was agreed that the first available college vacancy would be for the Centre. In September 1989 Dr Petronella Breinburg was appointed to a permanent Goldsmiths-funded post.

Petronella came to London from Surinam, formerly Dutch Guyana. She did her teacher-training at Avery Hill College, now part of the University of Greenwich. Perhaps best known for her Sean books currently translated into five languages, Petronella came to Goldsmiths from the University of Sheffield. As Co-ordinator of the Centre her role was to develop academic courses at all levels across the college and open to all students. Another aspect of the post was to encourage people of Caribbean

62. Petronella Breinburg, who gained her PhD in 1984. In her role as the Head of the Caribbean Centre, Petronella was the first African-Caribbean woman to be appointed at doctorate level at Goldsmiths College.

origin into higher education at all levels. Petronella set up a community support group to assess the needs of the centre into the 1990s, a period of acute financial constraints, growing demands for higher education and an increasingly professionalised black community. The tension over the academic-community focus remained.

> *If we are going to locate a centre within an academic environment like a university...one of the key functions has to be the development of curriculum and research because there is an issue around what constitutes adequate knowledge and how you get rid of a lot of racism in the curriculum. To some extent there is a difficulty in having this as a kind of ivory tower, an isolated thing without access to or linkage into the black community and it seems to me*

there is a balance that can be achieved. But you cannot afford to ignore the research aspect. GILBERT BROWNE

Cultural Responses

What were the cultural responses of Caribbean people to their stay in London? While dance, story and music have played key roles in keeping African-Caribbean people in touch with a culture rooted in the Caribbean, each of these developing in London has influenced and been influenced by contemporary local culture.

While dance styles have changed over the years with widespread impact on youth culture, forms that have been of historical significance also play a part in the cultural experience of African-Caribbean people living in London. Lewisham's Kon Kon Te dance group was formed in the mid 1970s. Led by Desmond Brown it has met weekly at the Albany to practise dances such as the Quadrille, taken into the culture of the African slaves in the Caribbean. The dances, executed in severe mock seriousness, carefully mimic and exaggerate the gestures of the slave masters of the period. Kon Kon Te perform locally and across the country.

Like the folk forms, popular forms travelled with younger people moving into the UK. In the 1950s dances such as Bogle and Hot Potato competed with the Twist and Rock 'n' Roll for young black people.

The Albany Theatre has played an important part in the expression and development of Caribbean performance art forms. Beverley Glean was a development worker there in 1985. With the support of her supervisor, Jenny Harris from the Combination Theatre, Beverley set up the dance group Irie! which performed throughout the country.

We're proud of developing a style which introduces cultural awareness, which actually says something to the local community and raises issues that they can identify with. BEVERLEY GLEAN, DEPTFORD KITE, NOVEMBER 1994

Many Caribbean folk tales, particularly Anansi stories, not only survived the passage from Africa to the Caribbean but travelled again with post-war Caribbean migrants. Those stories have been retold in collections widely available to schools and they have been passed on by word of mouth from parents and storytellers in the community and on children's television programmes.

Culturally, black music has had the greatest impact on the host community. When John Stewart came to London in the 1950s he remembers West African 'highlife' was the popular music among black people at parties. The popularity of highlife receded as blues and ska from Jamaica became more available.

When we came here the highlife was the go. We used to have parties, sometimes three or four times a week...so it was not difficult then to keep abreast.

Brixton was the place to buy records. Jazz was popular for those seriously interested in music. It was the era of the gramophone and the radiogram was a possession of which to be proud.

One of the cultural contributions that has influenced the wider community has been directly a part of the Rasta experience. The sound of Rasta, reggae music, hit the streets of London in the early 1970s and worldwide the influence of Bob Marley and his music has been itself a phenomenon.

Bob, as a Rastaman, ventured so far with his messages. The things he sung about was things that everybody could identify with. He sang about feelings in terms of the stresses of life in a particular community and even on a world level because he started to recognise how much and what was happening in Africa as a whole. Even now, you go to the States, you go to Jamaica, his music is probably the most played music anywhere in the world. HARRY POWELL

For many young black people, music is sound, art and news medium and the biggest name associated with black music for many years in Lewisham was Jah Shaka. From the early 1970s, Shaka provided the imported single discs, mainly from Jamaica, that have held an important place in cultural continuity for many black people.

Live performances continued to present choice to Caribbean audiences at events such as the 1986 Caribbean Christmas Concert which featured Victor Romero Evans as compere. Desmond Dekker, Roy Shirley, Seko 'Rapso', the Caribbean Folk Group, the Lee Choir and the Irie! dance company performed. Hazel Williams was Lewisham's Caribbean Focus co-ordinator. Local schools had a week of related activities offering a taste of Caribbean culture.

Another source of music which survives in the south east is that associated with carnival, Calypso and its derivative Soca. Patsy Steele has 'played Mas' at the Notting Hill carnival each year since it first started in 1970. Each year her costume changes and is inspired by the theme of the band. She travels with other players of 'mas' to take part in the carnival festivities. Still more travel to Notting Hill Gate from the south east to watch the spectacle or enjoy the sounds. Carnival has been part of a focus on the Caribbean for young visitors to the Horniman Museum.

Political Responses

The West Indians who arrived in the early 1950s found a post-war government in power of which they were largely oblivious. For many West Indians real politics centred on questions of federation and independence for the islands and territories in the Caribbean. However, as the years passed the black community became increasingly involved in local political issues, although representation in the mainstream political arena remained tokenistic right up to the 1990s.

LEWISHAM BOROUGH COUNCIL

In 1971 Orlando 'Ollie' Nurse was the only black person on Lewisham Council. He was an alderman which meant that he was appointed by the Lewisham councillors rather than elected by residents, an indication that members of the Council believed black representation to be important.

Born in Grenada, Ollie Nurse came to London in 1956 and moved to Lewisham in 1962. It was there that he was invited by a neighbour to Labour Party meetings and in 1970 elected to the General Management Committee of the Deptford Labour Party. When Labour won in the borough elections Ollie Nurse became an alderman, sitting on Housing and Health Committees. He became vice chair of the Ladywell ward Labour Party. He wanted to encourage more black people to become actively involved in politics in order to influence the course of public events.

Unless black people become more involved in politics, they are not going to effect any kind of change over their own lives. ALDERMAN OLLIE NURSE, 1973

Alderman Nurse found many black people to be disenchanted with traditional party politics.

Many feel that there is no difference between the parties...There is also considerable distrust shown of politicians as a group.

Russell Profitt's political career may be traced to his childhood experience of Guyanese politics. His grandmother was actively interested in politics and used to take him along to mass meetings in the large open spaces of Georgetown. Budding politicians such as Cheddi Jagan and Forbes Burnham would engage the crowds with the rhetoric of pre-Independence politics at these stimulating events held by the People's Progressive Party. For Russell politics appeared a normal part of everyday life.

Russell went to Goldsmiths College and played an active role in the Students' Union. In his second year he was Vice President and the following year he became President of the Students' Union for which he was allowed a sabbatical year. This was 1968-69, at the height of revolutionary student politics

At that stage, you could count the national black political figures on one finger and that was it. It was David Pitt. Now, I was part of, I suppose, a strong feeling among the black community that we should play a more active role in British political life which was a significant advance because, prior to the late 60s/early 70s the feeling was that we were an immigrant community and as soon as we had made our pile or achieved our ambitions we would be returning from where we came. However, as part of the men of the second generation – I was really first generation but I had grown up with a lot of young people who were black growing up in Britain – there was this feeling that it's not enough to say 'jam tomorrow when we are in the Caribbean' but that some of the jam should be spread today while we are here because we are making a contribution.
RUSSELL PROFITT

Russell Profitt became Lewisham's second black alderman in 1974 and served for four years before being elected as a councillor in 1978. He remained on the Council

63. Russell Profitt was an alderman in Lewisham from 1974 to 1978 when he was elected councillor. He served on the council for a further eight years. In Guyana he had attended mass meetings in Georgetown with his grandmother.

until 1986. He has also been a trustee of the Deptford Fund, the organisation which established the Albany Institute in 1894. He was one of the first on the scene when the old Albany building in Creek Road was gutted by fire on 14th July 1978. Greenwich police insisted that "the fire wasn't arson. It was either an accident or, more likely, natural causes." They did not mention the scruffy note pushed through the door the day after the fire. Letters cut out of a newspaper said 'GOT YOU' and the note was signed with the number 88. ALCARAF believed this was a reference to the fascist paramilitary organisation Column 88.

FASIMBAS

By the early 1970s a growing number of young black men and women had set aside traditional politics and assumed a militant stance. Alderman Nurse and JP Pauline Crabbe, like many of their generation, disapproved of this political path but black political organisations took root from around 1969. For many young politicised black people the lack of a credible policy on racism within traditional political parties was a significant factor in their rejection of mainstream politics.

Roy Forsythe, who was 24 in 1973 and studying law at the University of London, became an active member of the Fasimbas, a militant black political group based in Lewisham. Roy traced his political wakening to his schooling in Lewisham after he joined his parents.

> I could never understand why other black guys at school never used to bother much with studies, for I felt it was important to work hard to get better grades and thus get a better job. They used to laugh at my efforts saying it would not do me any good when I got out of school. It was only later on that I realised the validity of their comments.

It was at school that Roy first began to realise the inferior position to which black people were allocated in this society.

> After school I tried to get a job and learned the truth about what my black schoolmates had said. I applied for many jobs in the business field, mainly insurance companies, but it was always the same story. When I went for an interview they said I had the necessary qualifications but the next day there would always be a letter rejecting me.

Roy finally got a job as an insurance clerk for which he was overqualified. He continued with his studies and gained a Higher National Diploma but applications for stockbroking and business administration jobs were unsuccessful so he went on to study law.

Roy and the Fasimbas identified the real struggle facing black people not as a class issue but as a race struggle, pointing, for example, to the dockers who supported racist views and remained virulently anti-black. Focusing on race issues they drew attention to the central part played by racism in black history. Yet the Fasimbas made clear their willingness to discuss with and work alongside white people who understood the black experience in Britain and were seeking to achieve racial justice.

> We found in fact there were three classes: the bourgeoisie, the white working class and the lowest strata – the black working class. ROY FORSYTHE

The Fasimbas, like other black organisations undertook voluntary supplementary teaching at the weekends. They stressed the need to relearn black identity and get rid of derogatory conceptions of black identity derived from a racist curriculum as well as from the English language itself. The teaching of black history was given a central place and, contrary to colonial and English educational practice, pride in the connection with Africa was reinforced. The basic tools of literacy were given careful attention.

The organisation elected committees and held weekly meetings where Fasimbas from other areas could attend. New members were screened for their level of commitment and assessed initially by attendance at meetings. It was then put to a full meeting whether the prospective member was acceptable for membership. The Fasimbas were a variety of ages but there was special interest in young black people who felt alienated and frustrated with the system.

We are saying to them 'get politically involved' and the way to do it is not through destructive paths of petty crime but through the constructive outlet that we offer as a black organisation. The Fasimbas have given many young blacks a sense of pride and purpose. ROY FORSYTHE

One of Roy's younger brothers was recommended for ESN school at six years old. Told that it was a 'special' school where the child would be given extra attention and support, Mrs Forsythe herself suggested that his brother also went along. So the two younger Forsythe boys went to the same school. It was some years before it was understood that the children had been placed in a school for the 'educationally sub normal'. Roy was prominent in the fight to have his brothers transferred to a 'normal' school and they were finally transferred at the ages of 11 and 13 though they were placed in the bottom class after so many years outside of the mainstream.

My elder brother and I were educated in Jamaica and are both people with high qualifications and here are my brothers, born in Britain and they could hardly read or write. ROY FORSYTHE

Personal experience and stories circulating among the black community motivated students and young professional black people to give their time voluntarily to Saturday schools. The Fasimbas took an active role in promoting Bernard Coard's book about ESN schools to a national black audience.

Other practical involvement concerned relations between black people and the police and the setting up of defence committees. One such committee was established locally on behalf of the Oval Four who were members of the Fasimbas arrested and charged with trying to 'shop' two old people and attempting to steal a policewoman's handbag. They were all actively involved in the supplementary school and were carrying books with them for the school project when they were arrested.

UNIVERSAL COLOURED PEOPLE'S ASSOCIATION

The Universal Coloured People's Association was based in Stoke Newington at the end of the 1960s. The UCPA, Britain's first Black Power group, was founded by Nigerian playwright and poet Obi Egbuna. One young black Lewisham man who heard about it was Trevor Sinclair. The UCPA politicised black young people through meetings and study groups. The UCPA had a branch in Brixton and they were thinking of setting up a group in South East London early in 1969. It was at that time that

Trevor Sinclair met Ricky Cambridge and talked of the possibility of joining a local branch. The South East branch was short-lived and by 1971 UCPA had broken up. The core of its membership reformed as the Black Unity and Freedom Party.

BLACK UNITY AND FREEDOM PARTY

Ricky Cambridge was a founder member of the BUFP locally. The party was recognised in the local press as a 'black power' group but it was primarily a Marxist-Leninist organisation and did not have a 'race first' approach to politics. It was much concerned with the wider struggle but it recognised black people's special situation. In practical terms this allowed fraternal relationships with a range of other radical organisations.

The group was also very clear about the difference between tactics and long-term strategies so that members could work in any setting but retain a consistent analytical hold on political situations. Thus demonstrating against the police was not incompatible with operating confidently within the system. Organisationally BUFP was able to involve white allies in particular parts of specific programmes. For example, in publicising certain police cases they negotiated with the Ladywell Action Centre as well as with LCCR and Sybil Phoenix at the Pagnell Street Centre.

There may have been deeper disagreement ideologically, but there weren't disagreements at some of the level of practicalities and therefore there was a workable agreement. TREVOR SINCLAIR

The BUFP took the leading part in publicising the first clearly racial attack, the Sunderland Road bombing.

Every time I see one or two people, even today I actually can recognise them. The scars are still there and so is the horror of it all. We were very supportive of them and we paid the ultimate price of that which was the police attacking us. TREVOR SINCLAIR

Deaths in police stations was another issue raised by the BUFP both at meetings and in the publication *Black Voice*. They organised a number of campaigns on the issue of police brutality.

The BUFP had a very clear gender policy about the rights of women, how women should be treated and what their position should be. They were at great pains to ensure that the women involved in BUFP played as much as possible an equal part and assumed responsible roles within the organisation. The division of responsibilities was carefully monitored to ensure that women also had positions which allowed their expertise to develop. Women were encouraged to speak authoritatively on a range of issues.

The BUFP forged links with other black workers' groups such as the Croydon Collective and the Black Workers Co-ordinating Committee in the struggle against racism and developed a range of projects to empower black young people. The Mkutanto project which developed in about 1972 taught typing, photography and Swahili.

By taking an active part in the broadest aspects of community life – social, economic, educational, cultural and political – the black community had negotiated another stage of the journey.

14

INVISIBLE LEADERS

"I don't know how many projects in this borough have been born in my front room." Sybil Phoenix, 1994

The notion of 'the black community' has developed since the post-*Windrush* years of the 1950s. In the final decades of the 20th century with a number of identifiable black communities, the concept of a single black community in the south east inner city is severely strained. This chapter looks at the way in which the Caribbean community came together and held together. Grenadians, Jamaicans, Barbadians, St Lucians, Kittitians, Guyanese, Trinidadians and many more from a range of territories and social groups, came together despite their differences to make up the black community. Out of this collective emerged some who led in the limelight. Still more rolled up their sleeves and took charge where they were needed or quietly did what had to be done. Many women were among the latter category. They were largely invisible as leaders but their contribution must be recognised.

Sybil Phoenix: 'Young People Are My Business'

Possibly the single most visible Caribbean woman in Lewisham from the 1960s to the 1990s has been Sybil Phoenix. Sybil was born in British Guiana on 21st June 1927. She was educated there and came to London, a young woman with clear plans. Central to these was a six-month work placement in a Citizens' Advice Bureau. She was a volunteer in 1954, the first black person that her colleagues had ever worked with and quite a novelty in the office. Everyone asked what language she spoke. They were not sure whether she could read and write and do the jobs expected of such a placement.

In her second week, a client sought advice about fleas in the child's hair. Another wanted help with house bugs. Sybil was intrigued. She volunteered to visit the clients, sure that the house bugs and lice referred to could not possibly be the ones that she knew of at home. On her return, Sybil asked whether the Queen, living only 10 minutes away, knew of the conditions of poverty in which her subjects lived. The supervisor was mystified but explained that the Queen did not concern herself in such matters. The conditions of acute poverty for white subjects in the Royal Borough of Kensington and Chelsea were another important lesson that Sybil had learnt in her short stay.

At the next home visit, the client demanded to know where Sybil thought she was going. The supervisor explained that Sybil was a student working alongside her. The client refused to let her enter. Eventually, since the supervisor was adamant about not leaving Sybil outside and because it would be to the client's inconvenience to visit the office again for another appointment, she allowed 'the coloured' in.

Sybil's preparation for a lifetime of youth and community work in the inner urban south east lay in such early experiences. She had been four months in her placement when she first made a visit on her own. The client checked her identity card and hurried her roughly through the door, railing at the person 'from the jungle' sent to deal with her case and refusing her a seat. Sybil sat down anyway, beginning her interview by giving the client some valuable information on life in Georgetown, the capital of Guyana.

Such early experiences were a harsh grounding but Sybil's early foundation gave her the inner resources to persist. Her grandparents, who brought her up, were well known in Georgetown as pillars of the church. The young Sybil looked up to older people. She always had older friends. Religion was an important source of strength in her life even as a child. It helped to give her the courage to achieve the goals she set herself. An active and zealous member of the church, Sybil was one of the youngest youth leaders in Georgetown, trained in Guyana by the British Council of Churches. Nonetheless, her qualifications were not accepted in London. She was told that she would be required to retrain. Having only been trained to work in South America and the West Indies, she could only be employed as an unqualified youth worker. Marriage intervened but Sybil was undeterred. Her experience and training in Guyana had grounded her; she knew that community work was her field.

64. Sybil Phoenix, 1993. Possibly the most visible Caribbean woman in Lewisham since the 1960s, Sybil has pioneered a wide range of youth and community projects throughout Lewisham.

In 1962 Sybil moved into her home in Lewisham. The needs of the black community were immediately obvious. She 'rolled up her sleeves' and began a trail of projects which would make a difference to the black community and to Lewisham.

Sybil Phoenix? She was the pioneer, I think, in the borough of Lewisham for youth provision. TREVOR SINCLAIR

Known locally for her outstanding contribution to youth work in the borough, Sybil was involved in a range of projects meeting the needs of the Caribbean community as well as serving the wider community. In the process she came across Caribbean families whose adolescents were becoming more rebellious than their parents found acceptable. Fathers often dug in their heels in opposition to Sybil's social worker stance. As a black woman, her intercession on behalf of the young people was insufficient so she found allies such as Lloyd Grey, a 6'2" Jamaican and David Diamond, a white priest. Sybil and David came to know each other rapidly when their youth club members stood in opposing black and white groups before or after a fight with the two Christian stalwarts struggling for control. From these beginnings the idea arose for a local youth festival to bring the two groups together (Ch. 17).

Serving the Community

While women have undoubtedly made a steady contribution to the history of Black Lewisham from the 1960s, many have succeeded in doing so outside the glare of the public eye. In the 1960s and 1970s the priorities of the black community in Lewisham were focused on the family. Black women's mulitple oppression and their many roles as mothers, workers, partners could be expected to drain their energy, but Lewisham's black women have been at the forefront of developing services to the comunity.

Many women involved in the formative period of the West Indian community were instrumental in the development of key initiatives of the period. Beverley Campbell helped in the setting up of the library at the Moonshot. She came into contact with Hazel Williams, who had moved into youth and community work. Concerned with the cultural gap in the education of Caribbean children, Hazel began telling West Indian folktales in schools and at community events.

The Caribbean Women's Progressive Cultural Association was inaugurated in 1972 and officially launched on 24th March 1973 by Lady Joan Carter, wife of the Guyana High Commissioner. Its main aim was to establish childcare. This was a primary concern for the black population with experience of poor and minimal childcare facilities in direct contradiction to their needs as unprivileged workers.

Ros Howells came to London from Grenada in the 1950s. Her role in 1970s Lewisham reflected the concerns of that early period when the West Indian community was largely a young one with social needs exacerbated by racism. Ros was appointed as full-time development worker in the summer of 1974 to a project supporting young unmarried mothers at the Pagnell Street Centre. Her work expanded steadily as she became the vice chair of LREC from 1982 to 1988 and then its chair from 1989 to 1991. Ros was appointed Deputy High Commissioner for Grenada in London at the end of 1978. As the Director of Greenwich CRE, she was awarded the OBE in 1994.

Cecile Murray became involved with the LCCR as a private member in the mid 1970s. In September 1978 she was appointed with a community development brief. Her first report picked out the needs of pensioners and children.

65. Ros Howells. Director of Greenwich Council for Racial Equality, Ros was awarded the OBE in 1994. She has worked extensively with Lewisham Racial Equality Council.

1. I decided to concentrate much of my time in areas of work least well-covered by other agencies, e.g. ethnic minority pensioners and the provision of activities for children between the ages of six and 11 years.

2. Pensioners. I have now compiled a list of 50 pensioners around the borough. The list is still growing.

3. Clubs: The borough council's social services department and the staff of the Brockley Project have allowed me to use the project's accommodation for group work with the young.

4. Latchkey children: Preparation is being made to accommodate about 12 children of infant and junior school age after school between 3.30 and 6 pm.

5. Under-fives: Since the end of November I have been responsible for work with the under-fives; in part because funding for our liaison worker has been discontinued. LCCR ANNUAL REPORT, 1978-9

Cecile carried a large and diverse workload for a single community worker but the need was glaringly evident. She reported that over 140 children took part in the 1979 summer play scheme. Sixteen members of staff worked with the children during the three-week period. Outings were arranged for the children to places of interest outside London. For many of them it was the first time they had left the capital.

In early December 1975 the Pagnell Street Centre Women's Group held two days of activities to celebrate International Women's Year. Their souvenir programme drew attention to the stresses of many West Indian mothers in the multiple role of breadwinner, mother and housewife.

66. Cecile Murray became involved with the LCCR in the mid-1970s. Her work highlighted the needs of black pensioners and children within the borough.

> *Our women's group arose out of the realisation that the mothers of the young people of Moonshot Youth Club were coming to the Centre for help with problems not within the scope of normal youth club activity.*
>
> *Many thousands of women today are coping with the threefold role of wife, mother and wage earner, and it is not surprising that many mothers need support in order to come to terms with the stress of living in present day Britain.*
>
> *The aim of our group is to provide a relaxed atmosphere where women can meet and share their problems away from the pressures of home and work. We also aim to combat loneliness by offering friendship and provide information for those in need.*
>
> *But our fundamental role is to forge a new awareness in ourselves. This in turn will help us with the vital and all important work of giving more support to our children.* MAVIS STEWART

Mavis Stewart came to London from Jamaica in 1954 at the age of 18, having been recruited by the Colonial Office to train as a nurse. Mavis moved to Lewisham in 1961 after completing her midwifery course and has lived in the borough ever since. She was trained as a clinic nurse and later went into health visiting. Mavis became involved with the community when her professional involvement brought her into contact with the Moonshot Youth Club.

Her period with the Moonshot began in 1964-5 and continued into the mid 1970s. Reflecting on those days, Mavis recalls the impact of her unexpected immersion into the heart of the black community in Lewisham.

> *My initiation began there working with black people and coming face-to-face on a wider scale with problems that black youth were facing and so my*

exposure to a whole new learning began, especially with the Moonshot, with Sybil Phoenix and Asquith Gibbes. I have come through with those experiences, ever growing!

I felt a commitment from that stage onwards that no matter how busy I was with my young family – we had two young children by this time, my husband and myself both worked full time and you can imagine how busy our lives were – but I decided consciously that I would always find time for the black youths in this health authority, in this district and so my Moonshot experience took care of that.

Learning the Lessons

Within the black population a number of West Indians who emigrated as young people trained for professions. They were often the children of families who were well respected in their original home communities. They often owned or stood to inherit land. They held high aspirations for their families and lived by very high moral standards, a symbol of which was churchgoing. Many of their grown-up children now hold first and second degrees from British universities. Other Caribbean people were high achievers, with or without material or other support. Many older graduates found second chance routes to their academic goals. Many graduates have gravitated towards teaching, a trend which was already visible in the 1970s.

The Caribbean Teachers' Conference was held at Furzedown College in April 1974. The opening address was given by Rev Wilfred Wood. A paper presented by psychologist Waveney Bushell highlighted the plight of black children wrongly placed in special schools. The other item of particular concern was supplementary schools, viewed very much as an antidote to the ills of the established system. From this conference came the idea to establish a Caribbean Teachers' Association as an authoritative voice mediating between the established system and black children, whose education continued to be a source of concern to parents and the wider community.

Black teachers working in Lewisham, like those in other inner city boroughs, were required to make their own arrangements when the ILEA was dismantled. Paulene Grant became a deputy teacher in 1994, one of the growing group assuming management positions in schools.

Though heavily directed towards nursing at the end of her school career, Margaret Andrews went into teacher training. She had resisted the idea of teaching initially because so many members of her own family back home had been teachers. She recalls being the only black person in her year in a period when the subject of the black presence was being addressed in a thoroughly Eurocentric and offensive fashion.

The lecturers pathologised everything to do with black people and that was the way they saw us. Everything about black people was problematic in some way. Our family structures were problematic, our diets were problematic, our children were problematic, our countries were problematic, our design and perceptions and how we see and form our cultures were, our language was problematic. It just went on and on and on, so that whatever you learnt, whether it was something scientific, supposedly, or whether it was something intellectual around, say, literature, it was always a pathological look at black people and black families...It was tough, the process of being a student.

Margaret started teaching in secondary school in 1978. She now teaches adults.

Avril, who gained her BEd qualification in 1986, started her teaching career in a neighbouring borough. She co-ordinates 'Section 11' teaching, which refers to resourcing within education specifically focused on the children of New Commonwealth parents.

I think the term New Commonwealth came to be synonymous with black. When you look at the list of New Commonwealth countries you find they are ex-colonies of Britain...Caribbean countries, African countries, Asian countries and some countries in the Mediterranean.

With under-achievement of West Indian children occupying a prominent position on the community agenda, it was only a matter of time before the educational service was discredited in the eyes of many black parents. Bernard Coard played a major part in alerting the public to that damage in his publication exposing the plight of black children in ESN schools. A key section of the service directly involved in educational diagnosis recommending the misplacement of black children was the educational psychologists.

Despite being directed, in explorative discussions with her teacher, towards work in Woolworths, Jacinth went into teaching. In the West Indies many members of her family had been teachers and those role models were evoked in the summer following her final exams at school. She therefore applied for a teacher-training place. After qualification she taught in St Kitts for a year. The experience was a significant one which was to be a measure of professional expertise. She now works as an educational psychologist in Greenwich

I absolutely believe that my year in the West Indies made me a better teacher in the sense of how I prepared and planned my lessons and what the schools expected of me. JACINTH

When Petronella Breinburg gained her PhD in 1984 she was among only a handful of black women to reach such academic heights in the country. The first African-Caribbean woman to be appointed at doctorate level at Goldsmiths, she has inspired a wave of black women as well as other students to achieve academically. The number of Caribbean women achieving doctorates has steadily grown in much the same way that the medical, legal, scientific and other professions continue to find increasing number of black applicants for vacant jobs.

In the 1960s and early 1970s Caribbean job applications met with frequent rejections on the grounds of lack of qualifications. In the 1980s and early 1990s, as the group became more professionally qualified, still unemployment or underemployment remained a marked feature. New patterns of discrimination emerge. Lack of experience is cited as a barrier to employment. The glass ceiling remains overhead.

Extraordinary Elders

The term 'elders', referring to black people of pensionable age, retains elements of traditional African attitudes of respect towards older people. In Lewisham a network of elders' clubs developed offering an important source of leadership.

Yolande Newman was born in 1923 and came to Lewisham to join her husband in 1960. She raised seven children, worked as an auxillary nurse and later as a part-time postal worker. It was after a Senior Citizens' Day at Tanners Hill that she was introduced to Tony Ventour, black social worker for the elderly and she volunteered to help with the Rose Apple elders' club which meets weekly in New Cross. In 1991 she was asked to be the secretary and the following year she became the co-ordinator. Yolande is also involved with the Sweet Rose disability group. She disseminates information, arranges visits and co-ordinates events such as bowls, dominoes, seminars and so on.

The only time I am not at Rose Apple is if I am not well, not in the country, or such. YOLANDE

The club, an average of 25 elders, has an active reminiscence group which visits local primary schools. Beckett Turner, who came to London in 1955 from Jamaica, has been the club's secretary since 1990.

Metrina Mitchell was the oldest member of the Rose Apple group. Born in 1899 in Petit Martinique, she came to England in 1961. Unlike the usual pattern, her grown-up children came to London first then sent for her.

When I first came I didn't like nothing in this place. I used to cry all the time. I wanted to go home. After a year my friends who had been here years before me used to come to see me and they used to tell me that I just have to satisfy. But I got accustomed you know, or else I'd still be crying. METRINA IN SPECTRUM, WINTER 1982-83

Fiercely independent and a first class entertainer, Metrina's singing and dancing was legendary. She loved best to talk of 'home' and of her youth: traditional folk tales,

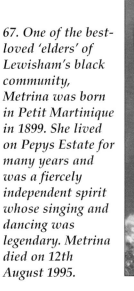

67. One of the best-loved 'elders' of Lewisham's black community, Metrina was born in Petit Martinique in 1899. She lived on Pepys Estate for many years and was a fiercely independent spirit whose singing and dancing was legendary. Metrina died on 12th August 1995.

singing and taking part in festivals. Then she would demonstrate her drumming skills, on the nearest table if necessary. When she was provided with bongo drums she was transformed, improvising with seasoned hands and the ear of an experienced musician. She was visited regularly at Rose Apple Club and at her home on Pepys Estate by two young musicians and at 96 years old she still became so inspired by music making that she would sing, beat out rhythms and, at times, push aside her Zimmer frame to dance! Unlike many elders who, through years of work in England, had forgotten or set aside traditional cultural forms, Metrina was a true keeper of the oral tradition. Metrina Mitchell died on 12th August 1995 and was returned to her home, as she had always wanted, to be buried.

68. Lilian Lewis was born in Guyana in 1891. She came to New Cross to care for her great great niece's daughter. This photograph was taken on her 104th birthday in April 1995.

Lilian Lewis was born in Essequibo, Guyana in 1891. She had no children of her own but in true African-Caribbean tradition she has shared in the raising of many generations within the extended family. She was brought over to Lewisham in 1976, first to Brockley and then to New Cross, by her great great niece Eveline Wharton to care for Eveline's daughter. Eveline herself is now an elder while Lilian celebrated her 104th birthday in April 1995 with her neighbour, black councillor Eddie Capone.

15

CROSSROADS OF FAITH

"When we were back home and we go to church that was part of the highlight of the week. But here!" RUBY ALEXANDER

"This European religion did nothing to affirm me as a black man and did everything to destroy me." PETER DENIS

In the Caribbean the measure of a 'civilised' black person, was, to a great extent, the quality of his or her religious belief. The established churches of Europe were the approved centres of religious expression. Though the most prestigious of these centres were in the capitals and more affluent areas, Sunday worship became embedded throughout West Indian culture. The extent of this may be glimpsed in the way in which migrants assumed a welcome in English churches in the 1950s and 1960s.

A Missionary Heritage

In 1835-6 the Colonial Secretary had distributed a Parliamentary grant of £20,000 among a number of religious groups to undertake the 'civilising' or 'Christianising' of Africans in the West Indies. Slavery had ended but the slaves were not quite free. They were in the marginal period called 'apprenticeship' designed to allow slave owners to become more used to the notion of abolition. There was much to be done in the interim years. Bringing Christianity to black people in the West Indies, a practice largely condemned during slavery, was now firmly on the agenda.

The grants were also used to build school houses for the 'emancipated negroes'. The Wesleyan Mission received £3,000 in 1835 for their West Indian programme. The religious group was required to raise £1,500 in order to qualify for the grant.

The 19th century saw a sharp increase in missionaries to the Caribbean. More than 70 of these were registered through the London Missionary Society, one of several missionary agencies operating in the West Indies and the areas newly opened up to British religious expansion. The register, held from 1796 to 1923, indicates that over 20 per cent were school teachers. The London Missionary Society was primarily interested in the black population and the majority of their missionaries took up posts in the Caribbean in the period after Emancipation.

W T Veness was a member of a well-established Deptford family, living in Hamilton Street. He succeeded his father as Sexton and Parish Clerk at St Paul's, Deptford in 1840. After taking orders Rev Veness served as a missionary in Berbice, British Guiana. Many missionaries expressed the view that in the West Indies the real work was about to be done.

When the legislator had finished his task, that of the schoolmaster and the missionary was to be begun afresh and indeed, in respect to large masses of yet wholly uninstructed negroes, absolutely commenced. MISSIONARY NOTICES

The missionaries were, by and large, pleased with their flock. Surprised at first by the enthusiasm for learning, some were stunned by the success of the infant schools they set up. This was widely reported within their networks. Some reports compared the children's progress favourably with that of their English peers.

So many negro children; and so improved! What a prospect for the next generation! It looks as if this little people were to come under a new dispensation of heaven. We know not how else to account for the success of the Infant schools. The like is hardly to be found even among children of a higher order in a more favourable clime. MISSIONARY NOTICES

Religion and Power in Post-Emancipation Years

In the post-Emancipation Caribbean, the Church held considerable power over the social mobility of the population generally and the black population in particular. The key to this power was education which the church provided. West Indians were systematically baptised and confirmed into the church. The priest's recommendation gave entry to further and higher education as well as into jobs and services. With missionaries and priests imported over a century into the Caribbean, the familiar face of Christianity was white.

African-Caribbean post-war migrants who had only known anglicised forms of Christianity took themselves, therefore, into the churches in Lewisham. Their reception was depressing. Those taking collection would often avoid the black visitors to the church. This surprised black Christians who, though not having an abundance of money to donate, expected to give proportionally as any other churchgoer. The white church members were unfriendly, largely ignoring their black fellow worshippers. This was Ruby Alexander's experience when she attended her local Catholic church in the 1950s.

We found out where the church was and started going but at the time I wasn't really welcome. RUBY ALEXANDER

Following such responses many black families dropped out. Their children were no longer made to go to church. Whatever the perceptions of Mrs Alexander's fellow Catholics, they were in no position to appreciate the groundedness of her faith. Within her family there was a nun and a priest.

The Black Vicar at St Lawrence, Catford

Reverend Wilfred Wood was vicar of St Lawrence, Catford from 1974 to 1982. Many parishioners remember him with special regard. A black priest in the Church of England was a novelty even in the mainstream churches in the Caribbean.

Though Rev Wood came to London as a direct result of the Church's response to racist violence, he was yet to learn about the pervasiveness of racism in British society and its part within the Church he served. He was training for the ministry at Codrington College, Barbados, with the intention to serve in the Caribbean. It was 1958, the year of the Notting Hill riots in London which culminated in the brutal murder of the Antiguan, Kelso Cochrane, by teddy boys.

Rev Wood's understanding of the racial situation in London came from British newspapers and English clergy. Lacking experience of the realities of African-Caribbean existence in England, he accepted the basic premise that Caribbean people were not

69. Bishop
Wilfred Wood,
vicar of St
Laurence
Catford from
1974 to 1982,
was made
Bishop of
Croydon in
1985.

used to living in cities and that there was an underlying unfamiliarity between the two
cultures. Because Wilfred Wood had a particular interest in reconciliation, he
volunteered to come to England. He planned to serve for three years and he hoped
that the time would be enough to help to interpret West Indians to English people
and English people to West Indians. He perceived his role as a kind of go-between.

*Needless to say, when I got here, I remember thinking in my first couple of
weeks, any West Indian who stays in this country longer than absolutely
necessary, needed to have his mind looked at. Really!*

Wilfred Wood faced a catalogue of difficulties so contrary to Christian practice as
to ensure that the West Indians left the church in droves. As if the unwelcome
reception was not challenge enough, attitudes at work brought chronic tensions which
exacerbated the difficulties.

Someone Rev Wood had known as a practising Christian at home tried to alleviate
the difficulties he found in the workplace by drawing on his religion for support. At
lunchtimes he got out his Bible to read. To him, this was an attempt at trying to live

up to the highest in him. To his workmates, it was provocation. They cursed and swore and were even more crude. His piety just seemed to annoy them. They made life very difficult for him but once he answered them back in their own language and to some extent behaved like them, he found that life became easier. However, such behaviour made him uncomfortable in church. He did not associate the type of behaviour he was now having to use with churchgoing. He gradually slipped away from the church.

Another person worked in a big car factory. Everyone in his section was stealing. Coming from a strict home, he had not been brought up to this. At first he held aloof but it became very clear that his job was insecure unless he behaved like the others. While he felt that it was not right, he made the decision to go with the crowd. That made him uneasy in church and he dropped out.

Rev Wilfred Wood left St Lawrence to take up a new appointment as Archdeacon of Southwark in 1982. Three years later he was the first black priest consecrated bishop within the Church of England in England, becoming Bishop of Croydon in the diocese of Southwark. His father-in-law, travelling from Barbados for the occasion, commented.

> *It has taken the Church of England 1,985 years to reach this point and I am not going to miss this occasion!*

Only Practising My Religion: Black People in Church

Black people arriving off the ships at Southampton in the 1950s were heralded as 'problems'. This was one stereotype fed to the nation. Another stereotype, which held sway within the Church, was of black people as objects of pity. It was fine to send missionaries out to foreign lands but incredibly difficult to share the communion cup in the same church.

Sybil Phoenix, who managed to maintain her religion and even strengthen her position within the Church, recalls being very ill with pneumonia a few years after her arrival in Britain. Denied access to decent accommodation, she was at the time living in what was actually a coal cellar. The place was so damp that her minister, visiting her there, feared for her life.

> *When I was that ill my minister asked a member in his church that he knew had two empty bedrooms to take us in during my illness. That Sunday after service she held on to my hand and she said, "Sybil, I know yourself and Joe, but I'm really very sorry...nobody on my street has taken in any coloured people yet and I've got to think about the children. So, I can't take you all in."*

While any such 'taking in' was, of course, completely voluntary, the clearly-stated hurdle for that member of the congregation was Sybil's 'colour'. Such incidents did not represent isolated cases. There were a great many instances in which black people pointed to the specific churches in which they were made to feel really unwelcome, in the 1950s and 1960s particularly.

Gracelin Arlett, raised as a Methodist in Grenada, has lived in Lewisham since 1967. At her Methodist chapel in Deptford she had no difficulties but when she moved to central Lewisham and went to church there she found that no-one would sit anywhere near her. As she left the priest mentioned that she had sat in somebody else's pew. She never went back. Sybil Phoenix also felt rejected in her local Methodist church but she determined to persist with her faith. No single denomination had a monopoly on the rejection of black Christians. Ruby Alexander experienced her deepest betrayal in a Catholic church in New Cross.

Word of this unchristian behaviour was passed on to new arrivals who questioned the ungodly habit of fellow West Indians not attending church. Yolande Newman recalled hearing of a pastor who told a West Indian that he appreciated his coming to church but would appreciate it more if he stayed away since the white congregation did not like it. Yolande herself avoided such an experience, by travelling regularly to a church in West London where she knew she would feel spiritually at home.

In 1976 Sybil Phoenix presented to the Southwark diocese a paper on racism in the church. She had also initiated schemes in which white clergy would spend a weekend living with a black family locally. Though some managed one night, few completed the weekend. Nevertheless, the scheme was thought to provide valuable experience for the clergy who participated.

Over and above the specific difficulties encountered, Sundays represented another day to be made to feel unwelcome for those African-Caribbean settlers. Many ceased the churchgoing practice they had always known and had been taught to see as spiritual support.

> *Frankly, you're coping with racism in situations where you haven't got any choice. You've got to work, you've got to go on the street; you've got to travel on the train and so on. You're coping with this all the time from Monday to Saturday. On a Sunday, when you do have some freedom of choice about what you do, you avoid exposing yourself to it yet again. Church is voluntary so you stay at home rather than face that.* BISHOP WILFRED WOOD

London-born Peter Denis was brought up a Roman Catholic and was very active in the Church. He attended church at least once a week and was part of church youth groups. When he began university he was still actively practising Catholicism. He was a lay member of the Caribbean Pastoral Service who met together regularly from 1979 to 1981 trying to understand their position within the Roman Catholic Church. They noted the rejection that many Caribbean people had experienced from established churches in the UK. Looking closer, they found that many priests were very racist, unwilling or unable to understand black people. It was the same pattern whether in England or the Caribbean.

> *My experience, and that of a lot of people of Afro-Caribbean descent, is that the white people lord it over us in every single sphere of our life. We allow them to do that because we don't really know who we are. We do not know who we are because we are not aware of our history as black peoples. We are not aware of the history of the Caribbean and so we have very little concept of self worth. That is reinforced through education, politics, economics, social justice. Even where you would find some enlightened white people within a European setting or within England there is still that tendency to look down on black people. It is because we have looked down on ourselves because of our history.*

Peter was sent by the Roman Catholic Archdiocese of Westminster in 1980 to represent the United Kingdom as a member of the Antinoges Liturgical School which was held in Trinidad. Members representing the entire English-speaking Caribbean were present. There were three black representatives from the UK. The other two were from the dioceses of Southwark and Birmingham.

At university Peter read of the African origins of Christianity and listened carefully to discussions about the African origin of man. He read of African saints and black madonnas. Serious doubts emerged as to whether his religion mirrored what he was as a black man. He asked himself whether his religion ever affirmed him as a black man and found it seriously wanting. He questioned deeply the authority of the Catholic Church then went in search of other means of spiritual expression.

I had deep-seated questions about it and the more research I did on religion, the more I was convinced that this religion was not for me.

Peter considered Islam but he found it difficult to reconcile the separation of women from men. Nor could he accept some of the fundamental tenets of the faith. Instead he took up Buddhism and joined the Deptford group of a lay Buddhist organisation called the Soka Gakai International.

In the battle between religious continuity and racism within English churches is that many Caribbean people set aside Christianity. Finding that English Christian practice did not square with the practice of those very English missionaries who taught a Christian code espousing tolerance and brotherly love, many Caribbean people left the church.

By the time you add that to what actually happened in church where black people go and they see how the white people shrink away from them, don't even want to touch them! It required considerable strength to persevere with churchgoing. BISHOP WILFRED WOOD

Not all black members left. Some arriving later, perhaps without families, found it easier to be accepted and stayed. Bonny Portes, born in Trinidad, was raised a Roman Catholic. He came to England in 1960 and moved to Catford in 1966. In his parish church in Lewisham he expected to practise his faith and remained single-minded in doing so for a number of years.

A few local black people were persuaded back into the Church. In 1975 when Ruby Alexander's sister-in-law, a nun, visited London, she was persuaded to set aside the early difficulty and return to church. Ruby found that more black people were practising and the Catholic Church was friendlier some 15 years after her early experience.

Growth of Lewisham's Black Churches

I always say to them they leave their God in the West Indies. When they come to me I say "well, which church you used to go to? What was your religion? You can't expect to leave your God in the West Indies and survive here without it. When you look up and there is the skies above and you look down and you have dirt under your foot, then you are living and wherever you are living that is home and you make the best of it." To a very large extent, not totally, but a very large extent, life is what you make it. SYBIL PHOENIX

Certainly for many churchgoers, it seemed as if they had left their God in the West Indies or had been abandoned by Him. While some gradually ceased churchgoing, for others the religious expression represented an important part of their lives. They met in twos and threes in the relative safety of the company of other black people. The seed of black churches in England had been sown.

As a child Yolande's family attended the Baptist church in Jamaica where her father was a fine tenor singer. Her mother Sarah Elizabeth Newman was an itinerant organist, playing in a number of churches. When Yolande's mother 'got saved' in 1933 the family saw a happier, more purposeful and less irritable woman. They began to attend the Brethren Assembly. For the rest of her time in Jamaica this remained Yolande's church and she was married there in 1943.

Though the elders of the church asked when she would be saved and baptised in the church, Yolande resisted this decisive step well into adulthood.

I wasn't walking the way I should and there were lots of things I still wanted to do which I knew wouldn't be conducive to the way the church would want.

It was Yolande's concern to bring up her children in a righteous manner which made her question in 1949 the spiritual dimension of her life. She experienced a sensation of having tousled with her faith, affirming her acceptance of the importance of faith in her life and so she made the decision to live daily by the Christian principles. She was 'saved' and 'gave her heart to the Lord'.

I had those kids. I was bringing them up. What was I bringing them up to? They must have a foundation spiritually. That was the thought that hit me between the eyes.

Yolande was baptised, as was the custom, by immersion in a nearby pool and she began to attend the Pilgrim Holiness church. There women were allowed to speak in the meetings and the singing was vibrant, in contrast to the Brethren's assemblies where women were expected to stay silent and the singing was far from lively. It was at Pilgrim Holiness that her husband Vernal Newman 'got saved' years later.

Yolande found that there was no Pilgrim Holiness church in Lewisham but, together with a friend from Jamaica who also lived locally, she travelled to a branch of the church at Harrow. One day in 1961, walking along Shell Road, she spotted a church with a gospel hall sign and recognised it as belonging to the Brethren sect. It was Loampit Gospel Hall Church. She attended the following Sunday and met a couple of fellow Jamaicans. Later that year she had her youngest baby. Ann Newman was the first baby to be dedicated at the Loampit Gospel Hall as the normal custom was to bless the baby at home. Yolande explained to one of the elders her determination to find a 'spiritual home' and asked if she could join them in fellowship so she became a member of the assembly.

Women do not speak at the assembly. The only time the women would speak is during the sisters' meeting when we are free to speak amongst ourselves but if a brother is in the meeting of course if you speak you usurp the man's authority because the man is the head of the church. Some of the sisters don't agree with that but then I was brought up in it.

Marcia Foster Norman came from Jamaica in 1974 determined to study for a professional qualification but though she held certificates from London and Cambridge examination boards they were not recognised. "Cast down but not destroyed", Marcia studied while working part-time at Peak Freans biscuit factory and for British Rail. Her first Lewisham home was on Milton Court estate in New Cross.

Marcia grew up a Christian in Jamaica but it was three months after her arrival before she met an elder in the church who saw her in Peckham High Street and commented on her sadness. She invited Marcia to join her 'big family' in the church and collected her regularly to take her to the United Pentecostal church. Since then the church has been Marcia's support through disappointments, hurts and traumas and has applauded her successes. When Marcia survived an attempted arson attack on her

70. *Marcia Foster marries Denzil Norman at the Calvary Temple, a United Pentacostal church. The church has helped Marcia "through disappointments, hurts and traumas, and has applauded her successes".*

home she saw in this God looking after her. The God known in the Caribbean was widely held to be benevolent, essentially a provider.

> *Where I'm from in the West Indies, the church is where you go if you have no food, if your kids are not behaving or if you want to be educated. In this country black churches don't offer that for organisational, financial or developmental reasons.*

So while black members seek out the inclusive community of black churches with its familiar West Indian style welcome and 'family' warmth, many are questioning what the church offers, especially to the young. The doctrines, invariably restrictive with their stress on discipline, are challenging to the young whose education in this country encourages questioning. Nevertheless the family is spiritually supported and attendance by all is the expectation. Choirs play an increasingly important part in church and community life. Both the New Testament Church of God in Lee and the Bible Way Church of God in Algernon Road have choirs taking gospel music into the community.

Rastafarianism

In the 1970s a popularised Rastafarian movement grew up. For many young black people it was an alternative to the strictly political black power movement. It offered a spiritual dimension. Rastafarianism, a distinctive socio-religious way of life to which the African-Caribbean experience is central, was catapulted to worldwide prominence through the music of Bob Marley and a host of other reggae artists. The symbols of African lifestyle – language, dreadlocks and lyrics drawing on folk wisdom – appealed as a movement of cultural resistance.

The attraction of Rastafarianism lay in the way in which it encompassed a positive political ideology on the one hand with a mystic/religious form on the other. In any event, the popularising of reggae through performers like Bob Marley brought the message of the movement direct to young people. From the early 1970s reggae music spread rasta culture worldwide.

Shana Stroud was attending the Moonshot regularly when the upsurge of Rastafarianism first started. Her family was Church of England and as a child she had attended St Stephen's church, Lewisham. Around 1973 the young people at the Moonshot were faithful followers of Jah Shaka sound. The wave of music coming in from Jamaica at the time exhorted black people to raise their consciousness. Burning Spear, another influential Jamaican Rastafarian musician who played with the Wailers, Peter Tosh and many others, offered the purer heavier sound of Fari favoured by the young people. Bob Marley was a 'lightweight' as far as the Moonshot members were concerned. The records played were imports straight from Jamaica. Through the music's powerful and appealing message many young people became interested in listening to Fari.

From such initial inspiration informal discussion groups were arranged and further meetings held in each other's houses. With greater freedom of movement and interest, the men managed to meet more regularly. When the Rasta styles emerged there was considerable disapproval from many families. This necessitated some separating away from home and family to regroup with those interested in practising Fari.

So we ended up being together, a people of like minds together. SHANA STROUD

By 1976 groups of Rasta were forming organised communities locally. There was the excitement of starting something new and a great deal of commitment. One group started a food co-op and a workshop making bags and clothes for other members. They looked into alternative lifestyles, changing diets and so on. The food co-op involved a communal kitty for bulk-buying and resold foods at reduced rate.

The religious aspects of Fari grew out of the wisdom of an earlier Jamaican sect of 'locksmen' and 'beardsmen'. Belief itself was thought to produce a change in consciousness. Together with the smoking of herbs and the pulsing of drums the opening-up of minds to Jah was achieved.

Let's say that you have a circle and that circle is your life. If you're going to be a spiritual person how can you link that with having, say, 10 women and not being a father to your children and not living a righteous life? SHANA

Having to search within your own self to find that part which is God was important. Of course, many converts were satisfied to play the drums and smok the herbs, not always prepared to seek any more spiritual level, to go further within themselves to find that part which shows believers how to live.

The herb or drug culture of Rastafarianism was simultaneously an attraction to young converts and a source of difficulty to observers of the group, including many black parents.

The thing about Rasta is that people associate it with drug taking, ganja smoking. For us growing up in the Caribbean – and I grew up in the hills – ganja was a normal way of life. When I came here and people were saying "Oh, that is illegal", we couldn't see that because, as young people out there, you

71. Ras Benjahi (Benji), Rastafarian poet and musician, based in New Cross

saw all the old people use it. They weren't going out cutting up anybody or stealing anything. That was how it was. However, many people associated the two together. So be it, I don't worry myself about that. But if you were among genuine Rastas you would find that they were people who care about their environment, who care about what is happening with them and to them. HARRY POWELL

So Rastas employed in public places adapted their lifestyle and learned rapidly a code of practice which was normal for the workplace and did not put them at risk of being picked up by the police for drug taking. From the earliest days the characteristic dreadlocks of Rastamen was an issue with parents, schools and agents of the status quo watchful for expressions of difference such as the dreadlocks signified.

Society knocked Rastas because of the rough looking hair style and a lot of Rastas suffered because of the locks, so many people tried to take it off in order not to be recognised, if you like to disguise themselves. But why should we have to do that? The Sikhs wear their turban. They don't disguise themselves and Rasta is also a religion. It's something that arrrived from the Caribbean, from Africa, from people like Marcus Garvey and Paul Bogle who died trying to get black people to realise who they are. HARRY POWELL

The demands upon Rastas to conform, at least in appearance, led to many shaving off their locks and finding a niche in the mainstream world of jobs and regular employment. The association with drugs also strongly influenced how Rastas were perceived when they applied for posts, especially outside of black communities. Even within the black communities Rastas sometimes faced the demands to conform, especially from parents worried about the opportunities which might be lost by such a rebellious statement.

Because the system put us under pressure, therefore we have to smarten up. You can get left out and the question is: am I skilled enough to ensure that I am part of what is going on. It's not whether I want to be left out. I want to be in it. Therefore you adopt the skills to ensure that you are contributing towards the system. Then again, why shouldn't we? Our parents spent money here, we got educated here, we have spent our money here, we have our children here. So we are part of the society and I believe that we should always be recognised for the contribution. I have not ever been unemployed so when people talk about claiming off the dole, for example, I don't know anything about that. I have never been given a penny by anybody. HARRY POWELL

Community of Many Faiths

While for the earliest African-Caribbean settlers the expression of spiritual needs was realised essentially through Christianity despite the difficulties, this has not been the case for the generation born or growing up in England. Since so many parents left the church, children gradually ceased to be christened and confirmed. Many younger black people, recognising a spiritual need, took up religions outside Christianity.

There are groups or districts of Buddhists throughout London. The Deptford and Hatcham Park groups meet and chant together, discussing themes of life, death, birth, suffering and sickness. These they discuss from the particular point of view of

Deptford and Hatcham Park: what is happening in the area, how members might contribute to the well-being of the area and so on. The practice of Buddhism is growing among local black people.

This group practises the Buddhism of Nichiren Daishonin. About 700 years ago a priest called Nichiren Daishonin started to collate all the Buddhist teachings, or Sutras as they are called. After long years of study he is believed to have said that one of the Sutras was the highest. That is the Lotus Sutra, the title of which, Nam-myoho-renge-kyo, is chanted by the group.

> *I know there are a lot of black people in Deptford practising Buddhism. Not just in Deptford but in Lewisham. I practice in Deptford, New Cross, Hatcham Park area. There's just been a major reorganisation. I'm now a young woman's district leader which fills me with trepidation because it means that I'll be responsible for helping young women in this district to develop their faith and to develop their practice of the Buddhism of Nichiren Daishonin.* JAN BLAKE

For some Buddhists of Caribbean origin the adoption of religious expression outside Caribbean cultural norms is a site of conflict. For others the situation is resolved in the first instance through the support of friends. Indeed the new religion is often introduced through friendship. Peter Denis came to Buddhism through a friend in July 1990. Like others he found the idea of chanting rather strange initially. Jan Blake remembers her introduction to Buddhism as a slow process.

> *A friend of mine was staying with me and asked me, when he went away for the weekend, to look after his gohonzon. Now a gohonzon is a scroll and on it is written Nam-myoho-renge-kyo and other characters from the Lotus Sutra. Anyway he told me to say nam-myoho-renge-kyo and change the water every morning and every evening. I did this and didn't think much of it, didn't think it meant anything significant at all. That was 1989. He'd given me a little card with nam-myoho-renge-kyo written on it which I'd pinned up on a cork board I had on the wall. I never threw it away. I didn't know why but it was always there and every so often I'd kind of say it. I didn't know why I said it, I just said it.*

An implicit criticism of Christian religions, particularly the older established churches such as Catholicism and Anglicanism is that it is only too easy to worship in church but effectively to insulate one's day-to-day lifestyle from the principles of that religion. Buddhism is seen in direct contrast to Christianity.

> *It's not a shallow faith at all. And if you try and deal with it on that level then you're barking up the wrong tree really. It's just driving home to me more and more that it's a way of life. Faith is a way of life. It's not something you just go and do on a Sunday and then forget about until the next Sunday. It's every single day.* JAN BLAKE

For black people the finding of other black people within the religious group serves to confirm the credibility of the religion. Even more affirming is the discovery of the particular religious expression being practised on Caribbean soil. Jan Blake, Deptford resident and practising Buddhist, visited Jamaica in 1992. There she found a Buddhist Chapter where she was able to practise.

I was a bit nervous about practising in Jamaica – especially as there are Christian churches on every corner, so I didn't think I'd find any Buddhists. Then I found out there was an actual Chapter of the Soka Gakkai in Jamaica as well, which really excited me. I thought, 'amazing, Buddhism is everywhere'. A guy called Clifton Brown is the Chapter Leader in Jamaica and they're affiliated to the American Soka Gakkai International. I practised there and I think that's what really pushed it for me. Because at first I thought it was alien even though I was doing it, but then the more black people I saw doing it the more involved in it I wanted to get. I'd never really made the distinction between a black person's religion and a white person's religion.

Soka Gakkai was founded in the early 1950s by Tsunesaburo Makiguchi. It is a lay Buddhist organisation founded on the principles of Nichiren Daishonin Buddhism through peace, culture and education. Jan Blake and Peter Denis are members of Soka Gakkai International UK.

Within the UK there is a heritage group called the Abibima, a West African term meaning 'children of black fathers'. The idea of the Abibima was to give opportunities to people from Africa and the Caribbean to practise together. The last national Abibima meeting in 1993 was attended by some 800 black Buddhists, and locally each of the Deptford and Hatcham Park leaders is from the Caribbean or of Caribbean descent.

In addition to the variety of religious practices, a number of self-healing belief systems are also finding a place in the spiritual lives of people of African-Caribbean origin locally. Some of these, like co-counselling, focus on the power within the self to heal and to live life to the full, whatever the circumstances.

The final three decades of the 20th century saw, then, a radical shift and increasing diversity in the range of religious practices taken up by African-Caribbean people in South East London. It has also been, for many black people, a period marking an historic break with Christianity.

16

THE URGE TO LEAVE

"There has been a kind of haemorraging of black people; more going out than coming in. When immigration is raised, it's always made clear that more people are leaving this country than are coming in." MARIA DALRYMPLE

When Tommy Martin, the disappointed 'Brown Bomber' of Deptford, disappeared from the public eye in Britain and was seen no more, few but his family knew where he was to be found. He had started a new life on the other side of the Atlantic. Thomas had met his wife-to-be in the United States and together they moved to St Croix in the Virgin Islands. There Thomas and Norma raised a family and made a new life.

72. Tommy Martin with his family in the Virgin Islands, where he went to start a new life after the war

'I'll Stay For Three Years'

African-Caribbean people travelling to the UK in the post-war period planned to stay a few years before return to their home countries. Whether they came as students, nurses, white collar workers or potential public transport workers, the stay in Britain was usually a temporary measure for a specific purpose: the gaining of further qualifications and experience or better access to jobs and wages. Time and again the African-Caribbean migrants recalled the original three or five years they had planned to stay or the course they had simply meant to complete.

I wanted to do three things. I wanted to learn Trubenising, mainly because we had a business of our own out there making shirts. I wanted also to learn

millinery and I wanted to have a holiday and see England. I was going to do those three things and go back home. SYBIL PHOENIX

The West Indian immigrant population of the 1950s and 1960s was largely a young adult population and it was not long before they started families. The planned years of stay were readjusted to children's needs. This meant a commitment to education and additional years in Britain. Invariably a longer stay followed and many deferred the time of return to a point in their lives when it seemed a more convenient option: the approach of retirement age with independent children fairly well established.

Returners

Harry Powell's mother returned to Jamaica in 1988. She had raised her family and the children were adults but in the meantime her husband had died. Mary Powell longed to return to Jamaica but habit and the desire to do the right thing by children and grandchildren held her in South East London. She delayed, wondering how going back home would work out. Would she settle? Would it work out as she wanted? Harry could see how badly she wanted to go home and finally he could bear it no longer. He went into Lewisham shopping centre and bought her a ticket for Jamaica. The ticket was due to expire in four weeks. His mother had just four weeks in which to make up her mind. Mrs Powell packed her trunks and together the family filled several barrels to be sent on to Jamaica. She had made the decisive step which would reunite her with family, land and the district of her birth.

There appear to be several categories of returners. The largest group comprises older people, like Mary Powell, at or near retiring age. Mr Wormington, a Jamaican who lived in Deptford during the 1950s, returned in 1994. He was the man said to be responsible for taking Father David Diamond of St Paul's church into the pubs where West Indian men drank, with the result that Father Diamond was fully at ease in the black community. David gained Mr Wormington's grudging admiration   when, as an impromptu visitor, he removed a piece of fried fish, uninvited, from his host's meal and ate it. While "dipping your hand in people's food" was frowned upon, the gesture of equal acceptance was appreciated. David Diamond was always given a separate plate when he appeared in the house!

Apart from older migrants, students who stayed longer than originally intended, make up another group of returners. The smallest group appears to be younger people who make the decision to go back, sometimes to a 'home' they have never known.
I just feel like I've come home. I think what is good is that people recognise that you have things to contribute. BEVERLEY BRYAN

Beverley Bryan belongs to the last group. Her parents returned in 1977 and the following year Beverley decided she wanted to go back to Jamaica. When she was 20 years old she had visited Jamaica for the first time since coming to South London in 1959. When she married, she visited Jamaica again, this time with her husband. On returning to London, they bought a large wooden trunk to remind them of their intentions. Beverley had completed her first degree and started teaching. With a view to enhancing her professional profile, she took a master's degree at Goldsmiths.

In 1983 Beverley applied for her first post at the University of the West Indies as resident tutor within the Continuing Education department. Her application was not successful. A post became vacant at St Augustine, Trinidad, in 1990. She applied but again was unsuccessful.

> *I always wanted to go back and help rebuild the country. This is kind of foolish in a way, kind of arrogant, but it is also the sort of idealism most people have, that you're going to make this great contribution.*

When internationally-known Jamaican writer and activist, Mikey Smith, was assassinated, Beverley nearly changed her mind about returning. She was attending a performance by Sistren, the Jamaican women's theatre collective, when the news broke. She had just applied for a post teaching reading development at the University of the West Indies but it occurred to her that she might not want to return to a country in the grip of such political turmoil and violence. However, five years later Beverley and her husband decided that it didn't really matter which government was in. They wanted to return.

Beverley did not give up her ideal. Her two children were not a deterrent to leaving London, but intensified her desire to move back to the Caribbean. She and her husband were clear that they did not want the children to grow up in Britain.

Schooling provided the crunch decision: the choice of private education within the independent sector or going through the state system. Each child had some private schooling before going to a Church of England school at six but the Bryans were not satisfied with the children's attainment. The oldest boy had been well supported at home and finally gained a place at Wellington School, one of the top 25 schools in the country. However, of some 800 pupils there were a mere eight or nine black children. In effect their son was going to an all-white school. They would be a curiosity themselves and be culturally isolated.

The Bryans considered carefully the two stark options. Having just seen the film Jungle Fever the possibilities of their boys surviving the urban jungle looked particularly bleak. There appeared to be only two ways open to black children and particularly to black boys. The local state school seemed to offer a disproportionate chance of a deviant route, becoming disaffected and engaging with the more distorted aspects of black culture, blind to the strength and rootedness possible within it. Alternatively, there was the prospect of becoming totally acculturised in an all-white school and alienated from all that is positive within Caribbean culture. Each choice seemed equally undesirable.

Six months later when another job in language education at the University of the West Indies was advertised, Beverley was teaching at the University of Greenwich in a comparable position to the West Indies post. By this time she had a track record of publishing. She applied and was appointed. She and her family have been living in Mona, Jamaica since 1991.

> *If you ask a child, probably just from a poor background, what they want to be they might say "I want to be an accountant". It's that kind of situation where nothing is seen as beyond them that I think is important. They see other black people. They see grey-haired black people doing things.*

In the Bryans' neighbourhood in Jamaica, deviance is not the norm for young black children. Beverley recalled asking a 14 year old neighbour what she wanted to be. Without hesitation or doubt, the teenager replied 'a surgeon'. She did not perceive the obstacles that a black child in Britain would invariably see. In addition, black role models reinforcing high expectations were everywhere to be found.

> *It was so nice when I went to Jamaica to see all those grey haired black women, looking so nice and smart and kind of rosy, healthy, sure of themselves, sitting behind their desks and being my boss. I used to think of myself as being a bit of an elder when I was in this country. I was 40 and I thought I was an elder!*

Jacinth was younger when she returned to St Kitts and her experience was different from that of the Bryans. She had just completed her teacher-training when she returned. She had never really felt at home in London. Perhaps because she was younger, she expected to be completely at home on her return.

Like the Bryans, Jacinth noticed the change that had taken place in the West Indies since she had left. She also recognised the changes in herself. It disturbed her most that, although in London she felt acutely West Indian, in St Kitts she was not accepted as such. Within a few years she turned again to South East London.

> *The fact is you don't fit in here but when you go back to the West Indies, it can be a very painful experience. I found that I didn't fit in as nicely as I wanted to. I wasn't seen by local people as being from there. I was an English woman to them even though I didn't perceive myself like that. It was very, very painful because I felt I belonged nowhere.*

Though it took more years than anticipated, some black people who migrated in the 1950s and 1960s have realised the promises to themselves and their families to return. Some of the children who joined them in South East London have also returned. Difficulties of 'settling in', emotional, financial or medical, sometimes lead to a less permanent return than planned. What is surprising, however, is the trend towards young 'returners', brought up Black British but moving to the West Indies to be educated in circumstances considered more nurturing.

There is little record of those who leave the area of Lewisham, whether to live in other parts of the UK or to leave the country. Patsy Steele has been filling the trunk in her spare room for years. The goods collected will furnish the home she is building in Grenada. The plan to leave became more real when the youngest of her family finished school at 18. Children are often cited as the source of the delay. This long process of returning is typical – very few make the decision overnight.

Travel To Other Lands

At every crisis within the black community, the option to return was constantly reviewed. There was also the option of leaving the UK and migrating elsewhere. The teacher recalled in the following instance is not untypical.

> *I remember reading an article written by a teacher, called 'Violence in the Toilets' and it was by a black teacher, one of the very few black teachers in schools in the 1970s. She was saying that she could see the future and she didn't like it. She was pregnant but she wasn't having her child brought up here, she was going back because she would rather deal with the struggles there than this monster that was looming here. I think there was a point that people who had gotten their qualifications had achieved what their parents had set up but found very quickly the barbed wire was making their lives totally*

unbearable. And they had options. Some of them went back to the Caribbean, some have gone to the States where there's an established middle class, where they feel they can live life, some have gone to Canada. So I think I would say it was those people who had acquired skills who found it very difficult to break through and get the respect, so off they go. MARIA DALRYMPLE

More is being done to document the returners trend but little is available about those who go on to other countries such as Canada or the United States, rather than return to their country of birth. Not surprisingly, Florida has been a popular destination for many.

Flight Out Of London

Much has been written about white flight from inner urban areas of cities such as London. Despite the problems of housing and employment, some South East London black people have also taken flight, not to return to the West Indies, but to live elsewhere in Britain.

When Deptford was bombed during the war the Martin family was rehoused in Wimbledon. While boxer Tommy Martin went to St Croix, his brother Gordon moved to the East Midlands after marriage in 1949 to Mary, a white woman whose family lived there. The couple have lived there ever since, raising their children.

Many other couples have made similar decisions. After 26 years in South East London, Amos Hurst and his family left the city to live in a small town near Glastonbury. He remains active in the Liberal Party and in the Harmony organisation which promotes black and white unity. Some black South East Londoners would find the relative lack of other black people in such towns difficult but Amos enjoys the country life and has always been able to mix comfortably with both black and white groups.

Turn and Turn Again

Sometimes the best-laid plans do not materialise and people find themselves back in Britain. Tony Ventour says that when he first came to London in 1960.

I thought I'd spend a few years, maybe five, perhaps 10 years at the most and then I'd go back.

In 1972 Tony returned to Grenada with his wife and children to resettle. They budgeted carefully but the country was going through difficult political changes which were reflected in an unstable economy. For example, the price of petrol rocketed from $1.80 to $5 per gallon. Prices of other commodities followed a similar pattern and wreaked havoc with the Ventours' budget. The children clamoured to return to their friends. In 1976 the family packed up again for London.

They lived first in Fulham, then Lewisham. Ten black people were needed to train in social work. 300 people applied but Tony was one of those chosen. He trained from 1983 to 1985 and then joined Lewisham Council's team of social workers.

In 1985 Tony began doing generic social work, working with families, adolescents and children. He also became a regular visitor at the Calabash Centre and eventually he moved into work with the elderly.

Elderly people appreciate what you do for them. They co-operate and you get a lot of satisfaction and joy when you work with them. So, for me, that's what I'd like to continue to do. TONY VENTOUR

Tony's return to the Caribbean has been postponed, perhaps to be taken up again when the children have grown up. While Tony's difficulties were very particular to the financial constraints of a young family, returners in other circumstances may also turn again to London.

Julia Jones' family returned to Gouyave in the north of Grenada when she was eight years old in 1969. They had lived in London since the mid 1950s and all the children had been born there. They needed to return because Julia's grandmother was ill and her aunts and uncles in Britain were employed on the railway or in the National Health Service so their careers were less 'transportable' than her father's. Friends warned that the move back to the Caribbean would be bad for the children's education but Mr Jones was a graduate and it was felt that his qualifcations would help him to find a suitable job back home.

Julia and her brothers and sisters found many welcoming family members but that also meant lots of people to get to know, along with moving to a new country and a new house. Altogether it was "a major adjustment". In school Julia attracted a lot of attention. She had not long since started wearing glasses and these were the National Health frames of the 'spindly' variety allowing them to be secured around the ears. Before long Julia's glasses as well as her 'funny' accent, were a focus of the other children's attention. Nothing could be done about her accent but one of the boys seized the distinctive glasses and smashed them. Julia and her sisters quickly learnt to stand up for themselves. They made friends and finally gained the respect of their peers. In 1971 Julia returned to South East London where two of her aunts still lived and she planned to study law. Since then she has lived in the borough of Lewisham.

Peter Denis' mother returned to London from Dominica. Peter was born in London but many London-born Caribbean young adults have plans to 'go home'. They refer to a five-year or other such fixed-term plan within which they make plans for settling into the Caribbean.

Most Caribbean people I have spoken to have expressed the wish at some time or another to return and live out their days in the Caribbean and it has been fraught with difficulty, great difficulty. PETER DENIS

Peter, with no immediate family of his own, has no such plans, particularly having noticed the drift of young people out of Dominica, his Caribbean 'home'. Dominica is the third largest English-speaking island in the Caribbean, situated in the Windward Islands group between the French departmental islands of Martinique and Guadeloupe. The islands share a common creole language and similar history.

Some people returning to the Caribbean have seen their resettling as unsuccessful. Sometimes this was because they had not sorted out their legal status. With the 1981 Nationality Act, British citizens were required to choose between British status and their island nationality, whereas on their arrival into Britain they had been both. To choose, for example, Dominican citizenship would lose them right of entry into Britain. Whichever choice they made, they have now been caught in a legal web. As British people, they have legal difficulties; as Dominicans they have restricted entry to Britain. For Dominicans the blow has been hard, not just from the recession but from the withdrawal of Britain's support for the Windward Islands banana market.

Most Dominicans express the desire to go back to Dominica but they haven't got the finances to build their house or it may be that land is disputed over in the family or their finances in the UK are tied up with homes here. PETER DENIS

In the meantime many family members have 'returned' happily. Their children grown up, they wished to be reunited with the home of their birth and with families missed over many years. They have also, in some instances, been joined by younger families who sought a nurturing environment for their children where to be black was completely the norm.

I really do enjoy it. I really love living in Jamaica. I love the mountains. I love when I wake up in the morning and I just look up to the hills. BEVERLEY BRYAN

17

BLACK YOUTH: MEN AND WOMEN OF TOMORROW

"We were very much aware of what was going on because literally the issue in the community was survival, and not only at school. We actually had to protect ourselves on the streets." TREVOR SINCLAIR

"Yet we are all people, never mind colour, culture etc, we're still people. The young black, the young white are the men and women of tomorrow." GEORGE DIXON

The issue of protection of young black people in a hostile environment evoked many responses from older black people in the local community and from the young people themselves.

Dancing and Fighting

One of the first bases organised for large numbers of young black people to meet locally was the Moonshot Club. The Moonshot grew out of the Telegraph Hill Neighbourhood Council formed in 1968 which found at that time that a third of the local population were children under the age of 14. In Deptford the black population was three times that of the rest of the borough. The Moonshot Club was the Neighbourhood Council's bid to meet the needs of the young people of New Cross.

The coming together of young black people predated the club. It arose from a social need but was also a response to hostile school communities and over-crowded homes at odds with values of the schools and the young people's own experiences.

There was actually low-level warfare in Lewisham and Peckham and lots of other areas where for our protection we had to be in black gangs, or groups anyway, out there. So, yes we were very much aware, even if we couldn't articulate it but just to walk home safely, we knew where we had to be. TREVOR SINCLAIR

Early attempts in the 1960s at formalising arrangements for young black people to gather socially fell apart for lack of a permanent base. At one stage the Moonshot group attracted some 200 young people but could not secure premises on a regular basis. During this period Sybil Phoenix emerged as a leading figure both within youth work and in the Methodist Church. Sybil's youth work through her church 'back home' had included everyone in the community. She operated on the same inclusive principle in Deptford but the gulf of racial intolerance was too wide for many, particularly when the Moonshot attracted unfamiliar black youngsters into the area. Black and white young people battled on the streets. Sybil says she got to know David Diamond 'through the fights'.

Himself and his curate would be on one side of the road and I'd be on the other

side and bottles and bricks would be flying...people were protecting their territory. SYBIL PHOENIX

From this experience David and Sybil began to plan the Deptford Festival, first held in 1970, to bring the two groups together. The Festival continues to be held annually, despite David Diamond's death in 1992. For many years it has been organised by a Festival group including Pax Nindi, who also runs Paxvision, a successful video training business at the Albany Centre in Deptford.

73. Sybil Phoenix and David Diamond responded to the fights between black and white youth by setting up the annual Deptford Festival in 1970.

The Moonshot group were constantly thrown out of church halls until 1970 when they secured the lease of Pagnell Street Centre from Lewisham Council. Several groups shared the Pagnell Street Centre but for the first time, the Moonshot had a fixed venue. Sybil was the first Director of the Pagnell Street Centre. By 1971 the Club registered 280 senior members and 60 junior members.

Both Sybil and Joseph Phoenix were involved in youth work and from 1965 they were also foster parents within the borough so that they were involved with young people on a number of levels. Sybil had opened her home to many children by being a foster mother. The Phoenixes own daughter, Marsha, died after a car accident in 1974 and in 1979 the Marsha Phoenix House was opened in her memory to provide a residential base for primarily black girls aged 15-20 in need of accommodation through difficult social circumstances at home.

Youth AID Lewisham

Another project which developed to cater for the needs of young people was Youth AID. The scheme grew in 1973 out of the New Cross Detached Work Project

A complex agency dealing with a wide range of issues and concerns that affect young peoples' lives. We explore with young people issues of their lives, search together for alternatives, try to introduce them to possibilities and ways of making use of alternative resources. We critically support them to take control of their lives and clarify with them the choices available in their relationships, work, leisure or where they live. HAROLD MARCHANT, 'LOOKING BACK OVER 20 YEARS OF YOUTH AID LEWISHAM', 1993

In 1974 Youth AID workers were involved in the Forest Hill Youth Project, which later became a separate unit, housed in Torridon Road where the name Hearsay was adopted. In 1977 Youth AID and Hearsay moved to a new base in Brownhill Road, Catford and Youth AID continued to spawn projects such as Downham Youth Project and the Longstop Project. Maria Dalrymple, resident in Lewisham since 1963, was Senior Youth Worker from the late 1980s.

Education and the Failing System

While one thrust of work with parents in the community has focused on the more isolated parents on welfare budgets, Positive Image Education Project (PIEP), an off-shoot of Youth AID Lewisham developed a parents' network with an extensive programme of regular talks and discussion groups as well as activities for young people.

The kids should be the main reason to pull us together. If we have an agenda about our children and most of us either have children or have nephews and nieces then we feel obliged to do something about it. That's how I'm working to find a solution. MARIA DALRYMPLE

Positive Image Education Project (PIEP) came out of a successful bid for three years funding from the Home Office submitted by Youth AID Lewisham for developmental work with African-Caribbean boys. The project, set up in 1992, involved a number of intervention programmes which addressed issues focusing on black males. Maria Dalrymple, manager of the project, who came from Jamaica in the early 1960s, worked for some 20 years in youth and community projects before undertaking the management of PIEP.

Though many reports had reinforced the need for such a project, three studies directly informed the application. The Lord Hunt Report in 1967 was one of the earliest to consider the lack of youth provision for immigrants. In 1968 the Select Committee on Race Relations and Immigration had drawn attention to the range of difficulties faced by 'coloured school-leavers'. Of particular significance within the black community was Bernard Coard's revealing work, How The West Indian Child is Made Educationally Sub-normal in the British School System.

From 1992 the project team ran a parent support group, seminars with teachers and teaching professionals and the wider black community. They also produced video-based work focusing on African-Caribbean boys.

PIEP made widely available within the Caribbean community very important details concerning the achievement of African-Caribbean children locally as well as national trends. A disturbing trend in the early 1990s was the high exclusion rate of African Caribbean boys from schools, even at primary level

In 1991 over 50 per cent of boys excluded from Lewisham primary schools were African-Caribbean. LB LEWISHAM EDUCATION COMMITTEE REPORT, 1991

The picture for the overall exclusion rate for African-Caribbean boys at all levels in Lewisham schools gave no comfort either. While only seven per cent of all schoolchildren were excluded from all levels of Lewisham schools, one quarter of those were African-Caribbean boys.

In April 1992 local management of schools was introduced in Lewisham. During the 1993-94 period the number of exclusions leapt from 39 to 72 in one year. Figures for 1994-95 indicated a similar upward trend. A "huge upsurge in exclusions" is how Leisha Fullick described the pattern in the borough. These figures refer to permanent exclusions. Fixed-term exclusions for a period of between five and 15 days show a roughly similar trend. Schools are not obliged to report exlusions of less than five days.

Lewisham's Director of Education, Leisha Fullick, announced at a conference in April 1995 that the borough now finds itself "in a position where over 50 per cent of the total exclusions taking place in the borough are of black children". Examined by gender, boys are excluded at about 3.5 times the rate for girls. The black population in Lewisham is 22 per cent but in schools the figure is 40 per cent. Black pupils are being excluded at about a third above the rate again. This pattern follows the 1993 Education Act which abolished the category 'indefinite exclusion' leaving, instead, fixed-term exclusion for over five days and up to 15 days. The reasons given for exclusions: disruption, offences against teachers, offences against pupils, were categories which meant different things to different schools. In 1995 Lewisham gave an undertaking to monitor the reasons given for exclusion.

Whilst African-Caribbean girls are generally performing well academically in relation to other ethnic groups, African-Caribbean boys are under-performing, particularly in areas such as reading. HANN REPORT, LEWISHAM PRIMARY SCHOOLS, 1992

On September 5th 1995 two black Lewisham parents publicly denounced the education system. Margaret Andrews said in The Guardian:

Generally expectations of black children – particularly of black boys – are lower than of white children.

The intervention programmes developed by the PIEP were part of its wider focus reflecting the concern within the Caribbean community over the position of young black men and the patterns of failure which so many experience. PIEP was not simply concerned with black males of school age but from its inception took a holistic approach to African-Caribbean male 'failure'.

Whereas African-Caribbean males comprise under 2% of UK population, they are 10% of those in the prison population. HOME OFFICE, 1991

Job Crisis for Black Youth

During the 1970s issues concerning young black people such as inadequate educational experience, housing, employment and leisure continued to be raised. Even by 1973 black unemployment was a prime concern and in May that year LCCR's magazine *Spectrum* reported on a survey of local unemployment. In the two comparable samples of black and white young people researched, the black group was found to fare much worse. Of 54 black youths interviewed, 37 (68.5 per cent) had jobs. In comparison, of the 55 white young people interviewed 53 (96 per cent) held jobs. The employment picture was more complicated than it at first seemed. Of the employed black young people, 73 per cent were in an apprentice relationship at work indicating lower pay and more tied conditions of employment. The figure for the white group, on the other hand, was 47 per cent.

Consideration of the qualifications of each group indicated an inverse relationship between qualification and employment. Forty per cent of the black young people had no qualifications. However, of the white group attracting more ready employment, a larger proportion, 58 per cent, had no qualifications. Gilbert Browne, convenor of the LCCR Employment Group in 1973, summed up the general attitude of employers.

> These employers were defensive and indifferent to the problems created by discrimination in employment. Only a small minority would be exempt from this criticism. As literature on the subject of Race and Employment has indicated, it seems more difficult to persuade these primarily small firms that it would be in their interest in the long term if they recruited and trained coloured labour. There is a severe shortage of skilled labour in the area and yet firms seem unwilling to train employees. A pool of unemployed black youth remains untapped and discrimination cases continue to be brought to our attention. It would also appear that the personnel responsible for recruitment and training are in need of a serious overhaul of their own attitudes to black labour. SPECTRUM, MAY 1973

Three years later, in 1976, John Fraser MP, then Parliamentary Under-Secretary of State for Employment, confirmed at a special meeting convened by the Race Relations Working Party that the Labour Government recognised that unemployment was hitting black youth much harder than white.

A survey of young people leaving Lewisham schools in 1977 showed that one in 10 white school-leavers compared to over two in 10 black school-leavers had been denied the right to work. Five agencies collaborated to produce the report: the CRE, LCCR, Lewisham Council, ILEA and the Opinion Research Centre. Among the unemployed young people the findings were 10 per cent white male and 10 per cent white female. While the figures doubled among the black sample population, in the case of black girls they more than tripled to a shocking 34 per cent unemployment rate. Further it was found that, at every level of educational attainment, black school-leavers found it more difficult to get jobs than their white peers.

At the end of the school year in July 1978 it was estimated that some 2,400 school-leavers were entering the job market. Hopes of employment were pinned to the Government's Youth Opportunities Programme. There were no reasons to expect improved prospects for young black people but the spiralling unemployment of the 1980s wreaked further havoc in a vulnerable sector of society.

> Given the global economy we now live in, with Britain more inclined, in social policy terms, towards policies directed by monetarist ideologies and practices, everything slimmed down. Institutions slimmed down, everything is 'value for money'. The patterns in unemployment are changing. We're now talking about fixed term contracts, if you can get a job. We're now talking about short-term contracts, a rise in part-time and low-paid jobs on the increase. The future out there for black folk looks pretty grim. The statistics, even for people with

degrees and such qualifications, are pretty grim. Now if you have educational practice which blocks opportunities for qualifications against black folk in significant ways and if you have employment that is diminishing all the time, people's perspective and notions of self worth and what society has to offer them will be pretty grim. GILBERT BROWNE

The pool of unemployed young black people continued to grow. As the young and the recently qualified battled with the difficulties of gaining work experience, they began to give up early expectations of full employment. Alternative lifestyles, including those involving drugs and crime, increasingly replaced the expectations that home and school had once reinforced of a place in the employment sector and legitimate financial reward. The crucial questions arose for the black community. What prospects are there for young black people and what stake do they have in society?

Voices of Youth

In July 1976 George Dixon, a young West Indian resident in South East London for some 10 years, wrote his perceptions of the situation for young black people and his hopes for the future.

In some cases it is a foregone conclusion that black teenagers are not treated fairly in comparison to white teenagers. The only reason being that we're black. We think black, we act black and most of all we're proud to be black.

Because of this, it's no surprise that we question the values of society. The only destiny we have found is in the colour of our skin. When we leave school we have no sense of belonging anywhere.

We are what integration is all about. A few years ago Mr Roy Jenkins MP, called us 'Coloured Britons', "dressing and speaking much as we do and looking for the same opportunities". Few of us have found them. We cannot share our parents' heritage, yet we feel apart from the society in which we grew up. We feel rejected where it hurts most: as individuals by the white children who were our friends.

My case is somewhat different. There is only a handful of blacks in the sixth form I attend. The white teenagers make jokes about blacks, browns, yellows, whatever the case may be, and then say, "I don't mean you, you're different!" But I know I am not.

Many black teenagers have lost faith in the law and in English justice. They do not believe that it applies to them. Black youths have grown cynical beliefs about the way society works and the way it shuns them. It leaves an enduring impression that the English are hypocrites.

Yet we are all people, never mind colour, culture etc, we're still people. The young black, the young white are the men and women of tomorrow. GEORGE DIXON, SPECTRUM, JUNE/JULY 1976

Towards the end of autumn 1976 plans were being made for a youth magazine aimed at black youth clubs in Lewisham and neighbouring boroughs. A pilot issue was planned for late December 1976 or, failing that, January 1977. Claudios Johnson and Norma Williams were contacts for the proposed magazine.

The Wire sold out its first print run of 500 copies within 10 days. The editorial team of local young black people were delighted with the response. Members of the team were interviewed by *Black Londoners* and the BBC overseas programme *Caribbean Magazine*. Priced at five pence, *The Wire* was financed through a special fundraising programme. An article in the first issue caused a stir with its criticisms of the *South London Press* Young Journalist award, won by Richard Woolveridge for features on Rastafarians. Ras Doogi and his editorial team on *The Wire* criticised the process of getting information and the perspective. The *South London Press* responded with an editorial attacking *The Wire* and a story the following week headlined "White Society Is No Longer Useful". The story led to a deluge of racist calls and letters to LCCR after a letter to the *South East London Mercury* wrongly stated that *The Wire* was funded by LCCR.

Police and the Moonshot

While many isolated cases occurred involving young black people and the police in the local area, it was at the Moonshot that many came face-to-face with the police. For two years Moonshot members were involved in regular discussions with Lewisham police. This was extended in 1975 to sports activities. Table tennis tournaments, football and other sports were arranged in liaison with P division and with a measure of financial support from them.

One of a series of incidents which soured relations was an unplanned weekend visit in 1975. A disco was in progress when the police arrived and insisted on searching the hall for a suspect who was said to have run in the direction of the youth club after an alleged offence. Despite the reservations of senior members of staff, the police attempted to stop the disco and search individuals with the result that disco equipment belonging to the club was destroyed. A number of arrests were made for obstruction and assault. The young people were angry and insisted on their right to press charges against the police. The warden, however, together with senior members of staff argued against such action and the matter went eventually to the police-community liaison group. Since, clearly the young people would not have the support of senior staff, they settled for compensation for the damage to their equipment.

In 1975 Commander Randall, head of the police division released 'statistics on mugging' in the area (see Ch.12). In the wake of this, the Special Patrol Group (SPG) assumed a high profile locally. Many members of the Moonshot, who had longstanding concerns about the involvement of the police at the club, became further alarmed at this turn of events. In May 1977 Lewisham police swooped.

On 30th May Lewisham police in a combined operation entered 22 homes between 6.30 and 7.30 am and arrested a number of black people. Twenty one of them were later charged with conspiracy to steal or being a person suspected of loitering with intent to steal. JOHN GUS

Only one of those arrested was charged with actual theft and Moonshot members responded with fury. Much of their anger was directed at the management which stood accused of conspiracy in the affair. Adding fuel to the angst of members, the press statements issued by the police implicated community leaders within the area with prior knowledge of their activities. Between 35 and 40 young people 'occupied' the office of the Moonshot. They demanded that the management explain the behaviour of the implicated community leaders and support those arrested. The following day a press release from the LCCR disclaimed prior knowledge of the police operations and, after threats of further action by the young people, a similar disclaimer followed from Sybil Phoenix.

In June 1977, two weeks after the arrests, Prince Charles visited the Pagnell Street Centre. The young people, still aggrieved by the questioning of young people under the age of 10, humiliating behaviour towards young black women during the operation and physical attacks upon suspects in custody, took the opportunity to express their concerns. Following the royal visit, the Prince invited community leaders and Commander Randall to Buckingham Palace to discuss the matter further.

74. Prince Charles visited the Moonshot in June 1977, after police raided local black people's homes. The Prince invited community leaders and the police to Buckingham Palace to discuss their concerns.

The Gender Trap

In the summer of 1978 Carl Foster was shot by an air rifle from a passing car in Loampit Vale. It was part of a pattern of random attacks on black people. The victims of those attacks were more likely to be male. No arrests were made.

While both males and females attended the Moonshot, single sex provision for young people was also offered in different parts of the borough. The less traditional groups, not modelled on militaristic youth groups such as the scouts or youth brigade, came later in the 1980s. Step Forward, funded by Lewisham Council Women's Committee and Lewisham Youth Unemployment Project, was originally based at the Rockbourne Youth Centre in Forest Hill and catered for black women of 16-25 years.

A small team of three black workers led the group, initially offering workshops, organising classes and outings. Project leaders at Step Forward noted the limitations of women's employment which clustered around clerical, social and community work. They

75. Chris Foster, Carl's brother. The New Cross Fire brought back memories of his grief.

hoped to build bridges to new areas such as technology and engineering. Before long, Elaine Burke was the lone youth worker, a reflection of the cuts in financial support for the project. The service ceased when the community flat utilised for the project was reclaimed by the Council.

Elaine's work was predominantly with young single women with children and the group she worked with consisted mainly of single mothers. The focus was strongly directed upon childcare and support for the single mother on low income. While young black men 'failed' at schol and faced danger on the streets, this was the crucial gender trap affecting young black females unprepared for motherhood and with inadequate financial or emotional support.

The Sounds of South East London

When, in May 1975, Jah Shaka's sound system at the Moonshot was damaged to the tune of several hundreds of pounds, the attackers had targeted the pulse of the young black community. Jah Shaka had become not only the sound associated with the Moonshot, but the sound associated with a large part of Lewisham.

> *In the music I play I bring to the people their culture and, in harmony with the Moonshot Club, I do a lot for black people. Shaka sound is a symbol for them.*
> SOUTH EAST LONDON MERCURY, 8/5/1975.

Jah Shaka came from Jamaica with his parents when he was eight years old and settled in South East London. His career began in the 1960s with an obscure local sound system called Freddie Cloudburst. By the end of the decade, Jah Shaka was based

76. Jah Shaka is an institution of British roots and culture. He came from Jamaica when he was eight years old and by the late 1960s had built up a renowned sound system in the New Cross/Deptford area. He continues to play at the Moonshot on a regular basis.

in the New Cross/Deptford area and his sound system was renowned for its promotion of roots music, music with a message. Shaka's live 'dances' were famous for their spiritually charged atmosphere and the acrobatic, stylised dancing of the participants. By the end of the 1970s, inspired spiritually by his interest in Rastafari and politically by the American Civil Rights movement, Shaka Sound became one of the top three in the country.

During the 1980s Shaka launched his own record label. Over the years the label has carried well over 50 releases by UK artists like Junior Brown, Sgt Pepper and Vivian Jones, Jamaican artists such as Horace Andy, Icho Candy and Max Romeo, as well as dozens of releases by Shaka himself. Shaka is not only a major force in the sound business, but also a talented producer and musician.

Today Shaka keeps hold of his strong South London roots and continues to play at the Moonshot on a regular basis, but he is also heavily involved in maintaining his African and Jamaican roots. Increasingly he returns to Jamaica to record albums with Jamaican veteran artists and musicians. He sponsors a football team and has ambitions to open two schools, one on either side of the island, to help with musical and cultural education, with possible exchange networks set up with similar projects in West Africa. He has visited Ghana each year since 1990, contributing time, effort and finances towards the establishment and upkeep of a clinic and a school.

Jamaicans are very close to Ghanaians. It's as if Jamaica just broke off from Africa and floated away! There's the obvious link between the two countries, dating back to the days of slavery, because many who were taken came from that region. JAH SHAKA

Jah Shaka, named after Jah, the African word for God as used in Rastafarianism and Shaka, the name of a Zulu warrior, is an institution of British roots and culture

77/78. Saxon Sound was started in Lewisham during the hot summer of 1976 by Francis Lloyd and Dennis Rowe (pictured right) and is now one of the best known 'sounds' in the country. Above: Many artists have aired their talent round Saxon's mike stand, including Tipper Ire (left) and Daddy Colonel (right).

who has inspired a whole generation of UK sound-systems, musicians and producers.

Saxon Sound started in Lewisham during the hot summer of 1976. It is owned by Lloyd 'Musclehead' Francis and Dennis Rowe. Denis learnt to operate sound systems by helping out at family parties from around seven years old. Later equipment for the sound systems was financed by friends 'chipping in' to buy not only such necessities as speakers and turntables but also dub plates and original acetates.

My family used to have parties...My Uncle Felix had a sound and I used to be with him all the time. If it was a family thing I would be there with him, learning how to play it. DENNIS ROWE

Saxon is now one of the best known 'sounds' in the country. The artists who have aired their talents round Saxon's mike stand include Maxi Priest, Smiley Culture and Asher Senator, Philip Levi, Tipper Ire and Daddy Colonel. Many of these were already involved with the sound systems of South East London.

What they don't realise is that every Sound has started off from little, from young men. When I was seven I used to play my cousin's Sound, stand on a little box putting the records on. People used to come round and say 'this little boy's going to be a musician'. I never got as far as being a musician, but I got as far as owning one of the best sounds in England DENNIS ROWE

Philip Levi, who joined Saxon in 1979, gets his themes for his 'chat' from a number of sources: from the news, from things he sees happen and from experiences of growing up in South East London. One of his songs talks about the New Cross fire, "13 dead in South East London, 13 blacks dead and the news was virtually nothing".

Saxon are also involved with organising MC clashes and were the first sound to hold an MC woman's competition. No other sound has pushed the DJ element in music 'to the fullness'. They are renowned for it.

You'll never find anybody chatting rubbish. Everybody on Saxon chats intelligently. The DJs are coughing up fire."

The source of the other essential element for a successful sound – original music – was essentially Jamaican imports but keeping sources secret was a key part in the originality of a sound system.

The usual sound just played one or two new records, after two weeks the record is old. We get music from anywhere, anyone, no partiality and that's what terrifies other sounds when we play them. DENNIS ROWE

Sound systems established themselves as the symbol of black youth in the mid-1970s and by 1981 there were well over 20 large sounds to be found in South East London.

New technology perhaps masks the cultural continuity of popular music with earlier forms. This is demonstrated at its best in the music of Rasta artists who used the medium in the manner of the oral tradition to teach black history and black pride. The influence of calypso, soul, rap and other African-American popular forms can also be found in reggae. Forms such as hip hop, "created out of re-mixing two records on a double turntable" competed for popularity among the young in the 1980s as Jungle, a mixture of a range of forms from reggae to classical, does in the 1990s.

18

BLACK LEWISHAM OF THE 1990S

"To see qualified black people taking responsibility; discharging those responsibilities well, being spoken of highly by white and black stakeholders, colleagues and staff; I think set me free a little bit." Joe Montgomery

In surveying the local scene in the mid-1990s there are some striking continuities of struggle and response. There are also some newer issues, but the focus on the old dreams of self-determination is as strong as ever. It seems as if some of the networks and alliances of the 1990s may have a chance to make a serious impact on achieving this dream.

Themes From The Past

The following three stories from 1990s Lewisham show how some of the main themes which have been traced through this part of the history continue to resonate: citizenship, police mistreatment, 'mugging', housing, racial harassment and attacks, and local authority responses.

At the end of 1991, Falklands veteran and local fireman Irwin Eversley was granted £20,000 by the Metropolitan police in an out-of-court award. Eversley, born in Barbados, alleged that he had been wrongfully arrested and mistreated by the police. Eversley was a paratrooper who saw action in the storming of Goose Green and was decorated for his part in the war. However, in the course of his own battles with the Home Office, he was required to pay £60 to register as a British citizen. He returned his medals in disgust.

The fight for compensation following Irwin's wrongful arrest outside his own home on Crossfield

Irwin Eversley celebrating with friends on Crossfield Estate

Estate in Deptford was long drawn out. An interesting feature of the story is that Irwin, a well-known and respected member of the local community, claimed that the support of his neighbours made all the difference. Irwin's face is familiar nationally through the fireman safety advertisement in which he features. The Metropolitan Police refused to accept liability but nonetheless made the out-of-court award for 'damages'.

In July 1994 the *South East London Mercury* revealed how Lewisham Council's policy punished victims of racial harassment. It was a full year after LREC's report 'Racial Harassment and Violence on Lewisham's Housing Estates' gave detailed accounts of disturbing racial incidents on a number of housing estates. Silwood Estate on the Southwark/Lewisham border, where the BNP put up a candidate in the May 1994 local elections, was considered one of the worst trouble spots in this respect. LREC's researcher, Richard Backes, reported 138 incidents of racial attack and harassment against 15 households in the year to March 1994. The families had suffered threats and physical attacks, racist grafitti and name calling, eggs and stones thrown, windows smashed and excrement smeared on doors and cars. Backes was shown a note which read:

> *How many times do we have to say it. Leave as quick as you came. Niggers are not welcome, especially when they drive fancy cars. BNP.*

Yet the Council insisted upon a 'transfer as a last resort' principle with the effect that distraught tenants were forced to remain on estates where they had been on the receiving end of racial violence.

Following the report, national press and television coverage ensured that the issue could not be ignored for much longer. In 1994 the Council began eviction proceedings against some of the perpetrators. This was after the victim had complained for two years with no response from the Council or the police. It still needed, however, a formal complaint via the CRE before substantive action was taken. In April 1995, the policy of transfer as a last resort was dropped. The previous year Lewisham Council's bid to central government for Single Regeneration Budget funding to tackle racial harassment on Silwood Estate had been successful. The money will be used over three years to enhance the estate's facilities, take legal action against perpetrators, build a self-confident multi-racial community and to develop practical projects like the 'Kick Racism out of Football' and the 'Uniting Britain for a Just Society' campaigns.

In the summer of 1995 the Chair of Lewisham Police-Community Consultative Group received a letter from Sir Paul Condon, Commissioner of Police, announcing the launch of the latest police operation against street robbery in response to the increase in 'mugging' indicated by crime figures. Two factors were said to cause this trend – unemployment and exclusion.

> *It is a fact that many of the perpetrators of muggings are very young black people, who have been excluded from schools and/or are unemployed.* SIR PAUL CONDON (LETTER)

The linking of black youth and criminality was further reinforced in September 1995 when Lewisham Crime Prevention Initiative was launched. On that occasion Labour Shadow Home Secretary Jack Straw began by spreading the blame for crime to include young white men but then went on to endorse Condon's Operation Eagle Eye. Black councillor Solomon Brown was among those who pointed out how damaging this blanket criminalisation by racial identification. Given that unemployment was a stated factor in the new orthodoxy on mugging, he described how police 'facts' about race and crime could cause further problems.

An interviewer interviewing a black candidate for a job, the first thing that comes to his mind: 'Oh, we've got to be very careful of these people because they are potential muggers'.

Networks and Alliances

One of the most positive feelings among many in Lewisham's black community at the end of the millennium is that the roots of that community are firmly planted, that it has the resources to nurture itself as well as contribute outwards into society and the locality as a whole.

The Black Childcare Network, a group of professionally qualified and experienced black childcare workers based in Brownhill Road, Catford, came together in 1984 from the experience of workers and mothers (often one and the same) of a history of unreliable and disturbing childcare arrangements.

The childcare was atrocious, really atrocious. It was very difficult to get good childminders even through the Health Visitors. They used to deal with you on the doorstep, not have you inside – 'what would the neighbours think'. So that was damaging our children and ourselves. SONIA STEELE

Sonia, who came to London from Jamaica in 1965 and lived on Pepys Estate from 1973 until the late 1980s qualified as an NNEB (childcare) in 1985. She now works for Lewisham's Early Years registering nurseries and childminders and helping them to provide high-quality childcare which is actively anti-racist and affirming for all children. Sonia has been a member of the Black Childcare Network since the start. In 1995 the Network celebrated ten years of "working for future generations" and many older parents wish it had been there earlier.

Another means of drawing together the community interested in the differing needs of the black family was established in 1994. Maria Dalrymple became an organising force behind the Black Parents Network which met weekly at the Hearsay project in the 1990s. It brings together black groups interested in education, leisure, youth, mental health and a whole range of other relevant issues.

In a different field, the Caribbean Women Writers' Alliance came out of the first International Caribbean Women Writers' Conference at the Goldsmiths Caribbean Centre in 1994. Courses on Caribbean women's writing were already offered by the college. Delegates debated the impact of the proliferation of new literature and a network of aspiring writers set up the termly publication *Mango Season* and a performance group 'Mango and Spice'.

The North Lewisham Law Centre in Deptford High Street has for years supported clients after racist attacks and with matters relating to immigration and nationality. However, during the 1980s it had only one black member of staff and was concerned about its role in the black community.

Law centres are meant to articulate the people who are disadvantaged and dispossessed and people suffering from lack of knowledge about their rights. I think the black community at the moment falls into those categories. JULIA JONES

The Law Centre reviewed its employment policy and recruited more black staff and by the mid 1990s it boasts a multi-racial staff and management which reflects the community it serves. Selma Williams, who came originally from Jamaica and has lived and worked in the borough for over 20 years, became the administrative co-ordinator for the centre in 1989 and another black woman, Julia Jones, was appointed as supervising solicitor in 1991. The centre continues to provide an essential service to local people including many black people. Alongside information on legal and welfare rights, staff advise clients on criminal matters, domestic cases, civil actions against the police and, since the 1993 Education Act, the legal aspect of children's 'special educational needs'. Much of the casework consists of 'petty matters' relating to youth crime which would be unlikely to be taken up by mainstream solicitors. Help in this field is essential to the individuals since a successful outcome may well prevent a youngster from having a criminal record which narrows so many opportunities.

Images of Black People

During the summer of 1994 Lewisham resident George Kelly, also known as Fowokan, presented his first solo exhibition entitled 'Beyond My Grandfather's Dreams'. George, who came from Jamaica to London in the 1950s and moved to Lewisham in 1987, had one day looked at one of his sculptures through the eyes of a forebear who had known slavery. It struck him that the expression of African beauty he was able to articulate in his work was beyond his grandfather's dream and so the piece and finally the exhibition was named. The exhibition of bold African-inspired figures was hosted by the Jamaica High Commission in London from 18th July to 2nd August 1994. Busts of Mary Seacole and Malcolm X were among the exhibits, along with stunning pieces which firmly reinterpreted African beauty.

George's experiences had taken him in many directions but finally led him to discover his particular creativity. He learnt to play the drums. He tried out photography, developing the images himself. He sampled a range of instruments, tried painting, drawing, pottery. In the mid 1970s George visited Africa. He has traced his specific interest in Africa to the mystic Rastas, known in his childhood as brothermen or beardmen who

Sculpture by George Kelly, showing the inspiration he draws from African culture

always made reference to Africa. George's father was a Garveyite and as a child the notion of 'back to Africa' was important. George attended meetings with his father and experienced something of the passion of Garveyism.

George noticed that he himself held conflicting ideas of Africa: ideas which contained elements of negative stereotyping he had picked up, as well as the more positive notions of brotherhood.

I had this kind of dual relationship with the idea of Africa but when I came here I met Africans for the first time. Real Africans! I was really freaked out. I met this guy Eddie. He was here studying from Sierra Leone and I couldn't believe how much like me he was. He even spoke a kind of Jamaican which I later found was called pidgin. I could recognise some of the words. I was totally fascinated by it... So I started going out looking for books on Africa. Then I discovered the culture of Benin and the Bronzes, the beauty and the majesty! So I thought, one day I must get to Africa.

The time in Africa in 1974 consolidated George Kelly's self-perception as a visual artist. He travelled widely across Africa with a group of musicians. In Benin he recalls having the strange sensation of having always known the place. After Africa came a confirmation of artistic direction. On reflection, George recognised his parents as 'makers and doers'. He recognised, also, the way in which the culture of 'making and doing' had influenced him as a young person.

Mum made all our clothes up until the age of about 13. My father was a master baker and he was always creating new recipes. His bread is special. At Eastertime he would put all kinds of special ingredients into his bun. So the culture of doing and creating and making was part of my life. I was always making things as a child. I made my own toys.

In 1994 the Black Childcare Network asked local photographer Jeni Mckenzie to display some of her images of the black family at their International Year of the Family event that September. In October the exhibition was used for Black History Month which took up the theme of the black family. After this Jeni approached Margaret Andrews with the idea of a symposium to address issues around the images used to portray the black family. Margaret Andrews, originally from Carriacou but living in Lewisham since the 1960s, persuaded George Kelly to donate one of his pieces towards the fundraising.

In Margaret's own teaching in child development and childcare, whenever the need arose for finding images of black families, she had always been in a position to budget for this. This was not the case for many other professionals with the result that they presented what was to hand. All too frequently the images projected were stereotypical and misrepresented the black family.

For me it was about making a statement about how we want to see ourselves...It was also about having a dialogue with other black people. Usually white people have that dialogue, then they write the book, they take the photographs and then we complain! The purpose of that seminar was to deal with it for ourselves...How often have we been able to take this option into the real arena? MARGARET ANDREWS

The symposium, which was held in Brixton in January 1995, aimed to set standards for the way in which black families are represented in published photographic images. The symposium was chaired by Vastiana Belfon, writer, parent and former editor of African-Caribbean programmes for the BBC. Speakers included Diane Abbott MP, Dr Kimani Nehusi and Jeni Mckenzie.

One of a series by local photographer Jeni Mckenzie. Jeni's approach has been "to embrace the still-unpopular theme of diversity within the community, and to celebrate black family structure, beauty and vitality". These elements are captured in this three-generation family photograph.

Black Teachers

Lewisham Black Teachers was one of a number of black teachers' associations in London set up after the ILEA was dismantled and education devolved to individual boroughs. Concerned specifically with issues affecting black teachers within the borough, it functioned as a vital support network. Lottie Betts-Priddy, chair of the group from 1990, returned to Sierra Leone in 1992 and Jackie Bygrave was elected in her place. Since Lottie had been employed at the Professional Development Centre at Kilmorie Road where the group met, the black teachers had to renegotiate for space at the centre for regular meetings. Jackie located over 100 named black teachers working in the borough at all levels of education.

The core group of 16 regular attenders were from a range of institutions locally. Creative tension within the group ensured debate as to its continued function and specifically whether the group should adopt a more anti-racist stance.

Jackie's objective as the new chair was to locate the black teachers in Lewisham's 45 schools. She worked closely with Gillian, another teacher at Deptford Green school, to enhance the way the association served the needs of black teachers. They were bedevilled by lack of funding and lack of a space to meet as the Professional Development Centre was at the time being reorganised and space was at a premium, but they found an ally in the centre's co-ordinator Bev Clarke-Brown. Jackie sent information into schools in order to reactivate the group. Although administrative assistance was still lacking, Deptford Green was given as a contact address and there began a programme of socials, audits, meetings and discussion groups.

In 1992 a number of black teachers, including some of African-Caribbean origin, felt that their jobs were under threat. They were among a group who had been given temporary contracts which looked likely not to be renewed. By 1992 the borough of Lewisham still had only two black headteachers. One of these was Keith Ajegbo who became the head of Deptford Green School in 1986 and was awarded the OBE for services to education in 1995. Deptford Green is one of the very few schools in the borough which does not conform to the usual patterns of African-Caribbean exclusions or 'failure'. This is certainly not only due to Keith Ajegbo himself. It is partly a reflection of Deptford's 'advanced' population demographics which mean that in a school with 48% 'non-white' children, African-Caribbean children are no longer the largest ethnic minority. However, the strong discipline and the overwhelming commitment to anti-racism within the school have undoubtedly proved successful in avoiding some of the worst failings of the state education system. In the rest of the borough:

> *The same appalling situation exists as regards Deputy Heads and the higher levels of the Education Department. No progress has been made in terms of increasing the numbers of black personnel within the Education Directorate as the Work Force Survey 1991 clearly showed.* LREC REPORT, 1991-92

A similar observation could have been made concerning teacher training. Despite over two decades of teachers being trained from within the African-Caribbean community, Lewisham still claimed a paucity of African-Caribbean teachers.

In 1994 the Black Teachers' Group was angered by the lack of early consultation in a local project which aimed to support black teachers being trained, and which sought partnership with black teachers. For over a term they had been planning a black mentoring scheme with a few black colleagues at Lewisham. They were therefore surprised to read in the papers that a British Telecom award had been given for such a scheme at Goldsmiths. They linked with black teachers' groups in the surrounding boroughs to protest. They were concerned that the project would be headed by someone with little or no expertise on black issues. They felt that their own scheme may have been usurped and they were concerned about consultation of black teachers in the spending of the money. They saw this as essentially yet another scheme 'doing good' to black people.

The Regenerators

One of the most prominent black people in the public sector in Lewisham is Joe Montgomery. Joe came to London in 1989 to take up an appointment for the Department of Trade and Industry running their inner-city Task Force in Deptford. He had been employed in the West Midlands for most of the time prior to that and he was brought up in Nottingham.

Joe's parents both came from the same parish, Clarendon in Jamaica. As a young boy growing up in Nottingham, Joe was expected to do well. Though he was not always completely co-operative in this, there were many relatives and friends of the family who took an active role in both exhorting him and supporting him to succeed at school. For reasons Joe did not understand, they had high expectations of him.

My elder brothers and my two elder cousins in particular tried their very best to encourage me academically. I was typically unco-operative in many ways but I managed to edge along and to make a little bit of progress.

Joe's school expected all its pupils to do well and he had little time to dwell upon his social isolation as the only black boy at his school. He responded to the school's expectations as he did to those individuals who were particularly supportive in the Catholic church which his family attended. Altogether, Joe thrived on the support which came not only from family and school but also from significant people within the community. Whatever hurdles stood in the way of his achievement, he was determined to negotiate them.

Joe studied at Birmingham University where he was one of a group of black students who supported and nurtured each other for the duration of the course. After completing their degrees, the group kept in touch. Joe had a major disagreement with one of his friends in the group when he noticed that she was applying for jobs for which she was overqualified and avoiding managerial posts which suited her qualifications and experience. Joe encouraged her to apply for the managerial position which was also vacant and predicted that she would be training the manager if she did not herself apply for the post. His prediction came true and the episode marked a turning point in Joe's life. Later he would himself follow the advice he had so freely given.

In the early 1980s Joe won a German Marshall Fund fellowship which allowed him to visit the USA to study his professional counterparts: the way they worked, the institutions that assisted in urban development and regeneration activities. The visit left a very deep impression, particularly having observed how black people in the USA ran businesses and major institutions at the most senior level beyond tokenism in an essentially white society.

Prior to this visit Joe had already broken through the barrier and had the opportunity, denied to so many young black men, to establish a track record in employment.

Any appointment is a risk and when you don't quite look or sound like the people on the other side of the table their perception of you as a risk can be heightened.

Joe Montgomery , chief executive of City Challenge, in Deptford Town Hall

Joe Montgomery's break came when he convinced the Cadbury Trust to employ him as financial adviser. By the time he left, Joe was responsible for a grant support portfolio of several million pounds. He arrived in Deptford with this experience and managed the Government's inner city Task Force, before taking up the post of Chief Executive of the new Deptford City Challenge to implement the regeneration of Deptford with a £37.5 million grant from the Department of the Environment. Joe's charming and easy-going style endeared him to many, despite the inevitable conflicts in a small, deprived community coming to terms with the seemingly vast sums being spent by an agency over which they had little control. However charming he could be Joe was proving himself a capable leader.

In 1993 Joe moved to Lewisham Council as one of its highest-paid officers. His new role was to lead the management of a newly-created department which had merged the leisure services, economic development and environmental services departments into one unitary force. This new super-department began life as DEEL (Department of Economy, Environment and Leisure), but soon recognised the inevitable "new deal" puns and changed to LEED; it covers most of the baseline services aiming to make the borough a pleasant place to be: street cleaning, refuse collection, lighting, quality of roads, leisure centres and libraries, play facilities, management and maintenance of council buildings and a host of other responsibilities. Joe took on the management of a staff of 13,000 including 800 full-time and a budget in excess of £15 million.

Up on Stage

The increasingly high profile given to freelance activity underscores crucial changes in the labour market and particularly the vexed question of growing unemployment in the final decades of the 20th century. Lennie St Luce's mother came from the Caribbean in the 1960s and Lennie has lived in Deptford since 1983. When she left drama school, she worked within the women's movement but had to leave that sector through lack of financial support. Her prospects looked bleak but she took a weekend break in

Lennie St Luce giving one of her many performances at the Albany

Amsterdam and discovered an affinity with the arts world there. Now a powerful poet and performer, Deptford and Lewisham have featured regularly in Lennie's writing though performing in London is less rewarding both financially and emotionally. Her six months in Amsterdam had allowed her to develop a network of support there.

With an acting background similar to Lennie's, Jan Blake of Cassava Leaf also lives in Deptford and also developed a European audience for her telling of Caribbean folk tales. As a professional storyteller she represents the professionalisation of a traditional role formerly with very limited scope for earning a living. The folk tales upon which Jan's profession is based are drawn mainly from the Caribbean and African traditions.

In autumn 1993 Jan Blake was both storyteller and workshop leader at a one-day conference hosted at the Goldsmiths Caribbean Centre. Among the delegates were a small Dutch group originally from Surinam, the Dutch-speaking Caribbean. Jan was invited to do storytelling in Amsterdam where the Dutch group was based.

Second Wave, a young people's theatre project, was set up in 1985 by Kathy Cucoi, a young white woman living in Deptford. The project offers a range of performing arts and creative work, dancing and writing for theatre. Originally based in a hut at the back of the Albany Theatre, Second Wave has helped many young black people to success not just in performing but also in creating material themselves. One of these is Kim Walker, who has appeared in *Desmond's* since the programme began.

In 1993 Second Wave began to offer accredited courses to young people in technical theatre training, specifically addressing the under-representation of black and female technicians in the industry. By 1995 Second Wave was based on Creek Road. The young people attending the summer school were predominantly black, an indication of how comfortable young black people felt in the environment.

The French Connection

The pioneering movement of individual African Caribbean people from Lewisham into Europe reflects the trend to freer movement between nations towards the end of the 20th century. Unlike the post-*Windrush* emigration to Britain and into the borough, however, the new trickle into Europe was not necessarily linked to former colonial ties.

When England finally entered the EEC on 1st January 1973, following the negotiations of Edward Heath's government, the debate signalled concerns about freedom of movement of black people into Europe and into Britain. Would black British people be as free to move into gainful employment in Europe as British whites? The argument appeared to favour those born in Britain above those born into British subject citizenship in the Caribbean ex-colonies.

The movement of EEC nationals across Europe became two-way. While Caribbean residents in Lewisham made tentative steps into Europe, despite an awareness of the prevalence of racism abroad, so Caribbean EEC nationals became associated with Lewisham, many through the Caribbean Centre.

Janene Altenor was born in the 1950s in Martinique, an island in the French-speaking Caribbean. The French colonial structure, of which Martinique remained a part, encompassed colonies as provinces or Departments of France. Thus, Martinique was still considered part of France and its needs were referred to Paris. Janene left Martinique with her family when she was 10 years old. She lived next in New Caledonia, another Department of France, this time in the Pacific neighbouring Tahiti. The Altenors had relatives already living in New Caledonia. After a few years there,

Janene's family moved to France. For French nationals in the Caribbean and Africa such movement was not unusual. Like the military service which brought recruits from the Caribbean to the UK in the 1940s, French military service took recruits from the Caribbean to the Pacific where France had a military base. Among them were many French African-Caribbean people.

For those in the French-speaking Caribbean, higher education and further training possibilities necessarily involved France, and extensive movement was the norm for Caribbean Francophones. Janene first came to London on holiday in 1985 and afterwards wanted to improve her English. Like many young French women she applied for entry to England as an au pair. When this proved unreasonably demanding, Janene returned to France and resumed her study. But she had made friends in Lewisham and when she returned in 1989 she took up residence in the borough.

During the first 'settling down' year, Janene returned constantly to France, an indication of the difficulty she found in coping with London. Gradually she discovered a French Caribbean community scattered across London. She describes a visiting pattern not dissimilar from her own. At first, there is the need to 'have a taste' of London life. Later, plans for further studies or training or settling come to the fore.

Without necessarily appreciating this role, Goldsmiths College and Lewisham College have both played a part in attracting Caribbean students from the Francophone Caribbean. Visiting students like Janene were intrigued to find a Caribbean Centre and the promise of a Caribbean focus within a London University. For Janene, it was a course in Caribbean Creole at the centre which first attracted her attention in 1990, a year after coming to live in Lewisham. As a result she became involved with the centre, attending classes and chairing events.

For Janene, the freelance culture provided an important financial lifeline. As a freelance journalist she contributed regularly to *Amina*, a 23 year old publication geared to the black French women's market and focusing on women's achievement. She has written for other, mainly black-oriented magazines and newspapers in French.

When Aurelie came to Lewisham she enrolled at Lewisham College. A French speaker, educated in French schools all her life, her tutors were unsure how best to draw out her knowledge. One of her tutors had visited the Caribbean Centre and knowing that the Caribbean link included French as well as Dutch territories in the region, made enquiries concerning the support available.

In the 1990s the Caribbean Centre could be identified as a 'pull factor' within Lewisham attracting the movement of a number of Caribbean students formerly resident in Europe. While for students like Janene the finding of the centre was almost accidental, for others there was an irresistible link. The Head of Centre from 1987, Petronella Breinburg, came from Surinam, formerly Dutch Guyana. It was no accident, therefore, that Dutch students involved in the development of Kwakoe, a community centre for the Surinamese in Amsterdam, regularly attended events at the Caribbean Centre and began in 1993 to develop a dialogue with black youth centres within Lewisham.

Two delegates represented Kwakoe at the 1994 International Caribbean studies Network Seminar. They were Jules Reijsen and Hady-Jane Guds. Hady-Jane Guds had attended the earlier Storytelling Conference in 1993. Jules Reijsen had attended the Network Seminar the previous year in 1993. Neither came as an academic but as community development workers hoping to strengthen the youth focus of Kwakoe.

The main impetus into Europe was to seek a means of generating income and the pursuit of a standard of living commensurate with qualifications and chosen lifestyle. Through it many incoming Euro-Caribbean nationals made new cultural links in Lewisham encompassing an appreciation of a wider, multi-lingual Caribbean. Others forged links based on cultures already held in common, as in the case of Suriname people, but keen to gain from the experiences of other Caribbean peoples with a lengthier personal knowledge of surviving within Europe.

Leading Lights

The 1990s saw increased participation within local government by black councillors and among these were African-Caribbean councillors. In the 1980s there were only two black councillors, Russell Profitt and Les Eytle. Les Eytle had been a council member since 1982 and in May 1984 he became Mayor of Lewisham.

Les Eytle
Blythe Hill Ward

Eddie Capone
Marlowe Ward

Claude Gonsalves
St Andrew Ward

Solomon Brown
Hither Green Ward

Angelina Simpson
Horniman Ward

Stephen Padmore
Marlowe Ward

My becoming involved in local politics was a conscious decision on my part. I have always been interested in politics and when the opportunity came to contribute positively to the community I took it. LES EYTLE

In 1995 Lewisham has 17 councillors from ethnic minorities. Of these Solomon Brown, Eddie Capone, Les Eytle, Stephen Padmore and Angelina Simpson are of African-Caribbean descent.

The political role of councillors in the local authority is in some ways paramount but the Council also has two other relevant roles. It is the biggest employer in the borough and it is the main source of financial support for community initiatives.

In 1988 Leroy Philips was appointed Head of Community Affairs. Born in Jamaica, Leroy had first started work for the borough in 1984 as Principal Grants Officer. He had a background in voluntary community work with ex-psychiatric patients, people with disabilities, black and white, young and old. In the mid 1980s local authorities were responding to community pressures. The 1981 riots in nearby Lambeth had taken their toll. Three units were added to Lewisham's structure of local government: the race unit, women's unit and a community development unit.

I always see myself as mainstream because I think you could do far more in the mainstream, although it's sometimes slower. LEROY PHILIPS

Leroy had 'a feel for community affairs' and found that his new post offered not only policy backing but the authority and financial base to implement decisions. Open and fair recruitment is an important aspect of the Equal Opportunity work that Leroy manages. Within the voluntary sector, groups frequently explain that equal opportunity cannot work in practice because of a lack of finance. For example, if a job becomes available, prospective employers might 'put the word about' rather than advertise widely. Community Affairs help to correct the inequalities arising from such practice by making funds available for wider advertising. Fair play is a central core of the decision-making process which Leroy's job entails.

I've been very fortunate in Lewisham because I have a high degree of autonomy and the councillor structure is very conducive to officers working together with councillors. LEROY PHILIPS

The Community Affairs Unit resource programme has given financial support for a host of projects such as training, support for self-help groups, advisory organisations and small businesses.

Kennie Williamson, Principal Race Equality Officer of Lewisham Council, was born in Grenada and came to London in 1962. He began working for Lewisham in the late 1980s as a consultant. He had worked for the GLC in the Ethnic Minorities Unit but it was not until February 1994 that he took up the race equality post. There had been two race advisors before him.

The Policy and Equality Unit where Kennie is based arose from restructuring when the two units were merged. Equality nonetheless remains one of the core values which Council policies continue to adopt. The principle of equal access to services informs the main functions which Kennie serves in his job. He advises the Chief Executive, directors and councillors on the issue of race policy. However, much of his time is spent dealing with instances of racism both within the Council and in the wider community. Racial harassment and exclusions in schools are two of the problem areas.

Another of Kennie's public roles is the distribution of small grants. Kennie took over this role when the Grants Liaison Officer post was deleted. The groups which qualify for grants are primarily black and ethnic organisations looking to redress inequality and eradicate discrimination, or putting on activities or events which undermine discrimination.

Black History Month, first established in Lewisham in 1993, has become an important part of the borough's annual calendar.

> *I would like to think that each year it gets better, it reaches a wider audience and we encourage more people in the borough to participate, and also in terms of quality and content. I think that one of the main things I've tried to do is to ensure that the ordinary black man and black woman in the street actually gets the opportunity to get involved in what is happening.* KENNIE WILLIAMSON

Racism remains in the 1990s a feature of the black experience in the borough of Lewisham, as virulent in pockets as it ever was, but structures to oppose the worst excesses of it are available to more black people than at any other time. With the continued cost cutting activity of local government, it remains to be seen how many of these remain in the new millennium.

Apart from the more global movement of black people, networks and alliances of the 1990s indicate a new trend in the local history of the black community in the area. They indicate too a new determined mood among that community to wrest from social forces of the day the responses to needs perceived by groups of black people. That movement is towards self-definition and self-determination.

Perhaps greatest of all the needs of the black community is that of economic opportunity, with unemployment having taken its toll of the qualified as well as the unqualified, the experienced as well as the inexperienced. For those in 'secure' jobs, equal opportunity, that is fair play not 'positive action' played an important and not-to-be-taken-for-granted part. It is not to be forgotten, however, that institutions responded – albeit late – to unrest in local communities. In Lewisham, preoccupied with laying the beast of racism, unrest did not surface in riot a decade ago. Nonetheless, many members of the black community perceived equal opportunity as 'the shadow but not the substance' of black people's development and independence.

> *I think that once we begin to understand that it is the economic base that gives us the autonomy and the ability to get into all the places we think we should be in we'll be dealing with the substance and not the shadow.* LEROY PHILIPS

Need for unity
where there is
one destiny

Epilogue

JOURNEY'S END?

*Fifteen years ago we didn't care, or at least I didn't care,
whether there was any black in the Union Jack. Now
not only do we care but we must.* STUART HALL, 1988

1995 was the end of an era for Asquith Gibbes, Lewisham's Community Relations
Officer, who had served for a quarter of a century. Five years previously *Outlook* had
called him "one of the borough's best loved and most respected sons".

Asquith's departure is
also the end of an era for
Lewisham, a time in
which the African-
Caribbean community
put down its roots and
fought discrimination in
every field. This has been
Asquith's battle. Whether
his official role was to
promote 'harmony' or to
struggle for racial
equality, he continued to
highlight issues of
injustice and needs
relevant to the black
community within the
borough. So, how much
has changed as the 20th
century closes?

One of the major
changes is the fact that
African-Caribbeans are no
longer the largest ethnic
minority in Deptford, an
area which usually
reflects the rest of the

*"As I rise for the last time to speak at an annual
meeting you will expect me to do so with mixed
feelings, having been at the crease for 25 years..."*

borough's population figures in advance. There are many omissions in this history:
there is no recognition of the substantial African community which completes the
triangular set of journeys, of Lewisham's pioneering role in the struggle against
apartheid, or of Bishop Desmond Tutu who is a freeman of the borough. Tutu roused
the children of Deptford to cheer for the release of their South African peers from

detention on one of his visits to St Paul's church. There are many more books to be written. This was simply the one that was longest overdue. This 'journey', the writing of this book, is really a beginning and there must be many more black histories, each contributing to a growing knowledge of ourselves as a whole community.

The story told in *Longest Journey* is a collective story. It is also my story, personal yet public. It has been as important to me to find Cornelius or Serica or Frances Lee in earlier centuries as it is for an adopted child tracing a family and, in places, as painful. In the post-war years, the stories of parents who came and children who followed were mine. When elders spoke of night shifts they worked or the drudge of factory work I heard my mother's voice, tired but determined that I would not suffer the drudge she had to endure. Those early parents named what they did. They called it 'sacrifice', but it was the foundation they built for us.

Our generation saw the situation differently. We saw submission and too great an inclination to accept the unacceptable. We wanted change and we acted on that. In the light of all we had to do, I laughed with Russell Profitt when he told the story of his first day at school as a head teacher. He was early, a young black man and smartly dressed with a suit, tie and a briefcase, but the caretaker ignored those signs and sent him straight to the boiler-room so that he had to explain. between embarrassment and subdued anger. that he was not a workman. I laughed because we have been there, regularly, and that is as familiar as the earlier stories.

We, the children who came, have a strong sense of 'home'. That, too, has been important on the journey. But we have been here a long time now and for so many reasons told in this documentation, we belong. Now with my own children born here it has become important to build on the foundation further so that they can operate in the world with the confidence of 'belonging' while understanding fully what that entails.

Since we are the direct survivors of slavery in the Caribbean, an institution unparalleled for its brutality and bestiality, we know, deep down, that the worst thing has happened. We have only to look forward to the future. We know, too, that the future belongs to the children.

Selected Sources for Lewisham's Black History

PART ONE

Documentary Evidence

Public Record Office: *Colonial Office Papers e.g CO 1/14 numbers 57, 59*
Parish Registers in Lewisham Local History Library and Greater London Record Office
Lewisham Local History Centre archives e.g. *Probate of the Will of William Coleman A62/6/273*

First Hand Accounts

Hakluyt, Richard *Principal Navigations*
Firth, CH (ed) *Narrative of General Venables*
Williams, E *Documents of West Indian History, 1492-1655*
Pepys, S *The Diary of Samuel Pepys*
Evelyn, J *The Diary of John Evelyn from 1641-1705/6*
Wesley, John *Thoughts Upon Slavery*

Secondary Sources

Andrews, KR *English Privateering Voyages*
Birchenough, J *The Manor House, Lee and its Associations (Transactions, 1971) and Two Old Lee Houses; (Transactions, 1968)*
Curtin, Philip D *The Atlantic Slave Trade: A Census (1969)*
Davies, KG *The Royal African Company (1957)*
Dews, Nathan *The History of Deptford (1971)*
Fryer, Peter *Staying Power; (1984)*
Ryder, Alan F *Benin and The Europeans 1485-1897 (1969)*
Rodney, WA *History of The Upper Guinea Coast (1970)*
Taylor, SAG *The Western Design*
Thornton, J *Africa & Africans in Making of The Atlantic World (1992)*

PART TWO

Documentary Evidence

British Library Miscellaneous Deptford Press Cuttings

First Hand Accounts

Equiano, O *The Life of Olaudah Equiano, written by himself (1809)*
Sancho, I *Letters of Ignatius Sancho*
Hoare, P *Memoirs of Granville Sharp*

Secondary Sources

Blackburn, Robin *The Overthrow of Colonial Slavery 1776-1848*
Craton, M *Testing The Chains (1982)*
Edwards, P & Dabydeen, D (ed) *Black Writers in Britain 1760-1890; 1991*
Fyfe, Christopher *A History of Sierra Leone (1962)*
Shyllon, F *Black Slaves in Britain*
Jennings, Gaile *The Campaign for Abolition of British Slave Trade: The Quaker Contribution 1757-1801 (Unpublished thesis)*

PART THREE

First Hand Accounts

Manley, Norman *Autobiography of Norman Washington Manley (Jamaica Jnl Vol 7 No.1) June 1973*
March-Ferron, E *Man, You've Mixed (1995)*
Ford, Amos A *Telling The Truth (1985)*

PART FOUR

First Hand Accounts

Oral accounts: collection of taped interviews by Joan Anim-Addo

Secondary Sources

Back, Les *Youth, Racism and Ethnicity in South London (Ph.D Thesis, Goldsmiths, 1992)*
Myers, Norma *Reconstructing The Black Past (Ph.D thesis, Liverpool, 1990)*
Ramdin, Ron *The Making of the Black Working Class in Britain (1987)*
Local Newspapers: *Outlook, South East London Mercury, Spectrum (LCCR), Lewisham Borough News, Lewisham Journal*
Occasional LCCR/LREC Reports including:
Backes, Richard *Racial Harrassment and Violence On Lewisham Housing Estates, 1994*

Greenwich Local History Library has a good collection of articles and studies on Black History. Lewisham Local Studies Centre has a 'Black People File'.

Index

academics, 147-51

Africa/Africans, iv-v, 1-9, 11-2, 14-7, 22, 25-8, 33-4, 40-1, 45-7, 51, 57, 65, 67, 69, 74, 105, 171, 174, 195, 200-1, 211

Ajegbo, Keith, 203

Albany, 103, 119, 151, 154, 187, 205-6

Alexander, Ruby & Noel, 94-6, 98, 166-7, 169, 171

Algernon Road, 118-9, 133, 174

All Lewisham Campaign Against Racism and Fascism (ALCARAF), 130-1, 133, 154

Altenor, Janene, 206-7

America, 34, 36-8, 42-3, 45-6, 50-1, 54, 56, 58, 70, 73, 75-6, 80, 86, 88, 94, 109, 117, 152, 179, 183, 203

Andrews, Margaret, 106, 162-3, 189, 201

Angerstein, John Julius, 31-3

Annesley family, 11, 22-3, 27-9, 49

anti-slavery movement, 45, 48-66

Antigua, 26, 81

apprenticeship, 37-8, 64, 66, 190

Arlett, Gracelin, 169

Armstrong, Louis, 70-1

Augustine, Avril, 106, 163

Australia, 42-4, 74

baptism, 40-1, 45, 52, 54, 63, 167

Barbados, 15-24, 26, 50-1, 58, 60-1, 68, 85, 157, 167, 169, 197

Baring, Sir Francis, 30-1

Belize (British Honduras), 81, 83

Benbow, Admiral John, 23-4, 49

Benin, 7, 8, 201

birth rate, 121

Black Childcare Network (BCN), 199, 201

black history, iv, 1, 116, 154, 159, 170, Black History Month, 201, 210

black power, 103, 107, 115-8, 147, 155

Black Unity & Freedom Party (BUFP), 107, 116, 124, 127 156

Blackheath, 31, 40, 47-8, 64

blacking, 71

Blake, Jan, 177-8, 206

Blanke, John, 3-4

Bligh, Capt William, 33-4

Bloody Saturday, 132-5

Blue, Billy, 42-44

Bogle, Paul, 65, 176

boxing, 73-7

breadfruit, 33-5

Breinburg, Dr Petronella, 149-50, 163, 207

Adinkra symbols are used throughout this book. They are traditionally carved from a calabash, giving a slightly curved printing surface which combines with the printing cloth to produce an individual message.

Photographs and illustrations courtesy of:

1 Joan Anim-Addo (Marie O'Connell) **2** Roman spoon-head (Museum of London Archaelogy Service) **3** John Blanke, Trumpeter (the College of Arms taken from the Westminster Tournament Roll) **4** The Gold Coast, (*Schwarz-Afrika: Black Africa* W, Hurschberg) **5** Africans repel European traders (*Schwarz-Afrika: Black Africa* W, Hurschberg) **6** Hawkins' crest (*Black Settlers in Britain, 1555-1958*, Nigel File & Chris Power, Heinemann, 1995, 2nd edition) **7** Cornelius parish register entry (St Margaret's church, Lee) **8** Map of Barbados (Richard Ligon, *A True and Exact History of the Island of Barbados*, 1673) **9** Slave ship (Library of the Religious Society of Friends) **10** Sir Francis Baring (thanks to the Directors of Barings Bank) **11** Manor House, Lee (LLSC) **12/13** John Julius Angerstein and Woodlands House (LBG Local History Library) **14** Breadfruit tree (RBG Kew) **15** The *Dreadnought* (National Maritime Museum, London) **16** Royal Hospital for Seamen (LBG Local History Library) **17** Billy Blue (State Library of New South Wales) **18** Granville Sharp (*The Slave in History*, William Stevens) **19** Ignatius Sancho (the National Portrait Gallery, London) **20** Duke/Duchess of Montague (LBG Local History Library) **21** Deptford Meeting House (LLSC) **22** Olaudah Equiano (Royal Albert Memorial Museum, Exeter) **23** Slave ship diagram (Library of the Religious Society of Friends) **24/25** Jospeh Hardcastle and Hatcham House (LLSC) **26/27** Mary Lloyd, Anne Knight (Library of the Religious Society of Friends) **28** Broken chains (Library of the Religious Society of Friends) **29** Samuel Coleridge Taylor (Croydon Local Studies Library) **30** Fisk Jubilee Singers (Black Cultural Archive) **31** Stephen Martin (the Martin family) **32** Gordon Martin (the Martin family) **33** Jack Johnson (Hulton Deutsch Collection) **34** Tommy Martin with weights (the Martin family) **35** Jack Johnson in the ring (Hulton Deutsch Collection) **36** 'The Brown Bomber' (Deptford History Group) **37** Greenwich beach (LBG Local History Library) **38** Deptford roadsweeper (Keith Cardwell) **39** Norman Manley (Jamaican High Commission) **40** Gordon Martin (the Martin family) **41** Eric Ferron (private collection) **42** Women's Auxillary Regiment (trustees of the Imperial War Museum) **43** 'Together' (trustees of the Imperial War Museum) **44** *Empire Windrush* (National Maritime Museum, London) **45** Immigrants at Southampton (Hulton Deutsch Collection) **46** Girl at Victoria Station (Hulton Deutsch Collection) **47** Basil Morgan (private collection) **48** Thelma Perkins (private collection) **49** Harry Powell (private collection) **50** Racist grafitti (LREC) **51** Coloured Club (Hulton Deutsch Collection) **52** Sunderland Road bombing (Time Out) **53** Bloody Saturday, New Cross Road (*South East London Mercury*) **54** ALCARAF march for peace (*South East London Mercury*) **55** Bloody Saturday, Clifton Rise (*South East London Mercury*) **56** New Cross Fire (*South East London Mercury*) **57** New Cross Fire tribute (*South East London Mercury*) **58** Day of Action (*South East London Mercury*) **59** Moonshot football team (LREC) **60** Burnt Ash Hill (LREC) **61** Sybil Phoenix at playscheme (LREC) **62** Dr Petronella Breinburg (Joanna Gore) **63** Russell Profitt (LREC) **64** Sybil Phoenix (Marie O'Connell) **65** Ros Howells (LREC) **66** Cecile Murray (LREC) **67** Metrina Mitchell (Marie O'Connell) **68** Lilian Lewis (LBL Press Office) **69** Bishop Wilfred Wood (Black Cultural Archive) **70** Marcia Foster-Norman (private collection) **71** Ras Benjihai (Marie O'Connell) **72** Tommy Martin in the Virgin Islands (the Martin family) **73** Deptford Festival (LREC) **74** Prince Charles at the Moonshot (LREC) **75** Chris Foster (*South East London Mercury*) **76** Jah Shaka (Tim Barrow) **77/78** Tipper Ire & Daddy Colonel, Dennis Rowe (Anna Armone) **79** Irwin Eversley (*South East London Mercury*) **80** George Kelly's sculpture (Eugene Smith) **81** Imaging the Black Family (Jeni Mckenzie) **82** Joe Montgomery (LBL Press Office) **83** Lennie St Luce (Marie O'Connell) **84-89** Lewisham councillors (LBL Press Office) **90** Asquith leaving LREC (LREC)

LBL   London Borough of Lewisham   **LBG**   London Borough of Greenwich
LREC Lewisham Racial Equality Council   **LLSC** Lewisham Local Studies Centre

DEPTFORD FORUM PUBLISHING was established in 1993 as a community publisher, aiming to bring the mysterious world of publishing down to earth. We create beautifully-produced books presenting high-quality research in a popular style and at an affordable price. Our publications include social history, oral history testimony, children's writing and historical source texts. Deptford Forum has pioneered innovative Publishing-in-Education projects and offers a Publishing Advice Service to individuals and groups. If you would like more information please write to 441 New Cross Road, London SE14 6TA.